BILL NYE'S
GREAT BIG
WORLD OF
SCIENCE

BILL NYE'S GREAT BIG WORLD OF SCIENCE

BY **BILL NYE** AND
GREGORY MONE

ABRAMS BOOKS FOR YOUNG READERS
NEW YORK

For today's students, who will promote
the progress of science and the useful
arts of engineering to create a
better world for all of Earth's citizens

Library of Congress
Control Number 2020936748

ISBN 978-1-4197-4676-5

Text copyright © 2020 Bill Nye
Illustration and photography copyright © 2020 Harry N. Abrams,
unless noted otherwise on page 247
Edited by Howard W. Reeves
Book design by Sue Boylan for becker&mayer!
Cover and chapter opener photographs by Sandy Honig
Illustrations on pages 4, 60, 97–99, 182–183 by Matteo Farinella
Experiment illustrations by Amelia Fenne
Additional drawings by Bill Nye

Printed and bound in China
10 9 8 7 6 5 4 3 2 1

The activities and materials discussed in this book may be potentially toxic,
hazardous or dangerous. We advise that children should only participate in said
activities with appropriate adult supervision. The author and publisher do not
accept liability for any accidents, injuries, loss, legal consequences, or incidental
or consequential damage incurred by any reader in reliance on the information or
advice provided in this book. Readers should seek health and safety advice from
physicians and safety and medical professionals.

ABRAMS The Art of Books
195 Broadway, New York, NY 10007
abramsbooks.com

CONTENTS

HOW WE KNOW

▶ **Look around.** You might be sitting in a chair, or on your bed, with an electric lamp or even a gas-burning lantern nearby. You might be outside on a sunny day, under a tree, or at a picnic table. You might be in the back of a car reading, while a grown-up drives you here and there. So much of what you see was created by people, and those people absolutely used science to design that chair, or bench, or lamp. In a modern city park, even the trees were placed by someone with a plan based on science. So what is this idea—this thing called "science"? It's the process by which we know and understand nature. And it's the process by which we change and improve our environment, and change and improve the way we live. It has become so much a part of the way humans think in the last few centuries that you might take it for granted. Science is both a collection of hard-won facts and a process that helps us understand our world. This process, what we call the scientific method, is how we have come to understand and know so much about nature. I'm tellin' you, the scientific method is one of the best ideas we humans have ever had. Even better than banana milkshakes and hot chocolate. Seriously . . .

You may already know or have heard that science starts with an observation. You notice something in the world around you, and that leads to a question. Why is the sky blue and not purple or green? How does a very small seed become a huge tree? How does a bird fly? Does an enormous metal airplane fly on account of the same science? How can a fish breathe? Why does one gear on my bicycle seem easier to pedal than another? Then you, as a scientist, come up with an explanation, what we

call a hypothesis [Hie-PAH-thuh-siss]. Next you devise an experiment, a way to test the hypothesis. Can I make something else fly—a paper airplane, maybe? You compare what you thought would happen in your experiment with what really did happen. And then . . . you start over. That's science. We build from one observation to another, one hypothesis to another, one experiment to another, and one conclusion to another. We fail, stumble, and keep asking questions. Through the scientific method we've learned about our world, the one right here in front of us (and behind us), and the larger universe—the distant stars and galaxies and mind-boggling black holes. And with every amazing answer we find to every amazing question about nature and the universe, we realize that there is so much more we don't understand, so many more questions to be pursued. For me, science is the most exciting thing humans do.

You may meet people now and then who aren't willing to consider or accept what scientists have discovered and proven to be true. They're often uneasy about science in general. They have trouble changing their minds, even when they're shown evidence and facts. You may also meet people who are very troubled by the idea that the universe presents us with countless unanswered questions and that there is so much about nature that we don't yet know. Well, don't be one of them. Instead, use your brainpower to learn about the cosmos and our place within it. Use your ability to think to push the boundaries of human knowledge. Science is the key to our future; it's the key to our health and well-being. It's how we've made countless discoveries about the cosmos, our fellow creatures here on Earth, and ourselves.

Here's something I think about every day. When my grandparents were born, there were about one and a half billion people in the world. When I was nine years old, there were twice that many, more than 3 billion people. Now, there are almost 8 billion on Earth. By the time you're as old as your grandparents, there will be nine, perhaps even 10 billion of us. In order for us to live comfortably, we're going to have to come up with new ideas and new ways to understand the world. Simply put, we're going to need science. So let's go!

Ideas Down Under

The word **"HYPOTHESIS"** comes from ancient Greek words having to do with the "foundation," or the "idea underneath."

1

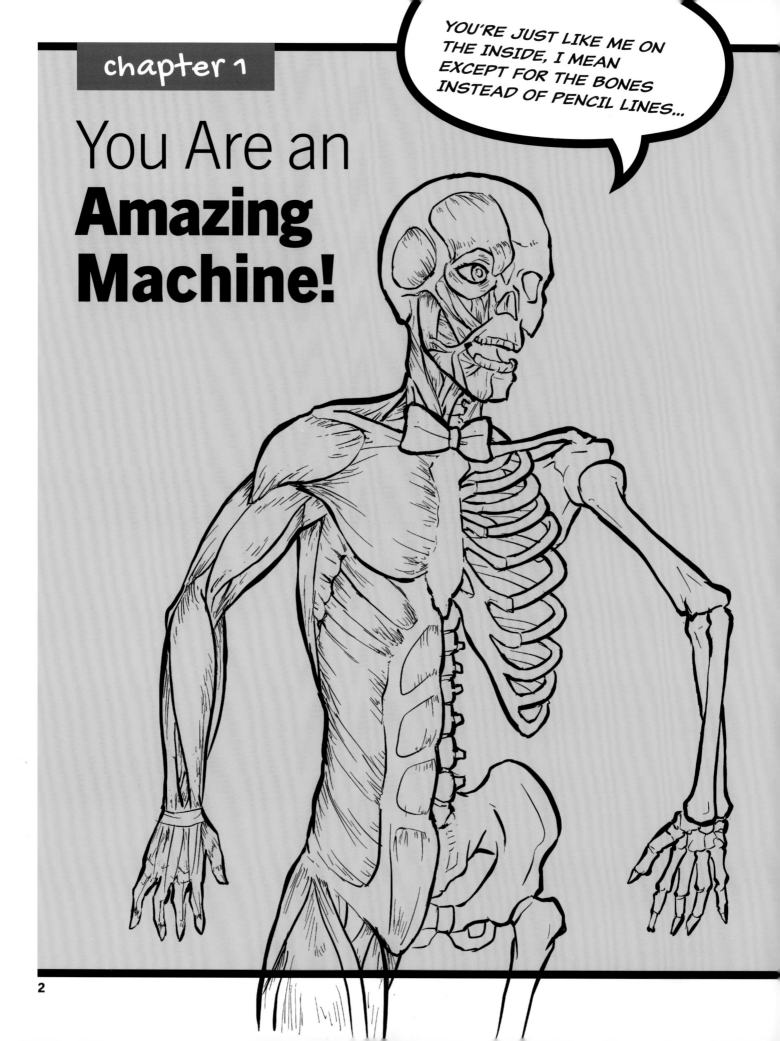

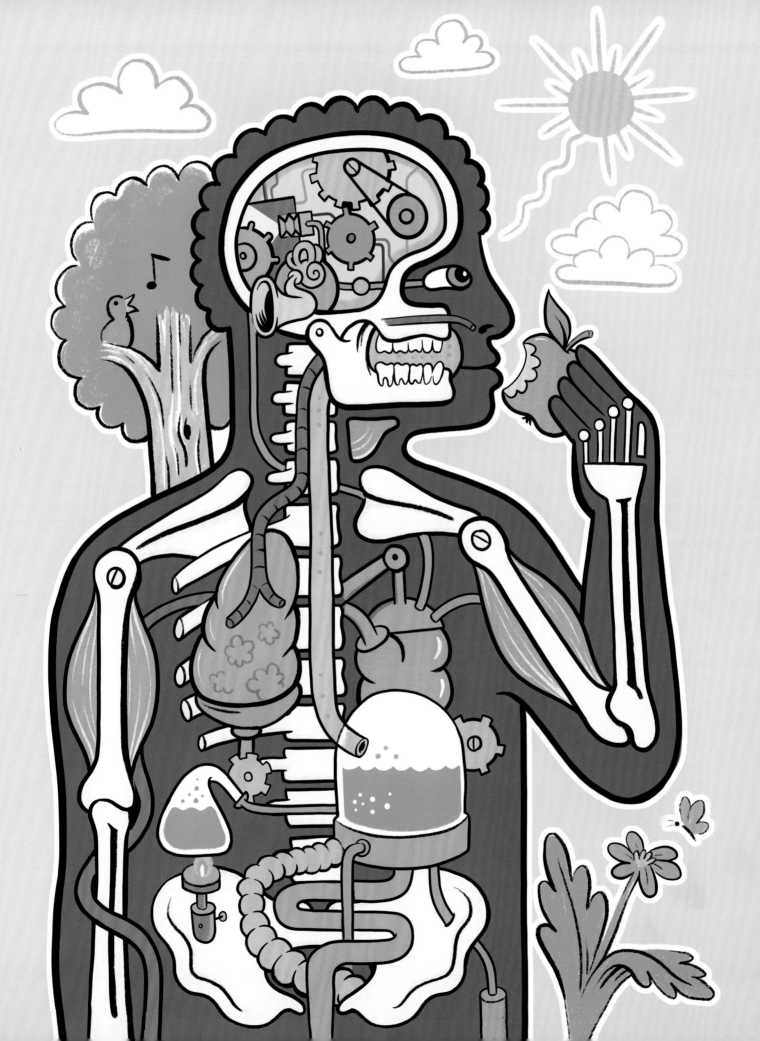

► **The human body is one of the coolest machines in the cosmos.**

It's probably the only machine on Earth that knows it lives on a planet, for example. Face it, fellow humans—we're amazing. We're complex. We think about complex things. We can walk, talk, run, dance, and build robots, just to name a few examples. All that moving around, and all that thinking, takes energy. We get that energy from the food we eat. That's right; apples, hot dogs, oatmeal, even broccoli have converted the energy of sunlight into food energy that we use to do our human things. We'll talk plenty more about sunlight, food, and energy in the coming pages. Right now, though, we're talking about us, us humans.

Our wonderful brains set us apart from the rest of the creatures and critters on our planet. We've used these brains to figure out how this planet goes round, how stars are born, and how the universe works. Try that, zebras! (Of course, I'll admit, all the zebras I've spoken with seem largely unconcerned about any of those things. They're usually quite busy eating grass all day, and looking out for lions—all day and all night. Creatures like these are coming up in the next chapter.)

The human body consists of a mix of biological machines and systems that help us grow, move, heal, eat, drink, breathe, and stay healthy. And all of these systems are built from cells.

Massively Important Point: You Are Made of Cells!

gut-lining cells

red blood cells

smooth muscle cell

skin cells

stem cell

bone cell

fat cells

nerve cell

>> The cell is the basic unit of all living things. Most bacteria live as just one cell separate from their neighbors, but plants and animals (like you and me) are what we call multicellular [Mull-tee-SELL-yoo-ler] organisms. You're built with 37 trillion cells—approximately. And there are about 200 different kinds of cells in the human body. Some cells build bone. Other cells help us think and store memories. Red blood cells pick up oxygen from our lungs, carry it around our body, and deliver it to other cells, so they can do whatever it is they're supposed to do.

White blood cells kill germs. Some cells are round balls. Others are flat. Still more sprout extensions in different directions and connect with thousands of other cells. Cells are busy—seriously busy.

Cells talk to each other (I mean in cell kinda ways). They divide and split into pairs. They carry that astonishingly important code that makes you you, and me me—our DNA. That's deoxyribonucleic [dee-OKS-ee-RIE-boh-new-Klay-ik] acid—yes, people, acid. Stay tuned for more on DNA in chapter 5.

We could go on about cells for pages and pages. Come to think of it, we will in the next few chapters. The cell itself is a wonderfully complex mix of fantastic tiny machines. In other words, we're made of tiny machines, which are made of even tinier machines. But now we're going to zoom out. We're going to explore some of the critical parts and systems built from all those tiny cells and the even tinier machines inside them. Are you ready? Good. Let's start with my favorite system. The one that's helping me write this book in the first place.

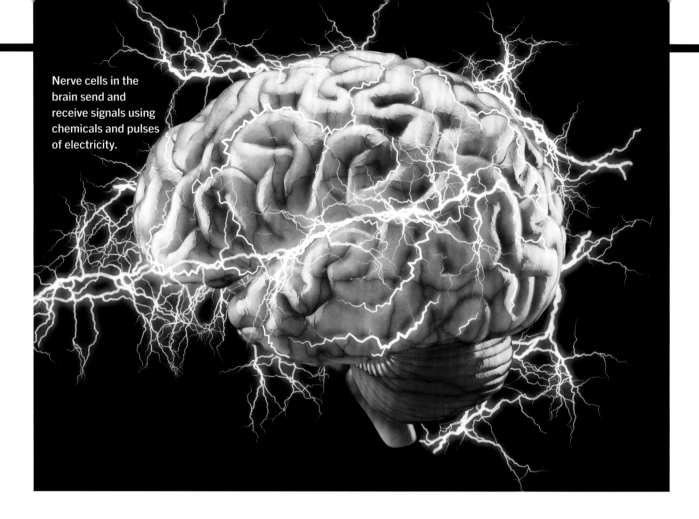

Nerve cells in the brain send and receive signals using chemicals and pulses of electricity.

The Brain and Nerves

➤ The one-and-a-half-kilo (about three-pound) human brain can store more information than the most powerful computer. It controls everything from our thoughts to our movements and heartbeats. The scientists who study the brain and the nervous system—the complex network of nerve cells that extend throughout our body and carry messages to and from the brain—are called neuroscientists [Ner-oh-SIE-inn-tists].

A brain cell is known as a neuron [NER-ahn], and our brains have somewhere between 86 billion and 100 billion of them. Why don't we know exactly? Sometimes it's hard to say where one neuron ends and another one begins, even under a microscope.

Neurons have some of the same machinery as the other cells in your body. But they're also delightfully weird. They sprout branches that allow them to send and receive signals—kind of like the electronic antenna inside a smartphone—only the ones in our brain spit out special chemicals and pulses of electricity, like tiny sparks. Neurons can connect with other neurons, too. A single neuron can link up with 200,000 other cells! Imagine a tangled kite string—with 200,000 twisted loops. Then imagine about a billion groups of those loops. The combination of the brain and the nerves that connect our head to our spinal cord and on out through the rest of our body is known as our nervous system. When you see, hear, smell, taste, or touch something, that information gets sent to your brain through your nervous system.

> "My favorite scientific instrument is the brain, fueled by imagination. Without that it doesn't matter what kind of instruments you have to work with. You need questions and you need time to think. I've formulated ideas about how birds regulate energy that are now in textbooks—just by looking at some data and letting myself think. The brain is the best tool we have."

—BIOLOGIST REBECCA HOLBERTON

TRY THIS!
Your Arm Doesn't Listen to You

WHAT YOU DO:

1. Stand next to a wall, or inside a doorway.

2. Lift your arm and press it to the wall. If your arms can reach both sides, press both arms against the sides of the doorway.

3. Press for 30 seconds.

4. Step away from the wall or the doorway, and try to lower your arms.

Results: Your arm(s) swing up without your brain telling them what to do. You might be begging your arm to do something completely different. Yet it won't listen! That's your nervous system at work. Once your brain has sent the "jam against the jamb" command, your nervous system keeps that command going for several seconds, even after you might have tried to tell your arm to stop. There's a lot that goes on inside you without you thinking about it, especially with your nervous system.

Let's say someone near you on the bus releases an unpleasant odor. Your nose picks up the scent, but it's your brain that identifies it. When you decide to move yourself away, your brain uses your eyes to scan the bus, then decides where you should go and gives orders to your muscles to stand up and hurry over to that other spot.

The nervous system controls sleeping, breathing, thinking, reading, balance, and more. Some of it is automatic. You don't have to tell your heart to beat, for example. That wouldn't be very effective, especially if you're distracted easily (like me). . . . Where was I? Oh yes: Other tasks require direct brain orders. You have to tell your body when to run, or jump, or reach for another cookie.

Our brains are crammed with billions of busy neurons.

THANKS, GUARDIANS, FOR THESE BIG BRAINS OF OURS!

It takes a lot of energy to grow a brain. The human brain grows for the first 10 years of life. On Earth, this is unusual. I mean—it's unusual for an Earth brain; we don't know about any non-Earth brains (not yet). With most primates, like the other monkeys and apes, brain growth stops earlier. Most animals need to start worrying about surviving at an earlier age than we do. They can't use up all that energy building a bigger computer in their skulls. And they don't need to. They need to build muscles and bones to help them find enough food in the first place and to hurry and scurry away from predators. Humans, meanwhile, just kick back and keep getting smarter (most of us, anyway). Some scientists think our human ancestors might have gotten big benefits from having bigger brains, as they struggled to survive through the changing seasons and learned to cooperate in a hunt. But the reason we can afford to spend the first 10 years of our lives growing our brains, and not our bodies, might have to do with our caretakers—our families, the people who raise us. Since they protect us and tend to our basic needs when we're growing up, we don't need to develop strong, mature bodies as quickly as other animals. Use some energy and have your big brain think about that; it's wild!

We Use Only 10% of Our Brains

WRONG!

> This idea is just wrong. Of course it sure seems like certain members of our species don't use much of their brainpower (if you know what I mean). But neuroscientists will tell you, if you're listening, that all of our neurons are used—all 86 (or more) billion of them.

MIND, BLOWN!

Your Brain Is Plastic

Okay, so I don't mean it's made of the same stuff as a flying disk or sports-drink bottle. The word "plastic" also means something that can be shaped—something flexible. For years, scientists thought the brain stopped changing after childhood. Three-year-old kids have roughly twice the number of connections between the neurons in their brains as adults do. But scientists eventually learned that the brain is constantly adapting as we learn and experience new things, even into adulthood. New connections between neurons are formed. Existing links are strengthened, which steadily makes it easier for all our connected neurons to send signals to each other, even when we're old. So don't stop thinking and challenging your brain. Ever.

WEIRD! SCIENCE

Your Hungry Brain

All this work means that brains are energy hogs. Your brain is only about 3% of your body weight, but it uses up more than 20% of your energy! Let's say you had 20 kids in your family and your mom or dad made 20 sandwiches. If your little sister were a brain, she'd gobble up four of them before you could even get one. That's the brain for you. It's always stealing sandwiches.

Most of this energy goes toward helping nerve cells send signals to each other. All that thinking and remembering and feeling that's happening inside your brain? It's really just a mix of chemicals and electrical pulses firing back and forth between your billions of nerve cells. But yes, it's exhausting. And you now have scientific evidence that thinking is difficult. Don't stop doing it, though. Our ability to think is what sets us apart from other critters and creatures—do you really think that hippo in your backyard knows her multiplication tables? I mean, just for example.

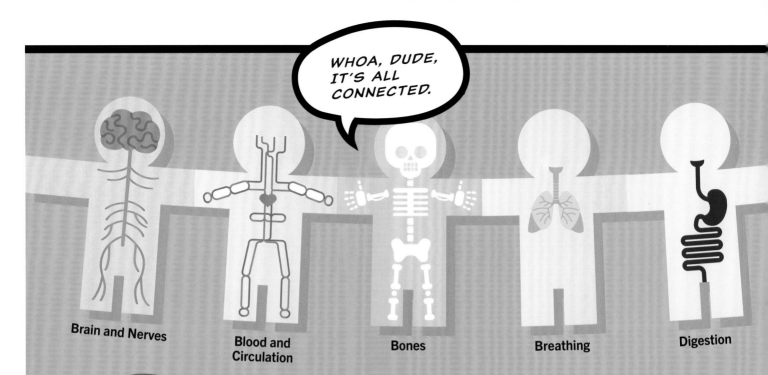

Brain and Nerves

Blood and Circulation

Bones

Breathing

Digestion

Skin

Breathing, Blood & Bodies

As I said at the beginning, our bodies are complex machines, made up of other machines. Let's start thinking (with our brains) about the different systems inside us. We just covered the brain and nervous system. Then there's the digestive system—or what our body does with what we eat and drink. The circulatory system, which moves blood around, is another. You've also got the respiratory system, which moves air in and out of our lungs. These systems work together to turn our food into action. Here are some of the body systems doctors and scientists like to start with.

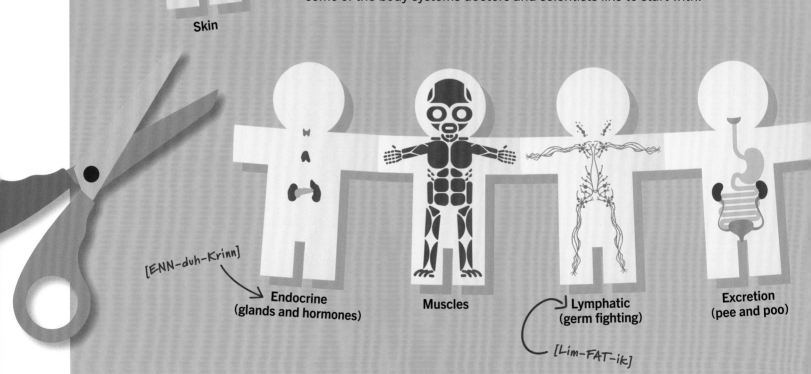

[ENN-duh-Krinn]

Endocrine (glands and hormones)

Muscles

Lymphatic (germ fighting)

[Lim-FAT-ik]

Excretion (pee and poo)

THANKS, GRAVITY: YOUR MUSCLES AND BONES IN SPACE

Your bones are alive and growing. Gravity keeps them strong and healthy. Astronauts who have spent plenty of time on the International Space Station, where gravity is close to zero, start to get brittle, weak bones. They even have trouble walking when they return to Earth. When you stand or walk around on our planet, gravity is pulling on your body. Your bones have to push against it to keep you upright. They have to work, and that work encourages the bone cells to make new bone and eat up or recycle old bone. In space, your bones aren't working as hard, since you're floating around everywhere, so the cells that eat away at older bone are busier than the cells building new bone. That's one of the reasons astronauts exercise a lot on the space station—they use special equipment to stress their bones and keep them as strong as possible. They have to work out two and a half hours a day just to keep strong enough to do their everyday jobs!

▼ Staying strong on the International Space Station.

NEED TO KNOW:

Beautiful Bones

➤ There are 206 bones in a grown-up human's body. But we're born with more, and as we grow, some of these bones fuse or join together. Most of our bones are in our hands and feet. Some help protect our insides, like our rib cage and skull. Others support our bodies so we can stand upright, lift and push objects, run and jump. But bones have a few other surprising jobs as well. They store most of the calcium in our bodies and some fat, too. They produce the red blood cells that carry oxygen around and the white blood cells that fight infections.

Three main types of cells make up the bones in our body. (Or maybe four, depending on whom you ask. And you asked me, so I'm saying three.) Some of them keep our bones in good shape. Some of them build new bones. And some recycle old bone cells into new ones. In other words, your bones don't just get formed and stay that way, like a Halloween skeleton, or a skeleton in a classroom. Your bones are always getting updated. It's like painting the Golden Gate Bridge in San Francisco. When they finish painting one area, they just start again somewhere else on the next coat of paint—so they're painting some part of that bridge day after day, all year round.

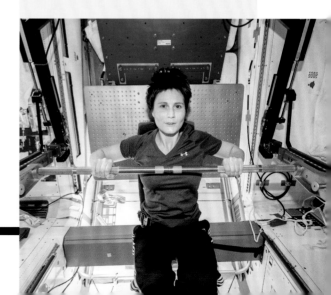

MIND, BLOWN!

Our Marvelous Muscles

Our skeletons wouldn't be much good if we didn't have muscles to move all our bones around. Humans have around 650 muscles, or maybe as many as 840, depending on how you separate and count them. Either way, muscles are made of cells, like just about everything else in our bodies. But muscle cells have a cool trick that allows them to fuse with each other and form long, thin fibers. Some muscles are small. Some, like my biceps, are enormous (just kidding).

Let's say I decide to pick up this 50-kilo (110-pound) barbell sitting beside my writing desk here in Nye Laboratories. Okay, maybe it's more like 10 kilos (22 pounds). The little muscles in my hand help all the little bones in my fingers wrap around the weight and grip it tight. When it's time to actually lift the weight and perform a few dozen arm curls, however, most of this work is done by the large muscle fibers in my biceps.

The biceps are the muscles stretching along the front side of your upper arm. At one end they connect to the shoulder bone. The other end connects to one of the bones in your forearm. As I perform my daily curls with this big barbell, the muscle fibers in my biceps contract, pulling that bone in my forearm—and the rest of my forearm with it—up toward my shoulder. When I lower the barbell, these fibers relax, and the muscles at the back of my arm, my triceps, take over, pulling my forearm away from my shoulder. **GRAVITY*** helps, too—on the way down. Someday, if you study science and engineering as long as I have, you might be able to lift giant weights, too. (That's a joke, people—but of course, exercise does build muscles, and studying does build brainpower—really.)

You know GRAVITY.
It's the force that keeps your feet on the floor, and makes balls fall to the ground. It's what makes "down" be down— and "up" be up. We'll get to all that in Chapter 11. Read on.

The Science of Superheroes

In the 2011 film *Captain America: The First Avenger*, a scientist injects a scrawny weakling named Steve Rogers with a mix of chemicals, and he's immediately transformed into a muscular superhero. While no such potion exists in the real world, scientists have discovered a gene that stops our muscles from growing too large. When they shut off this gene in mice, the mice ended up with superhero-like muscles. Now scientists are trying to figure out whether this could work in people, too. But they're not looking for a Captain America–style supersoldier serum. Instead, the idea is to develop a drug that could help people who suffer from diseases that weaken their muscles.

THE HUMAN MUSCLE HALL OF FAME

BUSIEST

THE EYE MUSCLES

Especially active when reading a book.

STRONGEST

THE JAW

The muscles around our jaws allow them to chomp down with 700 newtons, which is the same as 160 pounds of force. (More on newtons coming up.)

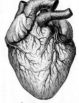

HARDEST WORKING

THE HEART

Not because it's broken now and then. This muscle beats day and night, billions of times during a human life.

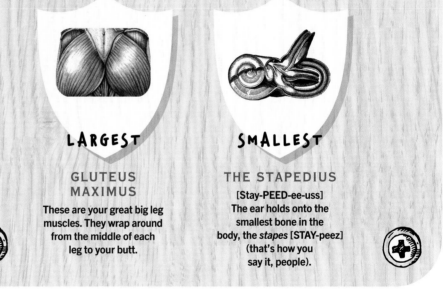

LARGEST

GLUTEUS MAXIMUS

These are your great big leg muscles. They wrap around from the middle of each leg to your butt.

SMALLEST

THE STAPEDIUS

[Stay-PEED-ee-uss] The ear holds onto the smallest bone in the body, the *stapes* [STAY-peez] (that's how you say it, people).

BEFORE WE MOVE ON...

That's it? No, no, no. There's so much more to the human body. The immune system, for example, fights off infections by bacteria and viruses. Other systems do things like regulate breathing and digestion and circulation. And there are weirdly enormous colonies of healthy and helpful bacteria that live in our guts. What I'm saying is: You, young scientist, are an absolutely fantastic machine. So amazing, in fact, that it kind of makes you wonder, where did we all come from? To understand that, let's talk about some of the other creatures we live with here on Earth.

chapter 2

Adventures in Zoology
The How and Why of Running, Swimming, Soaring, and Slithering

Life-forms like you and your friends move around somehow. We crawl, slither, swim, climb, stomp, skateboard, or fly all over our planet. We're birds, fish, bugs, beetles, worms, and humans. You, your friends, that hippo in your backyard—we're all animals—not microscopic one-celled creatures, and not plants. We're big, like buffalos, bison, and beetles. Seriously, just think of all the different insects you've seen! We've probably only discovered a fraction of them so far. Who knows what other animals lurk out there in the trees and the seas. There's work to do, young scientists!

The folks who research animals and learn about the habitats of different species—where the creatures live—are called zoologists [Zoe-AHL-oh-jists]. They do zoology. "Zoo" means having to do with animals. You probably know, an "ology" is the study of something. Zoologists find out what animals eat, how they find their food, and how they behave toward others. Zoologists explore how humans and climate change are affecting different animals, too. Are we helping them or hurting them? All of these things and more decide whether an animal species is going to thrive—like us— or be pushed toward extinction, like the black rhino or the orangutan.

Six Massively Important Points About: Animals

1. We travel.

We move around to find food, to meet other animals, and to escape from trouble. Plants do not move like that. A tree is not going anywhere, unless it's dug up and moved. A rock doesn't start rolling or sliding unless something nudges or pushes it along. But we animals—we can squirm, swim, run, leap, and even fly.

Monarch Butterfly

Electric Eel

2. We sense our surroundings.

Through our eyes, ears, nose, skin, and even our tongue and cheeks, we can see, hear, smell, feel, and taste what's happening in the world. Electric eels (which are a type of fish) use electric fields to sense what's going on in the very muddy streams where they live. Wild . . .

European Pond Turtle

3. We reproduce.

This is the fancy term for making babies. Some scientists say that everything animals do comes down to two goals: finding food and figuring out how to make more of themselves.

4. We share genes!

Genes [JEENZ] are the bits of information that living things carry in their cells. Near as we can tell, all life on Earth can be traced back to the same ancestor—the same ancient, ancient form of life. But animals split off from the other life-forms, including bacteria and plants, later. So even really, really different animals have way more genes in common with each other than they do with plants.

Siberian Chipmunk

Red-Eyed Tree Frog

Red Ant

5. We eat stuff.

Since we can't make our own food inside our bodies, we creatures and critters munch on plants, other animals, burritos, and so much more. (There are a few plants that trap insects, but that's a rare thing, and those plants aren't animals.)

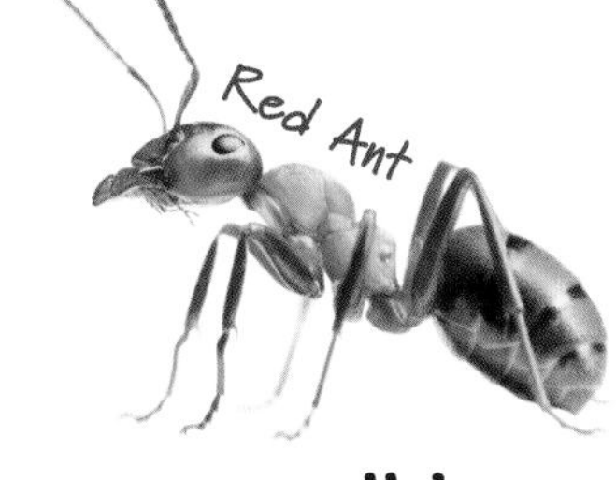

6. We are all important.

Even the tiniest creatures can be a vital part of the world because everything in nature is connected so strongly.

We Can Be:
ENORMOUS

A blue whale can grow to be 30 meters (100 feet) long. Even their babies are as big as adult elephants.

We Can Be:
HARD

The "ironclad" beetle has an outer shell so hard that scientists sometimes need to use a drill bit, rather than just a sharp pin, to poke through the exoskeleton when they want to study the beetle's innards.

We Can Be:
TINY

The frog scientifically named *Paedophryne amauensis* is so small that four of them could fit on a bottle cap.

MIND, BLOWN!

The Wide World of Creatures and Critters

Different animals are different. I know what you're thinking. Gee, Bill, what a brilliant statement! No one has ever said anything so intelligent in the history of the universe! But really. Some have spines or backbones. Others are fleshy and squishy. Our six-legged insect friends have hard outer shells called exoskeletons [EKS-oh-Skell-uh-tenz], but our skeletons are hidden beneath this soft, sensitive stuff called skin.

Yes, we're different, but we're all animals. You, me, and that friendly pet hippo of yours. (Wait . . . she belongs to your grandmother? How interesting. You should nudge her out of the flowerbed, though.)

We Can Be: SQUISHY

The soft-bodied octopus can squeeze through tiny crevices in rocks and coral, because it has a small, hard beak but no bones.

We Can Be: SLOW

The three-toed sloth would need about six hours to move a mile, and that's only if the sloth wanted to go somewhere.

We Can Be: FAST

Cheetahs have been clocked at around 100 kilometers (60 miles) per hour—that's as fast as a car on the highway—and sailfish can swim almost that fast.

WHOA, DUDE, IT'S ALL CONNECTED.

Zoology Department

About those giant blue whales: During their feeding seasons, they spend all day swallowing up small shrimp-like swimmers called krill. The type or species of krill that lives near the South Pole grows to be just 6 centimeters (2¼ inches) long and weighs only a gram (1/32 of an ounce). They eat tiny green plant-like organisms we call algae [AL-jee] that grow under huge blocks of ice floating at the sea surface. Whales, weighing 150 tons or more, arrive and gulp down tens of millions of these krill every day. It's amazing. Some of the largest creatures on Earth depend on tiny animals that eat tiny algae in an amazing icy garden on the southern side of the world. If one day soon there's not enough ice in the sea, there won't be a suitable place for the tiny algae to grow. Then there won't be enough for krill to eat, so we'll have fewer krill, and that could mean no more giant whales. We have to take care of our world, because we're all connected.

A baby bonobo sits in the grass; Democratic Republic of Congo.

NEED TO KNOW:

Why Different Animals Are So Different

> Beetles and bonobos, a type of ape, are both animals. How did they get to be so different? Tiny changes happening over many, many generations and long, long periods of time. The animals thriving on our planet today have changed in ways that help them survive in particular areas. Animal species finding themselves in a desert are going to end up looking different from animals that develop in a rainforest, a coral reef, or at the bottom of the ocean. To survive, a species has to adapt to its environment and territory.

Fish tails move side-to-side.

Dolphin and whale tails go up and down.

WHICH WAY DO YOUR LEGS AND FEET MOVE WHEN YOU SWIM?

MIND, BLOWN!

Olympic Swimmers Are Super Slow

Let's think about how habitat shapes a species in terms of swimming. The Olympic champion Michael Phelps swam at a top speed of around eight kilometers per hour (just under five miles per hour). He won more gold medals than he could carry (that's a joke; Michael can carry 'em just fine). He was fast. But only for a human. Dolphins can swim at more than 30 kilometers per hour (almost 20 miles per hour). A dolphin would destroy Phelps in a swim race! This doesn't mean Michael Phelps is slow. He's a human, and we humans have been evolving on land for millions and millions of years. Dolphins have been evolving in the water, adapting to that habitat. They have developed muscles and bones ideal for racing through the water via the up-and-down movements of their fin-like tail flukes. Their streamlined bodies slip through the water with ease compared to our big bulky human heads, wide shoulders, and skinny feet. So if you're at the beach, and a dolphin challenges you to a race, you can win—but only if it's on the sand. They're not much for rock climbing, either.

> " I was interested in animals from the time I was very young. I wanted to be a paleontologist, but at age seven I realized all the dinosaurs were dead, and I thought, what's the point of studying dead animals? So I decided to go into zoology. Now people pay me to fly to the South Pacific to swim in the water with humpback whales. How is that not fun?"
>
> —ZOOLOGIST FRANK FISH
> (yep, that's his real last name)

Be a Zoologist Right Now

Say you don't want to wait for college or graduate school. You want to be a zoologist right now. What do you do? Simple. All you have to do is look, listen, and explore.

LOOK

No matter where you live, there's a critter to study. If you're in the city, place a bird feeder on your windowsill or balcony and watch what sort of creatures visit. If you have a backyard, you might just be able to sit and look around. Lift up a rock; see what's underneath. Pick out an animal or a group of creatures. How are they interacting? Are they fighting? Over what? Why is the creature you're watching doing what it's doing, and how is it doing what it's doing?

LISTEN

Sometimes you might not be able to pick out a creature just by watching, but sitting outside and listening quietly is another great trick. The zoologist Mark Scherz once discovered a new species of frog just by sitting in the middle of a dried-out riverbed at night and listening. Every minute or two he heard a strange sound he'd never heard before—one that was a little different from all the other sounds in the area. Slowly he tracked down the source and found a tiny frog—a whole new species that had not yet been named. All by just listening!

EXPLORE

The best place to study the range of creatures and critters on our planet is to go out and explore beyond your neighborhood or backyard (with the permission of your parents or guardians, of course). Grab some binoculars and walk through the woods. Strap on a mask and snorkel and swim along the shoreline. If you don't want to swim, roll up your pants and check out a tide pool, pond, or creek. Hang around your own backyard and dig. Find out what's crawling, nestling, or slithering in the soil.

SCIENTISTS SAVING THE WORLD

ZOOLOGY DIVISION

In the past 600 million years, Earth has had five major extinctions. During each of these so-called extinction events, huge numbers of species get wiped out. Today, our planet is in the middle of a sixth major extinction event. But some scientists say this one is different. Species are disappearing 100 times faster than they did in the past, and we humans are probably responsible for the whole thing. Elephant populations are shrinking because people are killing them and selling their tusks. Orangutans are disappearing because we're cutting down their forests. Polar bears are struggling to survive because global warming and climate change are messing with their hunting grounds. Turtles, tigers, whales, dolphins, mountain plovers [PLUH-verz] (a type of bird), penguins—the list of both big and small creatures at risk of disappearing from our planet for good is frightening. Some zoologists, whom we call conservation biologists, focus specifically on finding ways to save and protect these species, and stop the people who are killing them all off. That's one of the reasons zoology is so important. By studying these creatures, we learn how to help them.

SOME OF OUR THREATENED FRIENDS
Left to right, top row: Bengal Tiger, Common Hippopotamus, Crowned Sifaka Lemur.
Center row: Yellow-Eyed Tree Frog, Shoebill, Saiga, European Honey Bee. **Bottom row:** Yunnan Snub-Nosed Monkey, White-Bellied Pangolin. **Images copyright © Tim Flach, from** *Endangered* **by Tim Flach.**

> 66 The same way astronomers want to explore new planets, I want to explore new species. When I was young, I wanted to be a marine biologist or work with chimpanzees, like my hero, Jane Goodall. But then I realized how little we know about insects, the most diverse set of creatures on our planet. You're never going to be disappointed studying insects because there are so many exciting things to discover. If I were to go in my backyard right now and dig around enough, I'm confident I'd find a new species with its own new story."
>
> —ENTOMOLOGIST
> [Ent-uh-MAHL-uh-jist]
> KATE UMBERS

ADVENTURES IN ZOOLOGY

THERE'S A SNAKE ON MY FACE!

When he was vacationing in the Bahamas as a kid, zoologist Graham Reynolds became obsessed with snakes after he spotted a small boa (a snake) trapped in the jaws of a cat. As a scientist, Reynolds has studied species on different Caribbean islands. During one expedition, when he traveled to a remote island, Reynolds and his team of scientists fell asleep on the beach after a long night of searching the jungle for tiny snakes. He awoke before dawn with a strange, heavy sensation on his face. A big ol' boa was slithering directly over him. Reynolds calmly sat up and held the specimen. Then he measured its head and length, took a sample of its blood, implanted a microchip so the scientists could track it in the future, and let the critter go. That's not just bravery. It's science!

The Bone Wars

> The study of fossilized animals and plants is known as paleontology [PAY-lee-enn-Tahl-uh-gee]. In the late 1800s and early 1900s, paleontology was a new field of study, and scientists were frantically rushing to beat each other to find the next interesting fossil. This race came to be known as the Bone Wars, and the researchers became so competitive that once they found something new, such as a fossilized skull, they'd rush to get credit by publishing a description and displaying the skeleton in a museum. They wouldn't even bother removing the rest of the creature's body. Naturally, this frantic rush led to a few mistakes. One of the famous examples is the dinosaur known as *Brontosaurus*. The skeleton of "brontosaurus" had been cobbled together from two quite different long-necked dinosaur species that were buried near each other. It was the head of *Camarasaurus*—which might have been a reconstruction and not an actual skull—on the body of *Apatosaurus*. Today some scientists are saying that *Brontosaurus* might have existed after all, but this particular specimen? No such crossed-up creature ever lived. Whoops.

Brontosaurus (*Apatosaurus*), 1918. Museum of Natural History, NYC.

The Tools of the Trade

Zoologists use all kinds of tools to help them study animal life on our planet. They might carry calipers—rulers with sliding cursors that help them capture accurate measurements—to record the size of a snake's head, say, or a flat folding kit to help them carefully collect and preserve delicate insects. We'd probably have to build an entirely new room at Nye Labs to house all the possible tools and instruments. But here are a few of my simple and not-so-simple favorites.

DNA SAMPLERS

How do you find out if some new creature you've discovered is really a new species? You study its DNA. Scientists have all kinds of DNA-related tools these days. One of my favorites is a new system called Environmental DNA (eDNA) analysis, which allows scientists to collect a water sample from a pond or lake, pick out the DNA, and figure out what creatures have been swimming or drinking in the area. Fish, I know what you're thinking: Where's our privacy? Long gone, my finned friends. Long gone.

BINOCULARS

Whether they're studying a known species to learn more about how it lives and survives or searching for a new species, zoologists have to look around. A pair of binoculars might seem old-fashioned, but they're still a fantastic tool for exploring the world. Especially the treetops.

SMARTPHONES

Many of us over the age of ten years old carry amazingly powerful computers in our pockets. They're not just for apps and posts, either. You can use your phone to photograph or capture video of an interesting beast or bug. When you get home, you can transfer that picture or video to a big screen and study the details. You can record the song of a bird. Conservation biologists—the zoologists who work to save species at risk of becoming endangered or extinct—say that smartphones can be powerful tools in their fight as well. Tigers, elephants, sharks, and other creatures are illegally killed around the world, but regular people can snap smartphone pictures of the location and the evidence, send it to one of the conservation biology groups, and help catch the bad guys.

TRY THIS!

Your Burning Love—for Your Food

WHAT YOU NEED:

Paper clip—large ones are easier to use

A peanut, an almond, a walnut, or a few of a few different nuts

Matches

Adult to keep an eye on things

WHAT YOU DO:

1. Bend a paper clip, so that it forms a base and a loop to hold a nut.

2. Crack open the nut. Separate the seeds or kernels. Rub the seed "coat" loose (if it has one). If it is indeed a peanut, separate the kernel halves. There are usually two seeds per peanut, and two halves per seed.

3. Place the seed half in the loop, so that its tip is pointing up and at an angle to the table. (This may take a minute to get it just right.)

4. Light a match; light the nut.

Results: Just like a regular wax candle, your nut candle combines its fuel (nut oil) with oxygen in the air and gives off heat. So do you and I. We combine our food with the oxygen we breathe. Animals like us are able to do our oxidation at a much lower temperature than a candle can, because we have special chemicals called enzymes [ENN-zimes] in our tummies.

BEFORE WE MOVE ON...

So we didn't quite have enough pages here to cover the millions of different animals that live—or have lived—on our planet. And so, so many of them are fascinating. But there's one animal I'm particularly fond of: us—humans. We're animals. We live in ecosystems like all the other species on Earth. But our relationship to this planet is different. Unlike any other animal you'll ever meet, we can affect and control the world's environments—on purpose. So here's something I'd like you to remember, young scientist: The more we understand how animals live and what they need to survive, the better we'll be able to shape the future for every species on Earth.

chapter 3

The Essential Science of Plants

They Don't Dance, but They've Got Moves

Don't turn the page! Not yet. Look, I get it. That last chapter got into hungry creatures and furry critters and, at first, that probably sounded way more exciting. Cheetahs run as fast as cars. Falcons pursue their prey at more than 300 kilometers per hour (almost 200 miles per hour). And plants, well, they don't move much at all. Or not quickly, anyway.

But we couldn't or wouldn't even be here without plants.

In its early days, our planet wasn't what you and I would consider much of a place to live. The environment of ancient Earth would have killed us pretty quickly because we wouldn't have been able to breathe. Then, in the early oceans, single-celled creatures were able to break the chemical bonds of that famous invisible carbon dioxide in the air and free the every-bit-as-famous oxygen. Eventually they passed this oxygen-freeing trick along to green plants, which have been pumping out fresh air ever since. Thank a plant after your next deep breath.

Do you like living on land, where you can breathe and keep warm? I know I do. Again, thank a plant. Any plant. Even the flowers that your grandmother's hippo just stomped or the geranium growing in that really old pair of sneakers over by the window. The ocean has been full of plants for billions of years. These watery plants put dissolved bubbles of oxygen in the water. Fish breathe it all day (and night). The first plants appeared on land around 500 million years ago. Animals wouldn't have survived on the ground if it were a big, barren wasteland offering nothing to eat. Plants created habitats in which animals could thrive when they crawled up out of the seas and started hanging around in dry air. And they still ensure that land is a nice place to live.

You Are Solar Powered

MIND, BLOWN!

You eat spaghetti, hamburgers, cereal, maybe even broccoli. In a way, it's as though plants eat sunlight. Our local star, the Sun, floods the Earth with energy in the form of light and heat. Plants absorb this light, pull carbon dioxide out of the air and water from the ground, then churn through this mix. In the process, they release a little bit of that water and plenty of oxygen back into the air. We've got more to absorb about this in chapter 8, all about chemicals.

Thanks to a process called photosynthesis (Foe-toe-SINTH-uh-siss), plants convert the Sun's energy into chemical energy, which is stored in different parts of the plant. Then we eat the plants, or the animals that have eaten the plants, and we grab this energy for ourselves. And it all starts with the Sun! The energy in our food rides to Earth on beams of light. So we're all solar powered.

> "Plants and algae are the only things that can harvest the energy of the Sun and turn that into the sugars and carbohydrates we need to survive. Plus, they provide oxygen. If we didn't have plants, we'd all die."
> —BOTANIST SHARON ROBINSON

SUPER COOL SCIENTIST:

Sylvia Earle

Sylvia Earle is known mostly as an ocean expert, and a very famous one at that. Her Mission Blue organization aims to protect the world's oceans. She has broken world records for deep-water dives, built and piloted submersibles, and was the first woman to serve as chief scientist of the National Oceanic and Atmospheric Administration. But she was trained as a botanist, or plant scientist. Earle studied algae. Much of the oxygen we breathe comes from aquatic plants, algae, and tiny little photosynthetic life-forms in the ocean. Botany is a blast.

BOTANY DIVISION

There are about 400,000 different types of plants growing on Earth, and the scientific study of plants, botany, is hugely important for several reasons. Botanists are some of the world's most valuable scientists. Seriously. Think about this in terms of three of the biggest problems facing our world today.

1. Food

How are we going to continue to feed our growing population? Only around 3 billion people lived on our planet in 1965, when nine-year-old Bill went to the World's Fair in New York. Today we're approaching 8 billion, and we're hungry. Growing food for all of us isn't easy. Plant scientists develop and cultivate crops that survive when there isn't enough water, or when there's too much water, like during a flood. Some plants can resist infections that would kill other plants. Some might be ideal for feeding us while our climate changes.

A field of mirrors concentrates sunlight, providing energy to raise crops thriving in the greenhouses of this indoor farm.

2. Energy

All the wonderful gadgets and machines and homes we humans love require electricity. Most of that energy comes from burning fossil fuels, stuff we dig up, like coal, oil, and natural gas. We convert the heat into electricity. Fossil, by the way, is from a Latin word that means "buried." To get fossil fuels, we have to dig or pump them up. And when we burn those fuels, we pump tons and tons of carbon dioxide into the air, which is causing our planet to get warmer and warmer. We have to stop that, my friends. Soon.

We have to get our electricity in other ways. Yes, we have solar cells, and they work okay. But we'd sure like them to be more efficient, so that they produce more energy for every second of sunlight that strikes them. Maybe we could borrow some tips from plants.

A ton of that invisible carbon dioxide would fit in 14 trailer truck containers. Or, imagine a huge cube as high, wide, and long as U.S. football goalposts are tall. Now imagine billions of those cubes spewing into the sky every year.

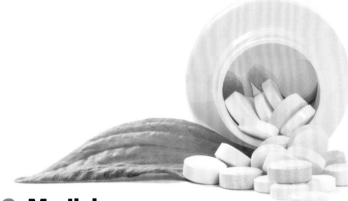

3. Medicine

Scientists are always searching for more powerful medicines. Botanists have found many new medicines by studying the chemicals that plants produce. After all, if a plant has an insect enemy, maybe it has developed a way to fight that bug off. Could that same sort of defense work for us, too? This is the kind of question botanists and doctors work on together.

HELP WANTED

None of these big enormous problems are going to be solved right away. We're going to need curious, eager young scientists to get out there and study plants to find new medicines, develop better technology to harvest power, and think up new ways to feed our billions of human neighbors. Are you up to the challenge?

Thanks, Botany!
Three **MORE** reasons to love plants!!

> "Botanists used to be seen as people who just went out and collected plants. Now we're working in climate change, evolution, even medicine. We're breeding new plants. It's really wide open. And plants are really cool. They start off as a seed, and unlike mammals, which are really needy as babies, these seeds can travel wherever you plant them. People have found seeds that are 30,000 years old and you can still grow them!"
>
> —BOTANIST E. HAN TAN

1. Food

In the simplest, most direct sense, plants are a great source of nutrition. Salads, broccoli, string beans, brussels sprouts—I devour them all. But even if you're on an all-steak diet, you owe that nutrition to plants, because cattle thrive on greens.

2. Climate

Our climate is changing because we're filling the atmosphere with carbon dioxide, trapping heat close to Earth's surface. But if we didn't have plants, carbon wouldn't make its way from the air to the seafloor and soil, then back to the air, very fast. All sorts of organisms depend on this pattern, the "carbon cycle." Life as we know it wouldn't exist without it. Plants growing and dying and growing again maintain the balance of carbon. Plants pull it out of the air during photosynthesis, then hold onto all that carbon in the form of stems, fruits, seeds, leaves, roots, and wood. Without plants, our climate would be warming and changing much, much faster.

3. Land

Plants don't actually create land, but they sure do hold it together. Their roots reach deep into the ground, spreading out and intertwining, holding soil in place. Without healthy plants, heavy rains and floods can wash away rich, fertile soil. Plants are tough, too, and they spread their seeds everywhere. After damaging fires or heavy rains, seeds that survive start sprouting and putting down roots, capturing carbon and restoring soil.

TRY THIS!

Grow Life!

WHAT YOU NEED:

Cups

Potting soil

A packet of seeds

Small plates or saucers

Water

WHAT YOU DO:

1. Poke two smallish holes in the bottom of each cup, allowing excess water to drain.

2. Put potting soil in the cups, leaving about a centimeter (½ inch) from the top.

3. Push a seed into the soil in each cup, so they are 2 centimeters (¾ inches) from the surface.

4. Place the cup on a small plate or saucer.

5. Add some water. Keep soil moist, but not soaked. We're not making a swamp here.

6. Expose your cups to some nice bright sunlight.

7. Add more water when the soil gets dry. Again, don't soak it.

8. Watch for a couple weeks.

Results: Look, I know the little demonstration above might seem simple. But I meet a great many people who have never grown a plant from a seed (city folk, not farmers). Everyone should try it, and try it again. Tend to your plant. Make sure it has water and sunlight. Move it around your home or yard and track how it responds to changes in how much light, air, and water it receives. Maybe you'll even fall in love—with botany, not the plant—and find a way to save the world one day—save it for us humans, that is.

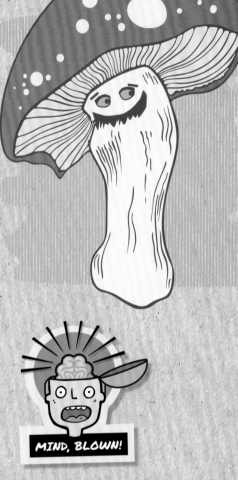

MIND, BLOWN!

MONSTROUS FUNGUS AMONG US

Botanists study fungi, too. When they're talking about just one, scientists say "fungus." When they mean more than one, U.S. scientists pronounce it like FUN-guy. Fungi aren't exactly plants. They don't make their own food, for one thing. Scientists have named around 144,000 different types of fungi on our planet. Mushrooms are a type of fungus. The largest living thing on Earth is a fungus. Last I checked, there was a honey fungus growing in the Blue Mountains in Oregon that measured more than three kilometers (two miles) wide.

WEIRD ! SCIENCE

Plants in Space

Cows in space sounds like a fun idea at first. But keeping a cow alive is tough! To grow, all plants need are water, carbon dioxide, light, and some nutrients from the soil or the sea. For years, scientists have been testing different ways of growing plants inside the big, orbiting laboratory known as the International Space Station—they're even harvesting green vegetables to eat! If we're going to travel to another planet, or set up a permanent camp on the Moon or Mars, we're not going to send cows. We're going to grow plants to give astronauts, space tourists, and other travelers the nutrition they need.

▲ NASA astronaut Jessica Meir cuts mizuna mustard green leaves grown aboard the International Space Station for the VEG-04B space agriculture study.

BEFORE WE MOVE ON...

Thank a plant the next time you see one. You and I depend entirely on plants to live. Every bit of food you've ever eaten came from plants. The oxygen in every breath you and I have ever taken came from a plant. We need it to run all our cells. No plants? No you. No me. Thanks, green machines!

chapter 4

Waterworld
How the Other Two-Thirds Lives

Five Massively Important Points About: Our Ocean

Our world is wet, very wet. Nearly three-quarters of the surface is covered by oceans.

If you were an alien staring at us through a distant, powerful telescope, you'd probably guess that any intelligent life on Earth would have to live in that water. Intelligent creatures, like (most of) us, would have to be oysters, or whales, or maybe "fish people," right? But you're not an alien. And you're not a fish. Well, you were kind of a fish at one point, which we will talk about next, in chapter 5, when we talk about evolution. Most of the living things on Earth live in the sea, because most of the planet is covered by an ocean.

So right now we're going to focus on all the beautiful water washing around our planet's surface. Some scientists like to think of Earth as having just one big ocean. But the ocean has distinct areas with different characteristics—the North and South Pacific, the North and South Atlantic, the Indian, Arctic, and Southern oceans. We find different creatures living in the different ecosystems in these different parts of the world's ocean, or oceans.

Now, I hope you're not shocked to learn that the study of the oceans is called oceanography.

1.
71%
of Earth's surface is water.

2.
97%
of the water on our planet is in the oceans.

3.
Ocean currents are driven by the warmth of the sun, winds, and the spin of the Earth.

4.
Ocean currents carry minerals and nutrients essential for life all over our world.

5.
The oceans exchange heat with the atmosphere every day and night.

We need water to live. Most of that water is in the ocean. We also need warmth. None of us would survive long on the Moon, even if it did have breathable air. It's too hot where the Sun strikes and too cold where it's dark! One of the reasons Earth has had such a nice, friendly climate for the last 12,000 years or so is that the ocean absorbs energy from sunlight and holds its heat. This heat is carried up into the atmosphere as water evaporates from the surface.

The oceans keep our planet warm, but they also prevent it from getting too warm—I mean too warm for us. The oceans store 50 times as much carbon dioxide as all the air in the atmosphere. If all that carbon dioxide were to bubble up into the sky, the planet would become too warm for creatures like us. Instead of being comfortably toasty, we'd be miserably roasty.

The Science of Ocean Motion

One key to being a living thing on our planet is the motion of the ocean. Currents move water, of course. But ocean currents also carry heat and chemical nutrients from one place to another all over our planet. Without currents, you wouldn't recognize the place. Oceanographers study how all this water and heat move around the world.

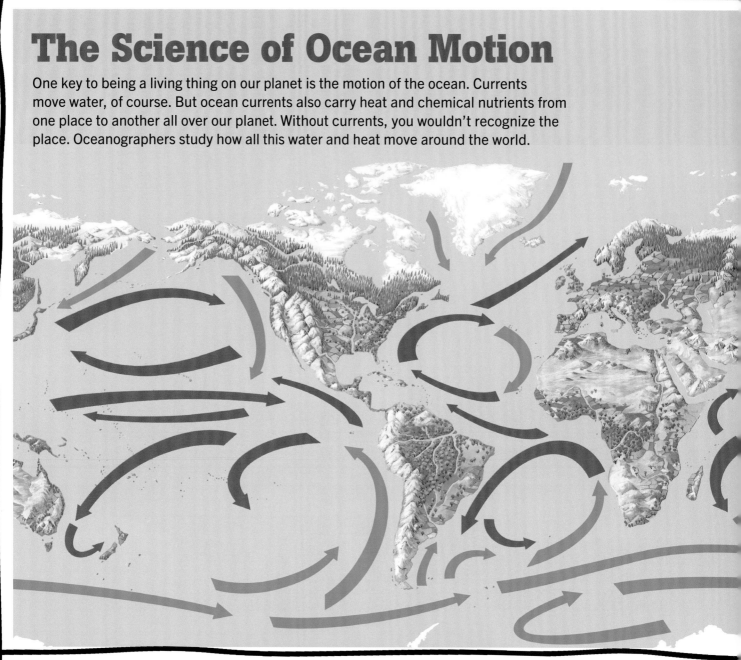

Sunshine

As the Sun shines on Earth, and the world turns, the heat of the Sun warms the ocean all day. But all night, on the side away from the Sun, Earth is cooling, releasing its heat into the atmosphere and toward outer space. The continuous heating and cooling make the ocean expand and shrink a little. This expanding and contracting helps create currents that move water around the globe, day and night, all year round.

ARCTIC CIRCLE: 670 km/hr

Bulge forms on side opposite the Moon.

EQUATOR: 1,700 km/hr

Water bulges toward the Moon and the Sun.

Tides

The ocean is also pulled toward both the Moon and the Sun by the pulling force of gravity. (See chapter 11; we'll go over gravity's ups and downs . . . ouch.) Because it's so much closer to us, the Moon's tug on the ocean is about twice as great as the Sun's. The pull of their combined gravity tugs the ocean so that it forms two bulges, one on the side of the Earth facing the Moon, and one on the side of the Earth opposite the Moon. As Earth turns through these bulges, we get high and low tides on shores the world over. When the Sun and the Moon are lined up, the bulges are big, and we get very high tides. At other times the bulges are not quite as big, and the tides are tamer. There are enormous vital ecosystems, involving tens of thousands of species, that have come into existence and rely on this tidal motion of the oceans. To live, they need to spend half their day high and dry and half their day underwater. We're talking all kinds of crabs, clams, and other creatures that can't thrive without the tides.

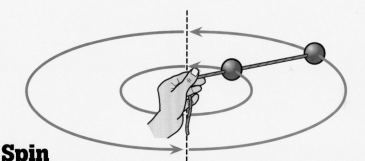

Spin

Then there's the spin of the Earth. Gravity is pulling every molecule of ocean toward the center of the Earth (what you and I call "down"). It never stops pulling. Now imagine you have a ball on a string—or just go get one—and you're twirling it in circles over your head (outside, please). The longer the string, the farther the ball travels each time it goes around. If you shorten the string, it travels a shorter distance, and it gets around quicker, in less time. If you stop twirling, the ball falls down—the string might end up wrapped around your arm (you might want to unwrap it sometime). For water in the ocean, the spin of the Earth acts like the ball on the string. At the equator, near Kenya or Colombia, Earth's surface is moving faster than it is near places farther from the equator, like Russia or Argentina. The difference in the spinning speed of different places on Earth's surface, combined with the pull of gravity, makes storms like hurricanes and cyclones spin. It even makes the ocean turn in huge circles or loops, what oceanographers call gyres [JIE-erz]. You may have heard of the Gulf Stream. It's part of a big ol' gyre in the North Atlantic. Please, read on.

Wind and Waves

Let's not forget wind. It's driven by sunlight and Earth's spin, too. As wind moves over the ocean surface, it drags up some water along with it. Maybe you've seen what sailors call whitecaps, when wind whips up waves. Those waves drive worldwide currents, too.

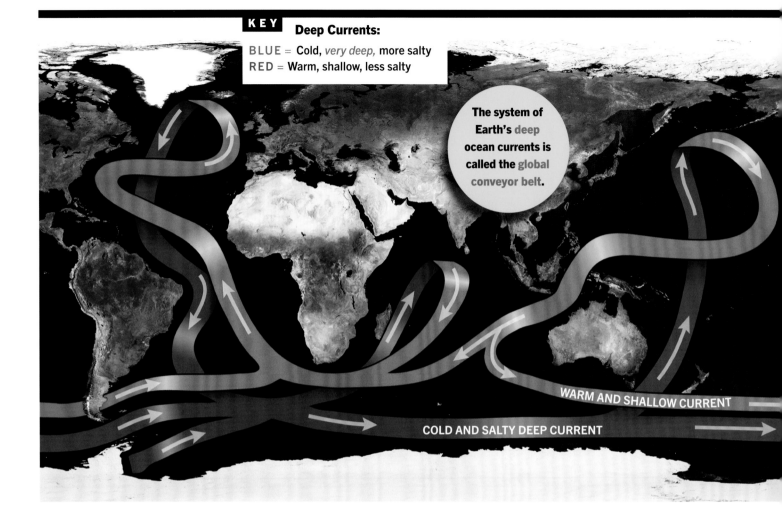

KEY
Deep Currents:
BLUE = Cold, *very deep,* more salty
RED = Warm, shallow, less salty

The system of Earth's deep ocean currents is called the global conveyor belt.

WARM AND SHALLOW CURRENT

COLD AND SALTY DEEP CURRENT

Salt

When it comes to cooking up currents, don't forget the salt. You've probably seen pictures of icebergs. At the North and South poles, the air above the ocean is cold enough to form ice. As the surface water freezes into ice, the salt in that water stays in the surrounding sea. And that extra salt left in the sea makes the seawater denser. Because it's heavier, this salty water sinks deep, deep down in the ocean. Less-salty water flows in to take its place at the surface. Meanwhile, the sinking, extra-salty water pushes the deep-down water out of the way. All this motion creates an enormous steady current that eventually makes its way around the whole world, from Greenland to Antarctica.

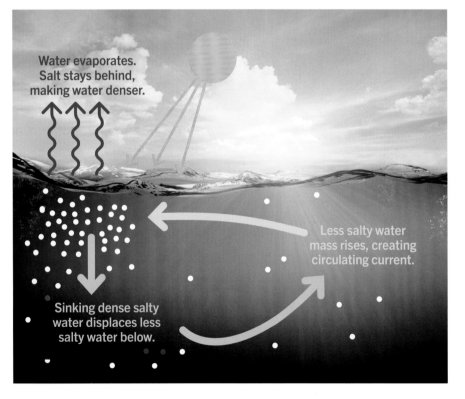

Water evaporates. Salt stays behind, making water denser.

Less salty water mass rises, creating circulating current.

Sinking dense salty water displaces less salty water below.

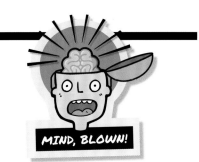

TRY THIS!

Sinking Salt Water

WHAT YOU NEED:

Salt

Drinking glass

Water

Blue food coloring

Clear baking dish

Pencil or stirring rod

Smartphone or other camera

WHAT YOU DO:

1. Dissolve 15 milliliters (1 tablespoon) of salt into a glass of water.

2. Add a few drops of blue food coloring.

3. Fill the baking dish partway with water.

4. Gently pour the blue salty water down the pencil or stirring rod, so it goes in slowly.

5. Observe! Photograph the mixture every 30 seconds or so.

6. Photograph yourself with the demonstration in the background, creating a scientist selfie.

7. After a few minutes, and after you've taken a few more pictures, pour your mixture down the drain.

Results: What did you notice? When you add salt to the water, this makes the water denser. The salty water sinks to the bottom and stays there. This is what drives the saltwater currents—the "thermohaline" [Thurm-oh-HAY-leen] currents—at sea. But why doesn't the dense water remain below in the ocean, as it does in your demonstration? Good question. Let's go there next.

The Rubber Duckies and Lost Nikes

In 1990, waves knocked shipping containers carrying 60,000 pairs of Nike shoes into the Pacific Ocean. Within eight months, some of the shoes started to wash up on the shore in Oregon. A year and a half later, more lost Nikes turned up in Hawaii. In January 1992, an accident onboard a ship dumped 29,000 rubber ducks and other bath toys into the Pacific Ocean between Hong Kong and Washington State. Over the next few years, the ducks turned up in South America, Alaska, and even Australia. Scientists learned a lot about the flow of ocean currents around the world from these duckies and Nikes! I wonder if anyone is wearing a pair of those traveling shoes right now.

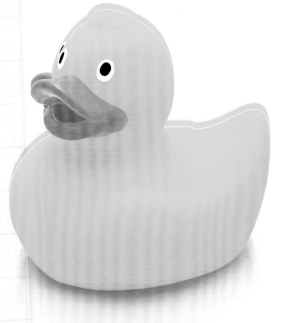

UNDERWATER WAVES

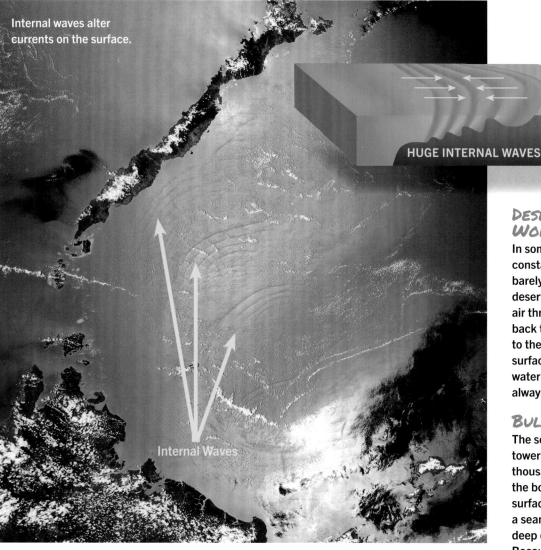

Internal waves alter currents on the surface.

Tides

River Flow

HUGE INTERNAL WAVES

Internal Waves

DESERTS AND WATER WORLDS

In some areas of the ocean, it rains constantly, but in other spots, it barely rains at all. These oceanic deserts send far more water into the air through evaporation than they get back through rain. They lose water to the sky. But the level of the sea surface hardly changes at all, because water from other parts of the ocean is always sloshing in.

BULGES AND DIPS

The seafloor rises in places to form towering undersea mountains. Tens of thousands of them are spread across the bottom of the ocean. The ocean surface bulges ever so slightly above a seamount, and it dips a bit above deep ocean valleys and trenches. Because of these very small changes, scientists can map the seafloor just by measuring the height of the ocean. They don't even need to look below the surface to know the shape of the seafloor down there!

UNDERWATER WAVES

That's right. Water waves rolling over water—underwater. They seem to happen where big rivers meet the sea, or where less dense warm water meets more dense cold water. Meanwhile, on the surface of the ocean, most waves are caused by wind and storms. Scientists are still trying to understand it all. Some think it might be the tides affecting ocean motion way, way far from any shore.

PALM TREES IN IRELAND

The vast, often frigid landscape of Siberia is the same distance from the equator as the southwest coast of Ireland. In Siberia, you can barely go outside in the winter, because it's so cold. But this part of Ireland has cabbage-palm trees. How is this possible? A branch of the famous Gulf Stream current carries warm water from the equator to the north and east, clockwise around the Atlantic. Part of the Gulf Stream runs along the southwestern coast of Ireland. The warmer water heats the air and keeps the climate mild. The summers are warm, the winters not too cold. And the Irish get palm trees, while everyone in Siberia is left shivering around their **SAMOVARS**.*

You've never heard of a **"SAMOVAR"**? Really? You need to catch up on your 19th century Russian novels, kids. A samovar is a fancy teakettle. It means "self-boiler" in Russian. Maybe keep one on your bicycle?

Floating sea ice caught in marine currents off the eastern coast of Canada.

UNSOLVED MYSTERY

What Stirs the Oceans?

➤ So the cold, dense, salty water that sinks at the North and South poles spreads out through the depths of the ocean, then mixes with the less dense, warmer water above. But how? If the water is cold and dense, it would tend to stay down there. Wouldn't it? But it doesn't. What brings it back up to the surface? In some areas of the ocean, tides force water to slosh back and forth over ridges and mountains on the seafloor, stirring up the sea and causing some cold deep water to flow up and mix with the warmer water above. Meanwhile, some scientists suspect critters. As the Sun appears over the ocean at dawn, and disappears again at night, all types of creatures swim down and up with the changing sunlight. Some researchers believe that all the little kicks from all these swimmers—some as small as one of your fingers—stir up the water enough to help mix the oceans; it happens every day—and every night. Critters? Animals? Oh yes, my friends. When you are ready, turn the page.

Marie Tharp

We still don't know enough about the deep ocean. Back in the middle of the 20th century, though, we really, really didn't know what was down there under the surface. The U.S. Navy developed instruments that could bounce sound waves off the ocean floor. Based on how long it took for the sound waves to return, engineers could figure out the distance from the surface to the bottom of the ocean (and back). They'd gather their data, then hand it off to mapmakers to create pictures of the ocean floor. Marie Tharp was one of these mapmakers, or "cartographers" (like the word "chart" without the "h"), and in the early 1950s, she discovered the Mid-Atlantic Ridge—a spot where two of Earth's huge rocky sections of the ocean floor are moving away from each other, allowing hot, gooey rock to well up and create a new underwater rocky mountain range. Despite her smarts and success, she wasn't allowed to travel on the research trips that gathered this valuable data because she was a woman. That's not the way it works anymore; progress has been made. Half the people in the world are girls and women. Why not have half the scientists be women?

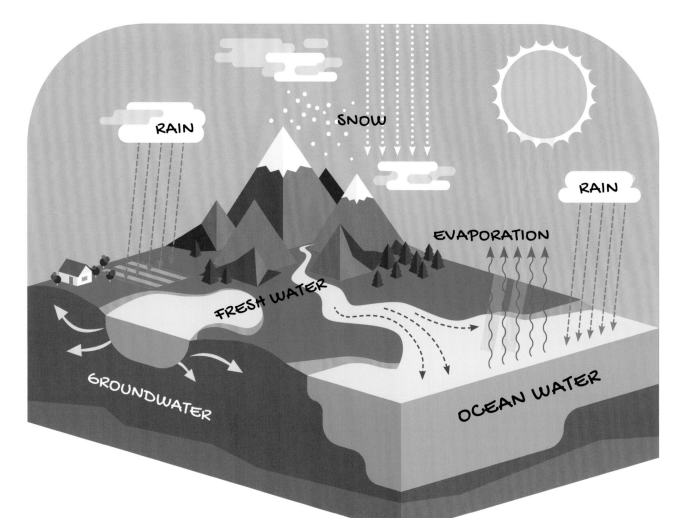

NEED TO KNOW:

The Global Water Cycle

➤ Have you learned about the water cycle in school? Sometimes, when you learn about the water cycle, which describes how water moves through nature, you'll be introduced to a diagram showing trees, soil, lakes, rivers, and streams. Maybe a mountain. A few deer on the hill. A friendly bunny or two. But some of my oceanographer friends get annoyed that many drawings of the water cycle show the ocean off in a corner of the picture, or even leave out the ocean altogether. The ocean, you know, 97% of the water on our planet. Go figure. Scientists aren't sure precisely how much certain areas of ocean contribute to rainfall over certain areas of land. But most of the evaporation (water going up into the atmosphere) and precipitation (water falling down as rain, snow, sleet, or hail) happens over the ocean. So when you learn or think about the water cycle, don't forget the oceans. The global water cycle? It's not just about what's happening near those bunnies.

Thanks, Plankton

What's the most common life-form in the ocean? Plankton! It's from Greek and German words that mean "drift" or "wander," and it describes all kinds of tiny living things that go with the flow of currents. They drift. Plankton deserve a lot of respect because they're the base of the ocean "food pyramid." Every living thing in the sea depends on plankton. And if not for the billions of tons of plankters (the members of the plankton), we wouldn't be here today. Some of them soak up sunlight and water and release oxygen into the air, filling our atmosphere with what we need to breathe. Others graze on this first group and in turn provide fertilizer for the ocean's whole system of living things. And if you don't think that's important, go hang around on Mars for a few days—well, for a few seconds. The Red Planet missed out on the plankton boom, so there's absolutely no breathable air. Here on Earth, half the oxygen we breathe was produced by a type of plankton! So if you get a minute later today, go thank your nearest plankter for its, her, or his generous contribution to society.

Copepods (Koe-puh-PODZ), like this handsome member of the plankton, make life on Earth possible.

BEFORE WE MOVE ON...

So the oceans are important. We wouldn't be alive without them. Almost all the water we drink comes from the seas. But we still don't know enough about them. For instance, where did all this water come from in the first place? Some scientists believe that icy comets and asteroids struck Earth after it formed, bringing enough water to fill the oceans. Others wonder if our water was here from the start, locked up inside rocks, and that it spread across the surface as volcanoes erupted. Do some science and find out for sure. Then tell the world about your discovery, okay? Great. Thanks. In the meantime, if you're thinking that ocean science might be in your future, I'll leave you with some words from a scientist friend of mine.

66 The ocean is the majority of the surface of our planet! But we understand it far less than we understand almost every other habitat or even other planets in our solar system. We still have so much to learn about the ocean. We still make amazing discoveries all the time, especially in the deep sea. If you're driven by curiosity, there's a lot to discover."

—OCEANOGRAPHER TESSA HILL

Evolution
The Fact of Life

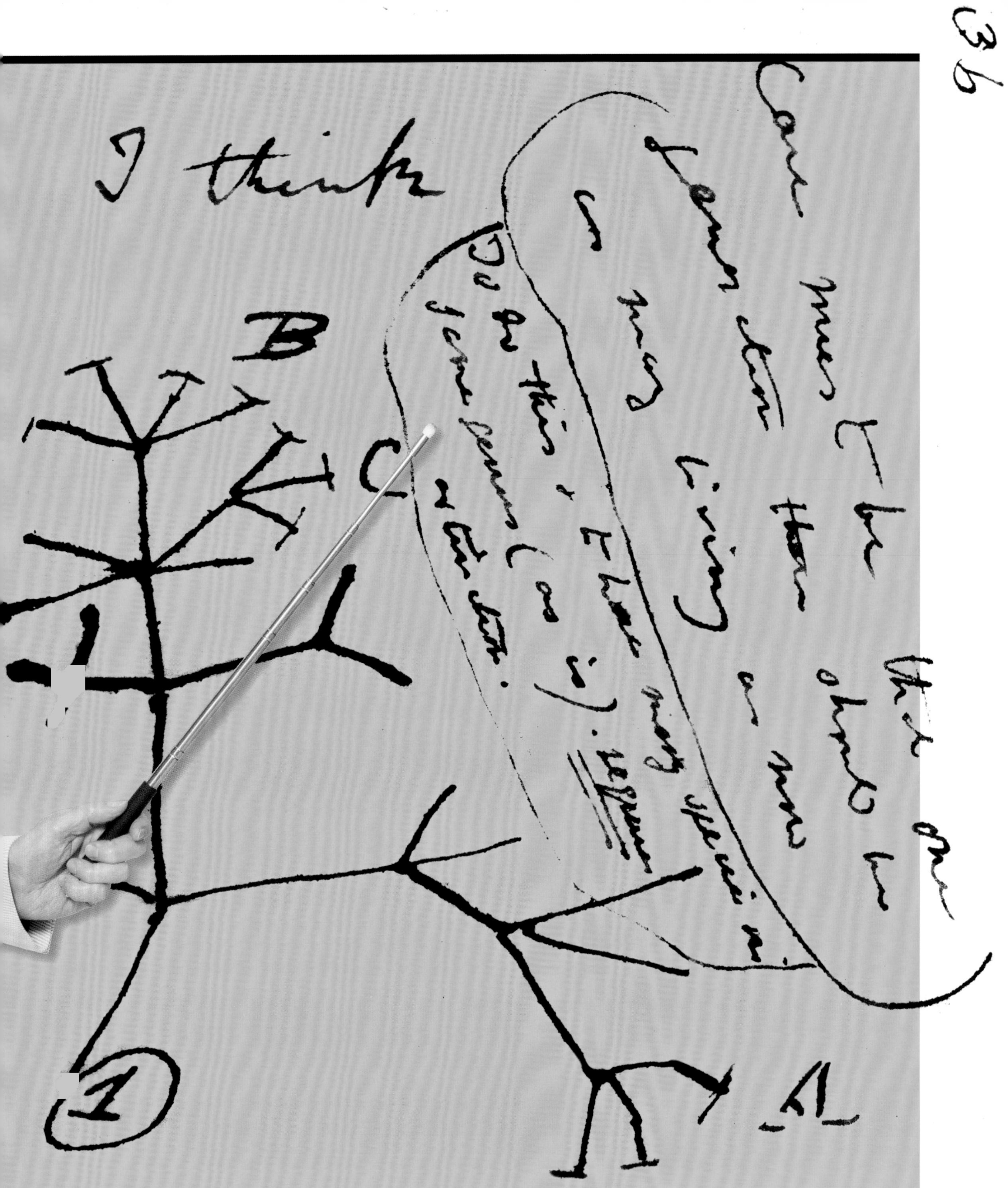
36
I think
1
A
B
C

Family reunion, summer of 1965.
Can you find me in this picture?

Mom and Dad

Mom and me at the beach.

Member, Troop 8 Hall of Fame.

> **This chapter is kind of a big one—**
it covers the main idea in all of biology, or the study of life. It explains the amazing mix of life on our beautiful blue planet. Yes, friends, I'm talking about evolution. Have you heard about it? I hope so. Stacey Smith is a scientist friend of mine. She studies evolution, and she says young people like you are much better than us older folks at understanding how evolution works. Not surprising. But maybe you've heard the word "evolution" thrown around a little, and yet you might not be sure what it means.

Let us start with a story. Every summer, the Nye family gets together for a big reunion. No, I'm not going to tell you where. And no, we do not launch rockets into space during the reunion. Not big ones, anyway. And not all the way into space.

So, the reunion. Many, many Nyes and relatives of Nyes come together. What makes us family? Well, my siblings and I shared the same parents. Our dad, Edwin, was a salesman who liked to be known as Ned Nye, Boy Scientist. Our mom was a pretty good mathematician and was a U.S. Navy codebreaker during World War II. (She hardly ever spoke of it. She kept military secrets till she died!) A few of my cousins usually attend the reunion, too. We're family because we share the same grandparents. My cousins' kids are all descended from that pair as well. We all look a little different and have different talents—I say no one can dance quite like I do (maybe no one wants to)—but we all share common ancestors. So we're family.

Well, here's what evolution tells us. Are you ready? You and I share a common ancestor, too. We also share a common ancestor with the bird that just flew past your window and the dog that just ran off with your socks—the trees outside in your yard, the weeds squeezing through cracks in the pavement, the worms in the soil, and even the hippopotamus that is now stomping through your neighbor's yard. (Maybe you should lure her back toward your place. Grandma's not going to want you to lose her. Actually, no. Keep reading. The hippo will be fine.) We are all related. No, not close enough for you to score an invite to the reunion, but still—we're part of the same big, big family.

< Previous spread: In 1837, Charles Darwin drew a diagram of an evolutionary tree. His later observations and drawings of birds played an important role in understanding how natural selection works.

➤ Your Ancestors Were Chemicals

Near as we can tell, all life on Earth traces back to the same ancestor. That ancestor's name wasn't Ozzie or Harriet, though. We don't know exactly what that original life-form looked like. It was probably a strand of chemicals made from minerals (rocky stuff) on Earth's surface that got a jolt from sunlight or ancient bolts of lightning, then naturally split in two, making copies of itself. Copying turned out to work well enough, and here we all are billions of years later. We don't even know whether it all started here on Earth, or if life hitched a ride to our planet inside a space rock from Mars. All sorts of chemicals and mixtures of chemicals have been in the nooks and crannies of meteorites that occasionally crash-land here on Earth, and in rock samples brought back by spacecraft from asteroids. Get this—the chemicals in space rocks are the same chemicals we find in all living things on Earth. Does that mean it's possible, or even easy, for life to get started just from the kind of chemicals we find in rocks? It's quite an idea to ponder.

➤ Changes and Changes and Changes

No matter where life started, when these ancient strands of chemical stuff made their copies, the copies weren't exact each time; there were changes. The changes kept happening. Some were helpful. Some were harmful. Some didn't do much at all. Each time one of these slightly changed life-forms had offspring—a fancy name for kids or babies—those changes were passed along to the next generation. They were inherited, the same way you might inherit hair or eye color from one of your parents—or your grandparents, or great-great-great-grandparents.

Over time, these changes started to add up. Living things became more complex and spread out all over Earth. Different life-forms started to look, operate, and act differently. Some survived and grew in number. Others faded into extinction.

After billions of years—an enormous, almost unimaginable amount of time—this process eventually churned out the amazing mix of life walking, crawling, swimming, scurrying, swinging, and soaring across our planet today.

Thanks to evolution, this planet of ours is one big, ongoing family reunion.

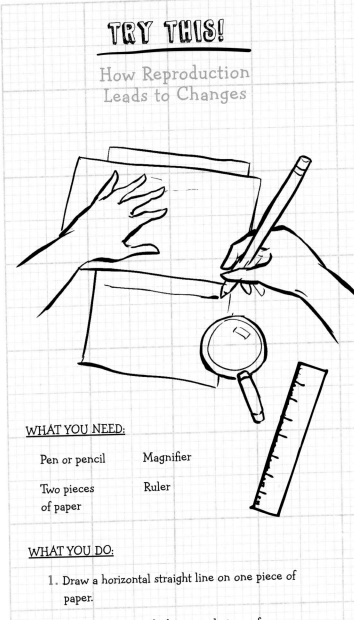

TRY THIS!

How Reproduction Leads to Changes

WHAT YOU NEED:

Pen or pencil   Magnifier

Two pieces   Ruler
of paper

WHAT YOU DO:

1. Draw a horizontal straight line on one piece of paper.

2. Cover the line with the second piece of paper.

3. Draw another line right below the first one.

4. Draw a few more straight lines, covering the ones above as you go.

5. Use the ruler and magnifier to see if the lines are really all that straight, and all the same length.

Results: No matter how hard you concentrate, you're not going to make those lines exactly alike. Sometimes a later line can sorta look like the first one . . . it doesn't turn into a square of anything. The same is true in nature, when living things make copies of themselves, or reproduce. The copies might be very similar to the generation before, but they're also going to be different in some way or ways. Slight changes happen. The more reproductions—the more changes.

A gecko with sand skin camouflage— it's evolution!

NEED TO KNOW:
Natural Selection

▶ This process in which small changes in the offspring of living things either help them survive, or keep them from surviving to have their own offspring, is called natural selection. Without any thinking involved, the natural world ends up selecting which offspring do well and live to reproduce, and which don't. The key is these changes keep adding up and adding up, changing and changing, getting selected and selected, over lots and lots of time.

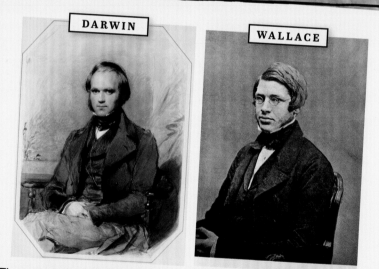

DARWIN   WALLACE

The expression "natural selection" was first published by a famous guy you've probably heard of: Charles Darwin. But he and another naturalist named Alfred Russel Wallace discovered the process, while they were working separately. Wallace wrote a letter to Darwin about it, while Darwin had been experimenting and keeping notes about the same idea for more than 10 years. They published a scientific paper together in 1858. You don't hear about Wallace as much as you hear about Darwin, probably because Darwin, living in Britain, managed to publish his famous book *On the Origin of Species* while Wallace was doing all sorts of research on the other side of the world, on the islands between Asia and Australia. These guys were deep thinkers. They discovered the key process of evolution without even knowing what goes on in the cells of all of us living things here on Earth.

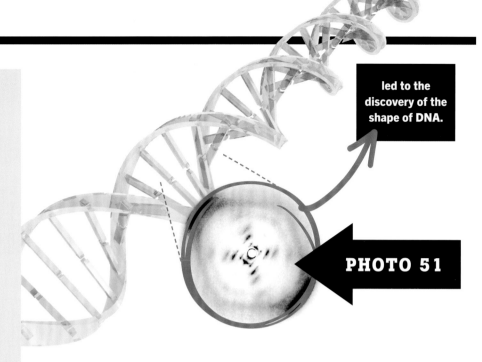

PHOTO 51

Rosalind Franklin

In the early 1950s, a young scientist named Rosalind Franklin and her student Raymond Gosling captured what she referred to as "Photo 51." It's one of the most important and famous scientific images ever produced—right up there with the Apollo 8 image of the Earth appearing to rise over the Moon. She used X-rays to see the shape of DNA. Her image showed that DNA has two strands wound around each other like two spiral staircases side by side. Two other young scientists, James Watson and Francis Crick, were also working to understand the structure of DNA, and they were shown Franklin's work without her knowledge. Many scientists feel that Watson and Crick wouldn't have been able to develop their idea without her images. Watson and Crick won the Nobel Prize. Franklin died young, of cancer, before the scientific world truly recognized her contribution. But these days she's known far and wide as one of the great scientists of the 20th century. The European Space Agency (ESA) named one of their Mars rover spacecraft after her.

NEED TO KNOW:

How Evolution Works

▶ All life-forms on our planet have a set of instructions built into their cells. These instructions are not on a paper page or on a website. They're strands and stacks of chemicals that direct other chemicals in your body to do their chemical jobs. We call groups of chemicals that provide an instruction or set of instructions genes. They help you grow and change into a walking, talking human. Genes are the reason your eyes are brown, blue, green, or gray. They help determine, along with some other things, whether you'll be able to resist certain diseases or be weakened by them. Can't drink milk or eat gluten? Blame your genes. Humans have about 20,500 different genes. They're all strung together and bundled inside that complicated molecule we call DNA. Once again, that's deoxyribonucleic acid. Try saying it again 10 times fast—please.

The common ancestor of life on Earth, that very first life-form, must have had strings of chemical instructions. I mean a gene—or maybe a few genes. Over time, making copy after copy, these genes changed. These little changes added up until we eventually ended up with the wonderful, wildly wild, beautiful mix of life we have on Earth today. Scientists have already identified millions of different types of plants and animals, or species, on our planet. But the total might be much higher, especially when we try to include all the different types of bacteria and viruses. We're talking about 16 million different kinds of living things, at least. Phew. This is yet another reason why we don't open our annual Nye family reunion to all the life-forms on Earth. That would be an event-planning nightmare. And I usually don't dance with wild animals. I've got two feet; most of them have four. We don't agree on which songs to play—it's always a problem.

Life on Earth:
A Very Brief History

>> Are you wondering how tiny changes in tiny genes could lead to a planet swarming with bugs and birds and hippos and humans? That means you're thinking like a scientist. So let's go deeper: While life-forms and their genes are making not-quite-identical copies of themselves, they might also be moving around Earth. A few members of a school of fish might get carried to another part of the sea, where it's warmer or cooler. A flower seed might get blown to a new meadow, or up a hillside, where there's less rain or more sun, or into a valley where there's less sun and more rain. A couple of birds flying over to the next valley to have a look around could be caught in a storm and never make it home again. Those birds could start a new population, and their babies are going to be a little different from the birds they left behind. With enough time, and enough generations, in the new environment, these life-forms will be very, very different from those ancestors and their descendants. We say the genes will "diverge." Every time fish, or flowers, or birds,

or beetles, or bacteria reproduce, their genes change a little (just like the pencil lines in your experiment). And because, in these examples, they're in new environments, some of the offspring will do better than others. Theirs are the genes that will spread. When some animals moved from water to land, and others remained in the oceans and seas, these once-linked groups couldn't pass changes back and forth to each other. They couldn't hang out together anymore, so they started wandering down different evolutionary paths. This big idea, divergence, is a key to producing the fantastic variety of life we see on our planet.

But we also need time. Time, time, time, time, and more time . . .

Normally, if we run an experiment in Nye Labs, we can finish it up in a few minutes or hours. Maybe a day. Earth has been running this experiment we call evolution for about 3.7 billion years. Those tiny changes in genes have had billions of years to multiply, spread, change, and change some more.

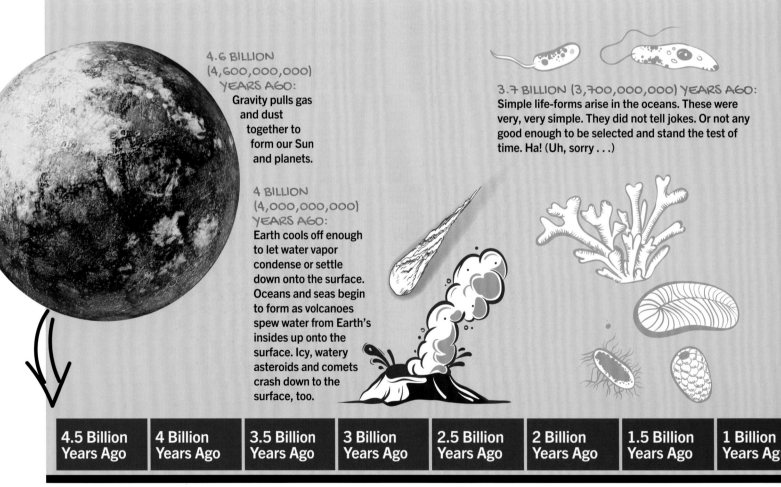

4.6 BILLION (4,600,000,000) YEARS AGO: Gravity pulls gas and dust together to form our Sun and planets.

4 BILLION (4,000,000,000) YEARS AGO: Earth cools off enough to let water vapor condense or settle down onto the surface. Oceans and seas begin to form as volcanoes spew water from Earth's insides up onto the surface. Icy, watery asteroids and comets crash down to the surface, too.

3.7 BILLION (3,700,000,000) YEARS AGO: Simple life-forms arise in the oceans. These were very, very simple. They did not tell jokes. Or not any good enough to be selected and stand the test of time. Ha! (Uh, sorry . . .)

4.5 Billion Years Ago	4 Billion Years Ago	3.5 Billion Years Ago	3 Billion Years Ago	2.5 Billion Years Ago	2 Billion Years Ago	1.5 Billion Years Ago	1 Billion Years Ago

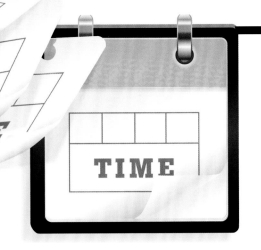

TIME

1,000,000,000

A BILLION is a hugely huge number.

Imagine counting one, two, three, four, five every second for days on end, no stopping for sleep or banana milkshakes. Even if you could stay up night after night, it would still take you a little more than eleven and a half days to count to a million. If you did it, great job. Nicely done. When you awaken from the nap you'll need after your first million, try counting to a billion. One billion is the same as 1,000 million. It wouldn't take you a few days, a month, or even a year. Oh no. Counting night and day, nonstop, it would take you 31 years and eight months to get to a billion! It would take over 117 years to get to 3.7 billion, and that's without sleep or milkshakes. What I'm saying is: 3.7 billion years represents an almost unimaginably long time. Earth has had living things reproducing and evolving for 3.7 billion years. So, evolution happens.

Sure, there are other forces driving evolution. Climate. Ecosystems. The changing surface of our planet. But the many different kinds of living things we find today, along with the fossils of ancient extinct living things, would not exist without the randomness of reproduction combined with time, time, time, and more time.

500,000,000 YEARS AGO:
Fish! Well, not fish, exactly. Not like the ones we think of today. But swimming creatures begin filling the oceans.

480,000,000 YEARS AGO:
Plants begin to grow on land, or maybe a few tens of millions of years earlier. Other life-forms later follow. Why? We don't know. Maybe the move was random, and they stayed for the salads.

225,000,000 YEARS AGO:
Dinosaurs, the ancient ones!

65,000,000 YEARS AGO:
A giant space rock hits. No more ancient dinosaurs.

4,000,000 YEARS AGO:
More animals and other species are roaming the planet including sorta human-like creatures. No people named Fred or Wilma yet, but they're a lot more complex than grasshoppers.

300,000 YEARS AGO:
The ancestors of modern humans, *Homo sapiens*, begin to thrive.

0 TO 130 YEARS AGO:
You were born. Hooray!

YOU ARE HERE

500 Million Years Ago

The Tangled Tree of Life

Think of life on Earth as an enormous tree with tangled, outstretched branches. That's how Charles Darwin pictured it. The trunk of the tree represents the first forms of life on our planet. The many branches, and the branches that split off from those branches into smaller branches and twigs—these all lead to the different types of life. The plants and creatures we see today, including us, are like the thinnest leaf-sprouting twigs at the very ends. Each split, where one branch leads off another, represents a huge change, when one group of a given organism became quite different from its former relatives. If we were to climb down this tree, and back through time, we'd eventually come to a branching-off point where we humans today split from other human-like creatures, such

as the famous Neanderthals (ancient almost-humans). Climb down farther and we'd find the point at which we split with chimpanzees. We wouldn't find chimpanzees, though. This spot would represent our common ancestors with chimps. That species would have some features like chimps, some in common with humans, and some we don't see around anymore today. Once again, the important point: We're not descended from chimps or gorillas or any other kind of ape you might meet today. We are descended from common ancestors. We're like really, really, really, really super-distant cousins.

Eventually, as we move toward the roots of the tree, and back in time, we'd bump into other animals that are less and less like us, and eventually we'd even meet

WRONG

The Sun's Made of Coal

> People studying evolution in the 1800s realized that evolution needed time, lots of time. Also, some scientists thought the Sun might be a big chunk of coal somehow burning in deep space. But as they learned more about heat and energy, scientists realized that a Sun-sized ball of coal (and air) would have burned out crazy fast—after about 3,000 years. William Thomson, a well-known professor and engineer, who later went by the honorary title of Lord Kelvin, imagined the Sun as a ball of rocks and gas getting crushed together by gravity— and getting really hot. With telescopes and math, he calculated how long a ball of rocks could keep the Sun shining. If his "model," or mathematical idea, was a good one, it would mean the Sun and Earth were about 100 million years old. That sounds a lot more like it, but still, Kelvin's model could not possibly provide nearly enough time for the evolution of the wildly diverse mix of organisms we see on Earth today.

Years later, other scientists discovered that sunlight is not produced by burning coal or crushing rocks. It's something completely different. We'll get to it in chapter 11. Although he did his best with the information he had, Lord Kelvin was off by more than 4.4 billion years. Whoops.

up with plants. As scientists study the history of life, and the branches and splits, they make changes to this story. For example, although Charles Darwin, in the 19th century, wondered if ancient dinosaurs and the birds we see today were related, we weren't sure of it until pretty recently. Scientists discovered new facts and relationships. They changed our view of this portion of the tree of life. But earlier thinkers were piecing the story of life together as best they could with the information they had. Science isn't just a stack of facts—facts are important, but it's the process of science, the scientific method, that helps us learn about the world around us. For example, when I was a kid, everyone figured dinosaurs had smooth skin like snakes. Later, we learned that most, if not all, of the ancient dinosaurs had feathers. It's part of the progress of our understanding. It's science!

WEIRD! SCIENCE

Evolution Is a Little Bit Random

DNA doesn't decide to suddenly try something new. DNA doesn't think or make decisions. It just is. Once a change in a living thing's DNA is passed along to a new generation, the whole question of whether it sticks or not, whether it continues to spread throughout the population of a species, well, that's far less random. Changes that help something survive—the long claws in a cheetah's paws that help it grip the ground as that cat sprints and turns, for example—generally stick around. The changes that hurt a life-form— like being unable to fight off a germ—tend to disappear, because the creatures or critters carrying them don't survive very long, either. That's evolution, the process of natural selection acting on the DNA in the cells of all of us living things. Whoa.

The Four Domains of Life

➤ The one thing all life on Earth has in common is ribonucleic [RIE-boh-noo-KLAY-ik] acid, or RNA. Even DNA is made with help from RNA. Down at the RNA level, all of us living things look pretty much the same. But c'mon, no one is going to mistake you for a mosquito. They're not going to confuse the kids in your grade with bacteria, either. Well, not all of them.

Scientists have thought carefully about what makes one living thing different from another, and that has helped us know more about us—you know, humans. Right now, scientists divide the tree of life into three or four different great big branches. All of us on the tree are made of one or many cells. Think of cells as tiny little factories or power plants. You're made of a few trillion cells. I am, too.

Far back in Earth's history, the trunk of our tree of life split into Archaea, Bacteria, Eukaryotes, and Vira. Then each of these branches split many, many times, in many, many ways, as tiny changes happened. But let's start with those four big "domains" of life.

Bacteria

Bacteria are single-cell organisms, and they have no nuclei, just like archaea. But their cell membranes are constructed a little different from an archaeon's. Bacteria are also everywhere. And I mean everywhere. They are on every surface you touch. They're inside your body, on your skin, thriving at every depth in the ocean, and doing very well in rocky spaces deep underground. Eight out of every ten species on our planet probably belongs to this family. Most bacteria don't affect us; they're just out there in nature living their lives. But you and I depend on certain bacteria to digest our food. And get this: If you count them all up, there are more individual bacteria in your tummy than there are people on Earth. Of course, you probably know there are a few kinds of bacteria that can make you sick, such as certain strains of *Escherichia coli* (*E. coli*, for short) that turn up in contaminated water. Oh, and bacteria were here on Earth before any of us were. They'll probably be hanging around long after we've fled Earth for our new home in some other solar system orbiting some other star—or somewhere. Show respect, people. Respect.

Eukaryota
[Yoo-KAIR-ee-Oh-tuh]

This is us! Humans like you and me are eukaryotes [Yoo-KAIR-ee-OATS]. But we're not the only ones. Worms are eukaryotes, too. So are butterflies and sea stars and cats and dogs. Oak trees and poison ivy plants, too. Basically, all large, complex life belongs on this branch of the tree of life. All the eukaryotes have nuclei in their cells (ours, too). And what binds us together are those fantastic cells, which are packed with miniature machines that complete all kinds of jobs within our bodies—whether that body is rooted to the soil, swimming in the sea, or kicking a soccer ball across a field of other eukaryotes (grass).

The word **"EUKARYOTE"** comes from Greek words meaning having seeds or kernels. Eukaryote cells have nuclei and a whole bunch of other tiny chemical machines inside.

The tree of life, in some ways, is more like a gigantic bush. But when we study the genes of all these different life-forms represented on this enormous bushy tree, scientists find proof that we're all related. We even share nearly 70% of our genes with sea cucumbers!

Vira
[VEE-ruh]

Around a million viruses are on your lips right now (no kidding). And look, with those particular viruses on your skin, you're fine. They carry genes, just like you and I do. But unlike you, and me, and squirrels, viruses can't grow or reproduce by themselves. Viruses, like the COVID-19 coronavirus that has caused so much trouble, need to invade or infect another living thing's cells to make copies of themselves. Maybe it's a little creepy, but they've been at it here on Earth for billions of years, doing their viral thing with the rest of us forms of life. Many scientists don't think viruses deserve their own branch on the tree of life. So far, we can't really trace them back to a single, common branch, and they don't work very well on their own. But neither do I. So I'm voting for the Vira. None of us other living things would be the same without the viruses out there mixing things up.

Archaea
[Ar-KEE-uh]

Each member of the archaea is a single cell, and each has no nucleus. They're microscopic. Archaea are everywhere. They're in the ocean, the soil, even inside humans. They might be the most common form of life on the planet, and their cell walls, what we call their cell membranes (the outer part that holds them together), are generally made of special types of sugars bonded to each other. The pattern reminds me of yarn in a sweater where the inside looks just like the outside.

Two Massively Important Points About: Evolution

1. Humans Are Not More Evolved.

Evolution does not have a plan or a goal. It's not trying to accomplish anything. There isn't anyone or anything telling living things to evolve. They just do. Tiny changes build up over time. The helpful changes stick around and are passed on through generations. Humans are the product of billions of years of evolution. So does that mean we're more evolved? Actually no—or NO! All the other living things on our planet right now are the result of billions of years of evolution, too. We're not even more evolved than the bacteria living in your belly. Sure, it's easier to see the changes with us. But other life-forms have evolved in less obvious ways. Take algae, for example. They've been here a while, and they're not driving around in cars like humans. But some algae have found ways to store energy using nothing but sunlight, carbon dioxide, and water. Scientists are now trying to figure out if we can use their tricks to make better fuel for our cars and airplanes. Algae don't build cars, but they could hide the secret to powering them.

Humans don't have the most genes, either! Even a tiny crustacean called Daphnia [DAFF-Nee-uh] has 31,000 genes compared to our roughly 20,500. Don't get upset. I'm not saying humans aren't amazing. We put people on the Moon. We might send them to Mars one day. And you? You're wonderful. Really. But all life-forms on this planet trace back to the same ancestor, and we've all been evolving for exactly the same amount of time. So from an evolutionary standpoint, humans are not that special. And we're definitely not more evolved. All of us Earthlings are still evolving.

2. We Are Not Descended from Gorillas.

Humans aren't descended from other ape-like creatures that are walking and climbing around today, like gorillas, chimps, or bonobos. We share a common ancestor, some prechimp, prehuman creature. You have to rewind millions of years of our planet's history, and climb quite a ways down the tree of life, to get to that creature. We're more like very, very, very, very distant cousins. I know. I said this already. Still, people make this mistake all the time. A source of the trouble may be those bumper stickers and T-shirts. There's a series of drawings of ape-like creatures that are supposed to show the evolution of humans. You follow the images from a chimpanzee on the left to a series of creatures standing straighter and straighter, until you get to the final modern human on the right, walking fully upright. Sometimes the image is closed with a joke—a figure sitting at a desk or dancing. But either way, it's wrong, wrong, wrong. We share a common ancestor with chimpanzees, but we are not descended from them or gorillas or any other modern ape. Evolution isn't a straight line leading from chimps or gorillas to humans. It's a branching, splitting bush!

Only Mutants Drink Milk

If you can drink milk without getting a stomachache, you can thank the flow of a mutant gene. We're not talking about flowing milk—not exactly. This flow is the movement of genes. Around 9,000 years ago, when our ancestors first started raising cattle in Africa and the Middle East, they also started chugging milk. This was long before grocery stores and vending machines and water fountains. Any reliable source of nutrients or fluids was a gift. Milk offered both. But there was one problem: The special type of sugar in milk can be hard for a human body to break down and digest. Back then, most adults couldn't really drink the stuff. But a few people had a mutant gene that made it easier to digest milk. This gene creates a protein that can break down those special milk sugars. Since these mutants had a more reliable source of nutrition, they were healthier than those who couldn't drink milk. As the milk drinkers had children, and those children had children, the gene spread. The ability to digest milk popped up in a few places around the world, and the genes flowed from one population to another around the globe as people traveled and raised families. Today, most people with this milk-drinking gene can be traced back to northern Europe, the Middle East, or Africa. Again, it's an example of what evolutionary scientists call gene flow. It amazes me every time I think about it.

MIND, BLOWN!

The Fishapod

Since evolution was discovered back in the 1800s, biologists have been thinking about which creatures came from which other creatures. They realized that land animals like you and me must have descended from ocean animals like fish. In 2004, one group of scientists went looking for, and then found, an amazing fossil of a creature that lived about 375 million years ago. This creature once had scales, and gills, but it also had a neck and front fins with thick bones that probably allowed it to prop itself up. Whether it could actually shimmy up onto the land isn't clear, but this so-called fishapod probably lived in shallow waters. They named it Tiktaalik [Tik-TAHL-ik]. It's a word used by people from the area where it was found, way up in the Canadian Arctic. It means "shallow water fish." And why should you care, young scientist? Because Tiktaalik is a creature that evolutionary biologists figured must have existed. They came up with a hypothesis about what its fossil would look like and where it must have lived. And then they went to Canada and found the creature's fossil! Their prediction was absolutely right—that's science!

All those hundreds of millions of years ago, plants had begun to grow on land, but animals hadn't made it out of the water yet. Eventually animals followed the plants. The Tiktaalik fishapod could be the branch on the tree of life that eventually—after a few hundred million years of change—sprouted the early versions of you and me.

For an idea to be called a scientific theory, it has to enable us to make predictions. Predicting that fossils of ancient fishapod creatures would be found, and where, because Tiktaaliks must have existed, is especially amazing.

BEFORE WE MOVE ON...

Look, I could write a whole book about evolution. Now that I think about, I already did. But rather than go into more detail about this fundamental scientific discovery, let's talk about some other discoveries that have changed the way we understand nature and our place in the universe. These next discoveries are kind of big deals.

chapter 6

Move!
How Everything That Happens . . . Happens

➤ **Here's a question for you:** What makes anything happen?
Put another way: What happens, when something happens? It means something
has moved; there's been some sort of motion. Plants and people move up and out as they
grow. A car is at one place, then it moves somewhere else. Water is in a cloud, then it
moves down toward us on the ground as it turns to rain or snow.

EVERYTHING IN OUR WORLD IS IN MOTION!

And it's energy that causes motion. Energy makes things go, run, or happen. Even big ol'
rocks that are sitting still got to where they are now somehow; something happened in
their past. There was motion and the movement of energy—guaranteed.

Nowadays, we call the study of motion and the science of the energy that causes motion
"physics." The word comes to us from the Greek word for "nature." I think of physics as
the study of nature's rules. There's an old joke: They say everything happens for a reason,
and when it does, that reason is usually physics. (Go ahead and laugh now . . . please.)
Many scientists think physics is the most basic or important scientific field of all. Ask any
physicist—the scientists who study physics. They think it's as important as science can get.

Because everything is moving, PHYSICS is everywhere.
The steps you take as you walk across the room? PHYSICS.
Birds flying through the air? PHYSICS.
Making a chair strong enough to hold you off the floor? PHYSICS.

In the 17th century, a scientist in Britain named Isaac Newton got to thinking about just what makes things move in the first place, and how something that's moving stops moving or changes direction. He narrowed it all down to what we nowadays call Newton's three laws of motion. By the way, when a scientist (like you, I hope) talks about a law of nature, they mean that no matter where you go in the universe, even to a distant planet orbiting some distant star, the same rule, or law, would apply, or be true. It's something to really think about. The three laws of motion that Newton discovered seem to be true throughout the universe!

66 Being a physicist is as close to being a magic worker as you can get in the real world. If you're a magician you understand how things really work. When people watch a magician, they see a miracle, but the magician sees how the trick actually functions. Learning about physics is similar because it helps you understand what's really happening even with everyday simple things. It's a very different way of looking at the world."

—PHYSICIST ROBERT BROWN

The Three Laws of Motion

THE FIRST LAW OF MOTION:

INERTIA

➤ Ask a book to jump up onto a chair. Won't happen. Objects don't move by themselves. Everything in the universe is going to keep doing what it's doing unless something or someone does something to make that thing move or stop moving. Scientifically speaking: Objects at rest tend to stay at rest, and objects in motion tend to stay in motion, unless acted upon by an outside force—something like a nudge, bump, twist, push, pull, or jolt. This is the first law of motion, and it works at the smallest level—on things you can only see with a microscope—and on stars and galaxies, even on the universe itself!

Your book, right now, is resting on the table or in your lap, and it's going to stay that way unless you give it a nudge. Or think about a bowling ball: Once it's rolling, it'll keep rolling and rolling. But it usually hits those bowling pins and changes direction. Come to think of it, the pins were happily sitting still until that rolling ball showed up, then they started bouncing and flying all over the place.

Physicists say everything has "inertia" [Inn-ER-shuh]. What this means is that stuff is stubborn; it just keeps doing what it's doing . . . or not doing. Test inertia yourself. Give this book a push. Don't get carried away—not too much. The book moved, right? In this case, your push was that "outside force" that set the book sliding along the table. And if not for the little force of the table and book cover rubbing on each other,* the book would have kept on moving—forever.

This little rubbing force is called **"FRICTION"** [FRICK-shun]. It turns the energy of the moving book into a tiny bit of heat. The relationship between motion and friction confused us human scientists for millennia.

Going, Going, Going...

In 1977, engineers, technicians, and scientists sent a pair of spacecraft called *Voyager 1* and *Voyager 2* out into our solar system to explore the planets. They gave each *Voyager* huge rocket boosts to get them out of our atmosphere—and all its air—and on their way. Today, decades later, those same two spacecraft are still traveling. They passed Mars. They flew past Jupiter and Saturn. They passed Uranus and Neptune. Out in space, there is hardly anything like air, and almost no dust, that could produce a force to act on these spacecraft to slow them down. So they just keep going farther and farther from the Sun, deeper and deeper into space. That's inertia!

TRY THIS!

A Coin, a Cup, and a Card

WHAT YOU NEED:

A card, like a playing card or a business card (if you don't have business cards yet, ask an adult)

A cup or glass

A coin (a quarter, a nickel, a euro, a yen, or a penny)

WHAT YOU DO:

1. Place the card over the cup.

2. Set the coin in the middle of the card.

3. Knock the card away with a flick of your finger.

Results: The coin drops into the cup after the card slid away, because the coin has inertia. It stayed over the middle of the cup even after the card was gone.

The Science of Seat Belts

The first law of motion is a great reason to wear a seat belt. When you're cruising along in a car, it's not just the car that's moving. You are, too. Otherwise cars wouldn't be especially useful. They wouldn't take us anywhere. Now, think about what happens if something goes horribly wrong: A car moving at 100 kilometers per hour (60 miles per hour) suddenly hits a very large wall. The car will stop, because it has been acted upon by an outside force . . . the wall. But you, my friend, will not stop moving. You will continue in motion at 100 kilometers per hour unless you encounter an outside force to stop you. Here's hoping the outside-of-you stopping force comes from your seat belt and perhaps a super-fast inflating air bag. But if you're careless and unbuckled, you'll keep going at 100 kilometers per hour until another outside force stops you—which might be force from smashing into the dashboard or the windshield. So buckle up, in the front seat, middle seat, or back seat. Gotta respect the first law.

THE SECOND LAW OF MOTION:
FORCE

(Psst!)

In the International System of Measurement (Système Internationale) the unit of force isn't a pound; it's a "newton." We usually just write capital "N." An apple weighs about a newton. In the United States, people still measure weight and force in pounds, like a one-pound box of butter. In Britain, they still measure a person's weight in "stones." A stone is 14 pounds. As an engineer, I can tell you: When it comes to forces, newtons really are way easier.

▶ Moving something requires a push or a pull, or what we call a force. If you push on this book, it's going to slide. But if you're reading this at a heavy table, and you give the table a push with the same force you gave the book, it probably won't budge. After all, the table is heavier than the book. The table has more inertia, and according to what Newton called his second law, you're going to have to apply a lot more force to move it.

Let's say you pick up a baseball and throw it as hard as you can—outside, please! The ball is going to travel pretty far. But if you grab a watermelon and throw it just as hard, I mean with exactly the same amount of force, it's not going to fly very far, and it's going to smash on the pavement and attract ants (and a few kids, maybe). But that would be wasteful—and we already talked about living things, like ants and kids, in the first few chapters. The second law of motion puts a little math in the mix. To get a book moving takes some force. To move a stack of 20 copies of the book will take 20 times as much force.

>> HERE'S ANOTHER THING.

If you were wearing a stylish space suit, and you were way, way out in space with that stack of books and a bathroom scale, something funny happens (I mean besides being in space with a bathroom scale). If you tried to weigh the books or yourself, the scale would say zero. The scale would say the books and you are weightless. But it would still take some force to push or pull the books around. You and they still have inertia. A scientist like you says the books have the same "mass," whether or not they're on Earth being pulled down by gravity. So do you. You have the same mass whether you're standing on Earth or floating in space. Think of it this way. Imagine trying to push an asteroid, or even the Moon, around (wearing a space suit, I recommend). They're not going to move—you are. Asteroids and the Moon have more mass than you do. So the second law of motion is really about mass and not about weight. On Earth, mass and weight may seem like the same thing, but now you know better. Way to go. (Weigh to go? Uh . . . sorry.)

Nothing shows off Newton's laws better than a big, beautiful rocket launch!

SpaceX Falcon Heavy rocket carrying 24 satellites, including The Planetary Society's LightSail 2, launches from Kennedy Space Center, 25 June 2019.

ACTION + REACTION

It's Rocket Science

Think about this: After you light a rocket engine, with every moment, with every instant of time that passes, the rocket weighs less, because there is a bit less fuel on board. It's been burned and shot out of the rocket engine. You know how much the astronaut or spacecraft weighs, so how much fuel do you start with? To solve problems like this, where one rate or speed is related or connected to another rate or speed, Isaac Newton in Britain, and at about the same time, Gottfried Leibniz in Germany, had to invent calculus, a new kind of math. In this example, it really is rocket science. Not bad.

➤ This one makes sense, but it may surprise you. Newton noticed that for every action in the universe, there is an equal and opposite reaction. If you can find a skateboard or maybe an office chair with wheels, try this: Stand on the board or sit in the chair. Now, using both hands, throw a basketball to someone. The ball will go one way; you and the skateboard or chair will go the other. This is how rockets work, too. When you see that flame shooting out of the rocket nozzles, the rocket is throwing burning rocket fuel down very, very fast, and the rocket is getting pushed up. The flaming fuel isn't pushing off the ground. It's the heavy fuel going one way that pushes the massive rocket the other way. It's also how an airplane gets around. Using a propeller or a very fast-spinning jet engine, planes push air backward, which makes the plane go forward. It's the third natural law of motion.

THE PHYSICS OF CONCUSSIONS:
HEAD SPINNING

>> Back when I played football for the Seattle Seahawks, in the year nineteen ninety never, I was always careful to avoid helmet-to-helmet collisions. But Newton's laws of motion can tell you that head-to-head collisions, and too many head-to-ball collisions, aren't a very good idea. Between your brain and your skull there's a thin layer of fluid. When the head of a sprinting football player smashes into the head of another player, or when a guy's head gets slammed down onto the solid turf, his skull stops moving, but his brain keeps going. The same thing happens to a soccer player when she takes a header on a long ball coming from the goalie out to midfield, or when you're in college, riding your bike on a sunny Saturday, and a sports car turns right into you, and the impact smacks your head against the pavement—before anyone wore helmets on bicycles. (I've been there and done that.)

The impacts squeeze that layer of fluid out of the way, as that player's or rider's brain smushes toward the inside of their skull. And, just like a twisting or rotating book on a desk (check the next page), the brain rotates, too. Once it runs out of room inside the player's skull, their brain rebounds and rotates back. That's the third law—every action has an equal and opposite reaction. All this jostling, moving, and twisting isn't especially good for a human brain; the damage can have long-term effects.

ACTION

For one thing: The brain crashes against the skull.

ACTION

For another thing: The brain rebounds, and rotates back.

The Twist

> We've talked mostly about forces that push and pull. But if you want something to spin or twist, it turns out you have to provide two separate forces, going in opposite directions. Take a look at that book on your desk. Place the fingers of your left hand at the upper left corner and your right hand at the lower right; better yet, use two pencils. Now push right with your left and left with your right. Two separate forces are working in opposite directions, and this turns or spins the book. The world isn't all push and pull. There's a twist to it, too.*

*

This twisting force is called **"TORQUE"** [TORK]. It's spelled with the "que," because it came to us from the Hawaiian word . . . I'm kidding, people. Torque was originally a Latin and then a French word. In Hawaiian, they have no q's, and their state fish is the humuhumunukunukuapua'a.

BEFORE WE MOVE ON...

These three natural laws of motion apply everywhere, to everything. You and I can't escape them. Neither can cars, trains, trees, flies, fish, rocket ships, or distant galaxies. But here's the thing. Physics isn't just about these three laws of motion. Not even close. Many other forces and laws and fancy mathematical formulas help physicists study everything from the smallest particles on Earth to the largest, most distant galaxies out there in the cold blackness of space. Speaking of cold, let's talk about heat. It's our next chapter.

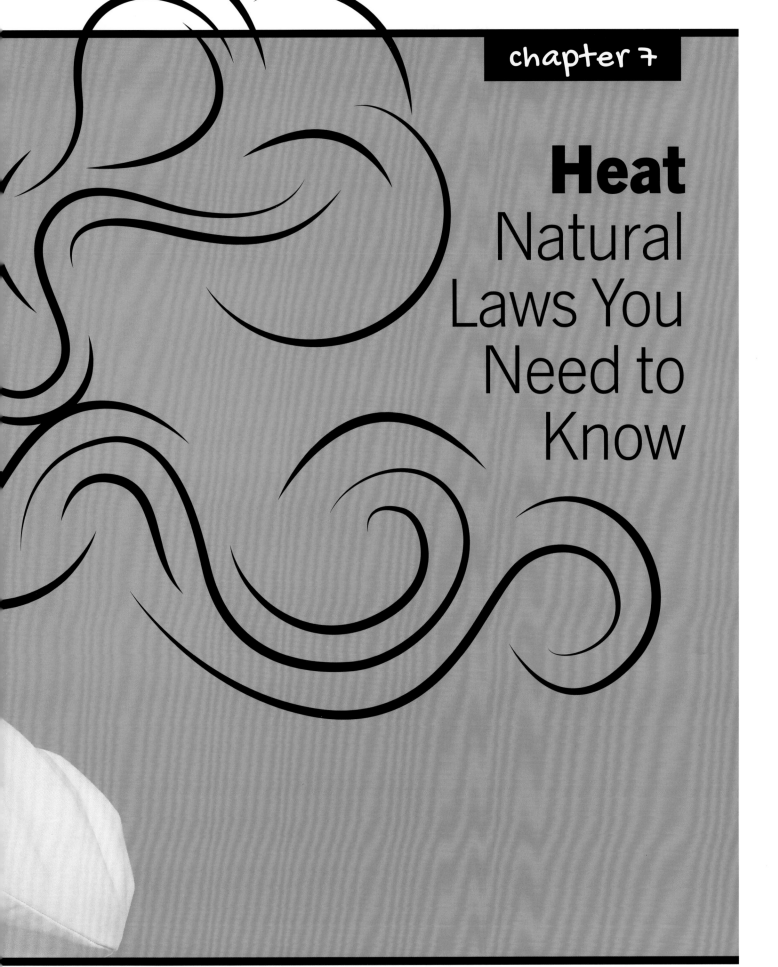

chapter 7

Heat
Natural Laws You Need to Know

NEED TO KNOW:

Natural Laws of Heat

> We all know heat when we feel it. The sun on your face. A mug of hot chocolate in your hands. The feeling in your armpits at the end of physical education class. A vat of warm green slime poured down on your head and shoulders as you try to climb the walls of your enemy's castle with ladders you made out of tree branches. You never forget these moments.

But what is heat, really? It's a form of energy. In science, we like to say energy is what makes things go, run, and happen. You can run because your body got energy from your food. Cars go because gasoline and batteries have energy. That hot chocolate is hot because your microwave oven or the burner on your stovetop added energy to that yummy liquid. Mmmm.

These all may seem obvious, and they are, I guess. But when it comes to heat, it's good to think about this big idea: Everything—the milk, the chocolate, the mug, and you and me—is made of fantastically tiny particles we call atoms. An ancient Greek deep-thinking guy named Democritus imagined cutting something, an apple maybe, in half and then in half again. He imagined that after a while, you'd reach a point where you couldn't cut the apple in half anymore. You'd have the smallest bit of apple there is. It would be the smallest bit of anything you can imagine. That's where the word "atom" comes from. It means "uncuttable."

Atoms, it turns out, hook or bond together in groups that we call molecules. And it's the motion or movement of atoms and molecules that we human scientists measure and feel as heat. That's right: Temperature is a measurement of the motion of molecules. We'll have more on molecules and atoms coming up in our next few chapters.

When you curl your cool fingers around that warm cup of cocoa, some of the heat energy gets transferred to the molecules of your fingers. Some energy makes its way from the chocolate to the cup, to your hand, and then you feel warmth. Same thing when you take those sips. The motion of molecules gets transferred to your lips, tongue, and tummy. When the fast-moving molecules collide with each other, you feel warmer. Speaking of hot chocolate, that does sound good. I'll be right back.

Three More Massively Important Points About: Heat

Heat is amazing! We're all familiar with it, but the way it moves around and changes from one form to another can be surprising. There are three main ways heat moves around.

1. Conduction

When heat moves between objects that are touching each other—like your fingers wrapped around that warm mug of hot chocolate—it's called **CONDUCTION**.* Or let's say you jump in a cool pool on a hot summer day. The cool water conducts heat away from your body. Energy goes from you to the pool.

"CONDUCTION" comes from the Latin words that mean roughly "to bring together."

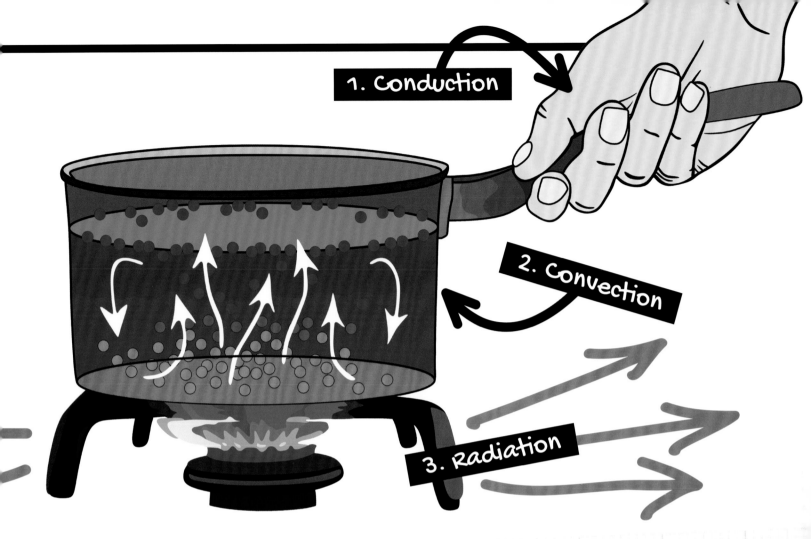

1. Conduction

2. Convection

3. Radiation

TRY THIS!

Conduction

WHAT YOU NEED:

Cup of hot water

Metal knife

Plastic knife

Stick of butter

WHAT YOU DO:

1. Get a cup of hot water, like you might use to make a cup of tea. You may need an adult to help you.

2. Dip the metal knife and the plastic knife in the water for 15 seconds.

3. Try cutting a slice of butter with each knife.

Results: The metal knife goes through the butter easily, because the water conducted heat into the metal. Heat did not conduct into the plastic knife very much. By the way, the metal knife can conduct electricity like a wire. The plastic knife cannot conduct electricity, like the rubber coating on a wire. Coincidence? Probably not.

I wish we didn't have to mention this, but for the 0.0001% of you who don't know: Do not ever put a knife (or a fork or a spoon) in an electrical outlet.

2. Convection

This is how heat moves when liquids and gases get in on the molecular action—when heat is being carried with the flow of a fluid. In science, anything that flows is a fluid. That means liquid water, milk, air in a hot-air balloon, and helium in a birthday balloon are all fluids.

Let's take a moment and think about a hot-air balloon. (I hope you get to ride in one someday. It's so quiet; it's amazing.) When air is warm, its molecules collide and push each other apart more than they do in air that's cool or cold. There are fewer air molecules in a hot-air balloon than there would be if the balloon were filled to the same size with cold air. The hot-air molecules collide with the skin of the balloon to make it hold its graceful shape. When its burner is running and keeping the air inside quite warm, a hot-air balloon gets squeezed up by the cool air around it. It's true to say that hot air rises, but only because cool air squeezes hot or warm air up. Not bad. We call this way of moving heat around natural convection.*

Now back to that cupful of hot chocolate—I couldn't keep writing without making one. But I accidentally made it too hot to sip. So I'll gently blow across the surface. The moving air molecules, and the molecules that sweep in behind them, will pick up some of the heat of the chocolate and carry it across the table toward my robot, which is sitting, watching me sip. (Of course I have a robot. I'm Bill Nye, people.) Some heat moves from the cup to the moving air. The drink cools. When you blow over the cup, you're forcing the air to move, so sometimes we say it's heat transfer by forced **CONVECTION**.*

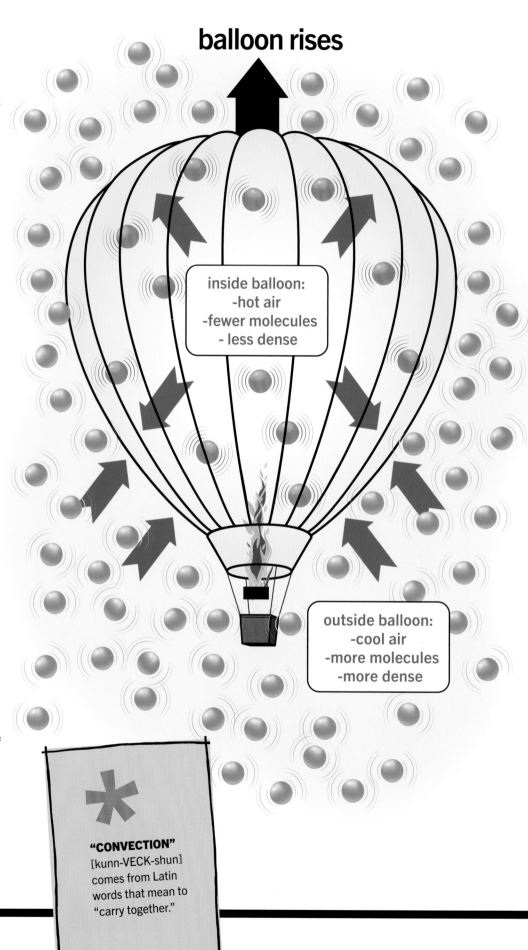

balloon rises

inside balloon:
-hot air
-fewer molecules
- less dense

outside balloon:
-cool air
-more molecules
-more dense

"CONVECTION"
[kunn-VECK-shun]
comes from Latin
words that mean to
"carry together."

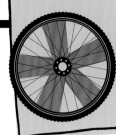

"RADIATION" [Ray-dee-AY-shun] comes from a Latin word that describes the spokes of a wheel. On a bike wheel, the spokes all go out, or radiate, from the center.

3. Radiation

Matter can lose heat without touching anything. If an object, like a mug of hot chocolate, is hotter than everything around it, it gives off some heat, even without your cool hands there to help. We say heat "radiates" away from the warm mug. The Sun's heat gets to us by **RADIATION.*** You get warm when the Sun shines on your shoulders, but you're not touching the Sun (ouch!). The heat radiation gets here right through the emptiness of outer space.

The remote control for your television uses a very small heat-producing lightbulb to beam tiny pulses or bits of invisible heat to your TV or cable box. With the right electronics, different patterns of pulses of radiating heat can change channels or adjust the volume.

Radioactive?

Some people are scared of the word "radiation," because we use the same word to describe atomic or nuclear radiation. That's when pieces of atoms (which turn out to be cuttable after all) come shooting out, or radiating, from the materials that we call radioactive. This is the kind that frightens some people. Radioactivity is not the radiation of heat. Radiant heat is a completely different thing.

So these are our first big ideas when it comes to heat. Temperature is a measure of molecule motion. Heat moves through conduction, convection, and radiation. I hope it makes you feel all warm inside (uh . . . sorry). Once you get that heat is another form of pure energy, the science of heat comes down to a few major rules. So let's lay down the laws for heat—what we call the laws of thermodynamics.

TRY THIS!

Radiation

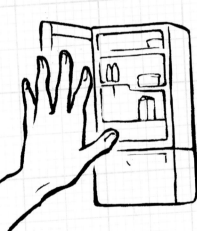

WHAT YOU DO:

1. Stand a couple long steps away from your refrigerator.

2. Open your hand, and face your palm toward the refrigerator door.

3. Have someone open the refrigerator door—better yet, the freezer door.

Results: The change in temperature you feel isn't the cold air inside—not if you're far enough away. Heat from your hand is moving from you toward the cool refrigerator. We say the heat "radiates" from your hand. It's heat radiation.

THE LAWS OF THERMODYNAMICS

THE **FIRST** LAW:

Energy anywhere in the universe stays in the universe.

➤ You can't create energy. You can't destroy it, either. It just moves from one thing or system to another. If you rub your hands together to produce a little heat, your muscles get their energy from chemical energy in your food. You converted it into moving energy, which in turn became heat energy. When we're thinking about **THERMODYNAMICS**,* the biggest of the big ideas is that energy can change from one form to another, and when it does, there's usually some heat involved.

ONE MORE BIG IDEA: Energy in all of its forms has been moving around the universe since the universe was formed 13.8 billion years ago—really. I'm the first to admit that that right there is amazingly amazing. Or maybe I'm second. I don't know. It's still amazingly amazing.

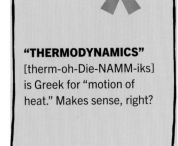

"THERMODYNAMICS"
[therm-oh-Die-NAMM-iks] is Greek for "motion of heat." Makes sense, right?

DEPARTMENT OF HEAT

BACK IN THE 1840s, the British scientist James Prescott Joule devised a brilliant experiment to measure heat energy and test this first law. He attached a small weight to a thin, strong wire, and connected the wire to a paddle wheel, which was in turn immersed in a carefully insulated—so the heat wouldn't sneak out—container of water. He ever so carefully measured the temperature of the water, then he let the weight fall and the paddle spin. The temperature of the water rose a little. He converted the energy of motion into the energy of heat—and he measured the relationship precisely. Thanks to his work, we now measure energy in units called joules. In the coming years, you'll see nutrition labels on food items with joules or just "J" on the package instead of calories (they're old-fashioned). Either way, we're measuring the chemical energy in your food. Burn it well!

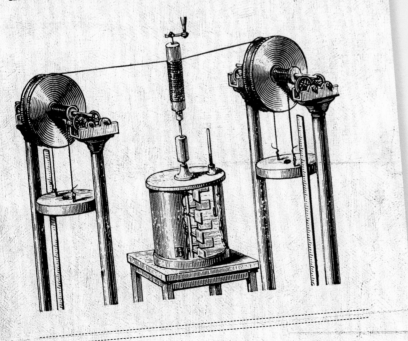

Tri·bol·o·gy

>> I'd like to take a moment and talk about . . . tribology [trih-BAHL-uh-jee]! No, it's not a scientific term for someone who studies tribes of people or trilobites. And don't worry if you've never heard of tribology. I think most people haven't. Tribology is the study of friction, or how surfaces rub and slide against each other. And friction is all about turning motion into heat. It's the essence of Joule's experiments. Although he may not have ever brought it up over a pizza, Leonardo da Vinci was one of the first tribologists; he carefully studied what happens when wooden blocks rub against each other. Of course, maybe Leonardo did discuss it over a pizza. I know I have.

Say you take a running start and slide across a wooden floor. If you have sneakers on, you won't slide. There's a lot of friction. Try this same test wearing only a pair of socks. Well, and clothes, too, probably. Don't want to scare people. You slid farther, right? That's because there was less friction between your happy socks and the smooth floor. Of course, if your socks and the floor had no friction at all between them, you wouldn't stop sliding. You'd smash right into the wall. You might crash through and end up outside, which could be interesting if you ended up in a garden or on a playground. But if the outside wall you crashed into was a few stories up in an apartment building, well, you'd be in midair looking for some friction. So stay inside, grounded, and study up on the first law, my adventurous future tribologist.

THE SECOND LAW:

Heat energy spreads out.

▶ The first thing to know about the second law is that heat only goes one way, from hot to cold. It never, ever goes the other way, from cold to hot, on its own. Never. This is the main idea, the very essence of the second law of thermodynamics. Heat energy spreads out.* You can bet that a lake will not freeze over on a warm summer day. If it did, somehow heat energy in the lake would have to have flowed from the cooler water in the lake up and into the warmer air above—which it just does not, cannot, ever do. This is a feature of our universe. Nature is not going to produce ice on a warm summer day, unless we provide or expend some energy to make heat move in the other direction. We can, and we do—with refrigerators and air conditioners—but that takes putting in some extra energy that we can't get back. While we're at it, in a way, there's no such thing as "cold." There is only the absence of heat, I mean, in a science kinda way. Whoa . . .

SOLID   **LIQUID**   **VAPOR**

COLD ⟶ HOT

The key word to describe this scientifically, and especially mathematically, is the word **"ENTROPY"** [ENN-truh-pea]. It's from Greek words meaning roughly "change within."

HELP WANTED

Of course, this idea is based on all we know right now. Who knows what new type of science and thermodynamics will be discovered soon? Maybe the universe will go in some new nonentropy direction. Maybe you'll be the scientist who figures it all out.

UNIVERSE ON

OFF

Uh-Oh: The Utterly Dull End of the Universe

This idea that some energy is always lost to heat may lead to a very dreary end to our universe. Billions of years from now, if all the heat from all the stars (and bicycles and air conditioners) is somehow completely spread out evenly through the vastness of outer space, so far apart that we can't use it in any useful way, then the universe will end up as a dull, lifeless void, with nothing going on. It's weird and very hard to imagine. But if this does happen, it's not happening soon. Our world has its troubles, but as long as the Sun and the stars are shining, there will be plenty of energy moving around to keep all of us moving around.

The Science of Bicycles

When we use any kind of energy, or change it from one form to another, some of that energy is always transformed into some heat. This usually isn't a good thing. It means we have to come up with a little extra, a little bit more energy than we're going to be able to use, to do just about anything. Like every other living thing on Earth and probably out there in the cosmos, you and I fight all the time against entropy, the second law of thermodynamics—the spread of heat.

When you pedal a bicycle, for example, the rubber in the tires is getting flexed and squeezed as the wheels go round. The pins and links in the chain are rubbing against each other a little. The metal or glassy balls in the axles of the wheels and pedals are getting squeezed. So is the grease and oil. All that rubbing and squeezing energy turns into a small bit of heat. This heat radiates off into the air and eventually out into space. That may seem weird, because you hardly notice it. But where else would that energy go? Why else do you slow down when you stop pedaling? Anyway, the point is that some of that hard-spent energy is always lost. But keep pedaling. Really. It's good for you and for the planet, for reasons we'll discuss later along about chapter 14.

THE TEMPERATURE GUYS

WE HAVE A FEW DIFFERENT STANDARDS FOR MEASURING TEMPERATURE, AND ALL OF THEM ARE NAMED AFTER SCIENTISTS AND ENGINEERS.

CELSIUS

The Celsius temperature scale is named after the astronomer Anders Celsius, who had his heat-measuring idea in Sweden back in the 1740s. He suggested that we call the temperature at which water freezes "0 degrees," and the temperature at which water boils "100 degrees." Most people around the world use Celsius temperatures. And degrees Celsius used to be called "degrees Centigrade." Either way, it's "degrees C."

FAHRENHEIT

The Fahrenheit scale is named after Daniel Gabriel Fahrenheit, a pioneer in measuring temperature. He published his big idea in 1724. He started with the coldest temperature he could produce in his laboratory using ammonium chloride (a type of salt), ice, and water, and then worked his way up from there. Looking back, it might seem a bit strange to have freezing be 32 degrees and boiling be 212. His scale caught on, though, because he also invented the mercury-in-a-thin-glass-tube thermometer. It was the best kind of thermometer you could get for more than 200 years.

KELVIN

William Thomson (good old Lord Kelvin, who tried to calculate the age of Earth, but missed) did some very important work concerning the nature of heat and how it spreads out. So we named a temperature scale based on absolute zero in his honor. A Kelvin is the equivalent of a degree Celsius, but measured from absolute zero. We don't say "degrees Kelvin"; we just say "Kelvins." Absolute zero is 0 Kelvins. The room you're sitting in is around 295 Kelvins. You may see lightbulbs that say 2700 K or 6000 K. It means the light given off is the same color as something heated to one of those super-hot temperatures. Our star, the Sun, glows at about 6000 K.

RANKINE

And oh yes, my friends, there is an old-fashioned absolute temperature scale that uses Fahrenheit-sized degrees. It's named after the Scottish engineer William Rankine [RANG-kin]. Absolute zero Rankine is also -459.67 degrees Fahrenheit. Early in my career, as a professional engineer back in the 1980s, I used the Rankine scale, but just a few people use degrees Rankine anymore. It's kinda clumsy.

When you read temperature with a thermometer, you're measuring the energy of those tiny molecules in motion. Moving molecules hit against the bulb of a liquid thermometer or against the metal rod of an oven thermometer and transfer some of their energy to the instrument. When molecules in the liquid of a liquid thermometer start moving faster, they make the thermometer's molecules bounce into each other and move farther apart. The liquid expands and moves up the tube.

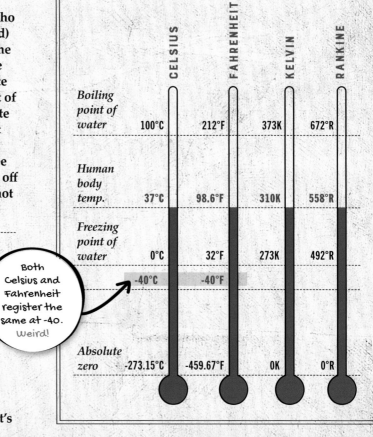

	CELSIUS	FAHRENHEIT	KELVIN	RANKINE
Boiling point of water	100°C	212°F	373K	672°R
Human body temp.	37°C	98.6°F	310K	558°R
Freezing point of water	0°C	32°F	273K	492°R
	-40°C	-40°F		
Absolute zero	-273.15°C	-459.67°F	0K	0°R

Both Celsius and Fahrenheit register the same at -40. Weird!

Almost Zero

To understand heat and matter, scientists zap lasers at atoms with just the right amount of energy to make an atom stand almost completely still. They've gotten atoms to just 0.00000002 degrees above absolute zero (degrees Celsius that is, read on)! That's pretty close to having absolutely zero motion. You might wonder why anyone would want to get anything that cold in the first place? Well, it turns out that under these super-cold conditions, clouds of billions of atoms become locked onto one another like a swarm of robots controlled by a single brain. This condition is called a Bose-Einstein condensate [KAHN-denn-sate]. Yep, that Einstein—the one with the wild hair and the wilder ideas we find in a few upcoming chapters. Albert Einstein and a brilliant Indian physicist named Satyendra Nath Bose predicted that if you could cool a group of atoms enough, they'd behave this way. Bose and Einstein made a prediction, and decades later, it turned out to be true. We learned a little more about molecules and the universe and the weird way our world works.

THE THIRD LAW:

You can't ever get to absolute zero.

▶ This last law is cold. Seriously cold. Heat is really all about moving, jiggling, vibrating molecules. Hotter molecules are moving faster than cooler ones. But do or can they ever stop? Suppose we got things really, really cold—colder than an iceberg. The molecules would move slower and slower. What if we could get the molecules so cold that they just about stopped moving? Well, the temperature at which motion stops, the coldest of the cold, is the temperature we call absolute zero. It's -273.15 degrees Celsius (-459.67 degrees Fahrenheit). That's 273.15 degrees below when water freezes. At this temperature, there would be absolutely no vibration. No movement. No nothing. The third law says, well, it says you can't ever get to absolute zero. If you try to get there in your kitchen (or your lab), the lab or the kitchen would not, could not, be that cold. There will always be some heat moving toward the thing you're trying to get to stay absolutely still—I mean molecule moving-wise.

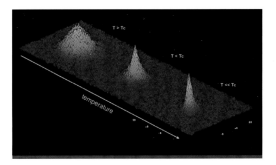

BEFORE WE MOVE ON...

So there you have 'em . . . the laws of thermodynamics, the science of heat. If you haven't yet grasped heat's importance, consider this: Away from any star, out in the middle of deep, dark outer space, the average temperature isn't absolute zero. There's just enough star light and heat to keep it a comparatively toasty 2.7 Kelvins! But compared to your 295-Kelvin room, that's cold. Real cold. Remember, heat moves from hot to cold. If it weren't for the air in our atmosphere holding in the heat surrounding our planet, all of our lovely heat would radiate away, out into space, and the top of your head would be exposed to the bitterly cold cosmos. But it's not. You're warm, or warmer than you would be if you were drifting through the endless void of space.

So while you're sitting, standing, or floating there all nice and comfortable, let's return to our warm and very busy planet, and learn more about how all these laws and tiny particles work together to make our corner of the cosmos so interesting.

chapter 8

Chemicals
and Their
Reactions

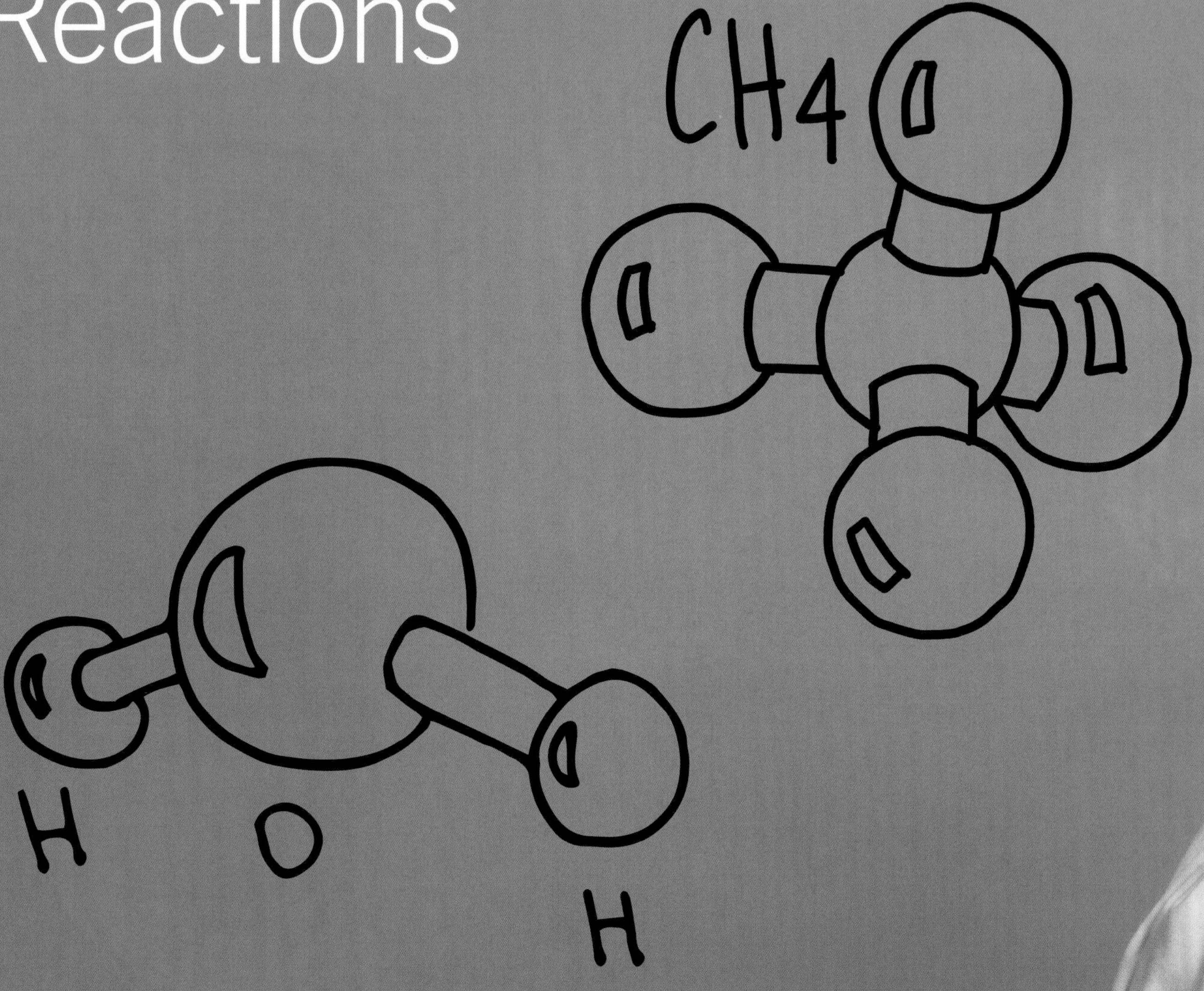

CH4

H   O
      H

O_2

➤ Everything in our world is made of chemicals.

You are a mix of chemicals. So is your shoe. And your sandwich. Your bicycle? The one with the tassels on the handlebar and the pink wicker basket on front? Chemicals. That sippy cup you used as a very young person, the one you probably should still use once in a while? Chemicals again.

All of these chemicals are built from atoms, those tiny particles we mentioned in chapter 7. When people first started using the word "atom" centuries ago, they may have thought an atom was the smallest thing in nature, that there was nothing smaller, that an atom really was "uncuttable." Well, it turns out that atoms are made of even smaller particles and those particles are made of even smaller, smaller particles, which we will talk about in chapter 10. To do chemistry, though, we only need to think about a few of these particles. You may have already heard of some of them. Here we go.

> " Someone once asked me if 99% of what we eat and drink is made of chemicals. I said, You're close, but no. It's 100%. Everything you eat and drink is made from chemicals."
>
> —CHEMIST GAVIN SACKS

Particles of Particular Importance

Electrons

Much, much smaller and lighter than protons, these particles zip around outside of the nucleus. They carry an electric charge that's just as big as the charge of a proton—only exactly the opposite. Electrons have a negative charge.

electron orbitals

Scientists describe electrons as being in one area but never in one place. Areas where the electron might be are often represented by puffy patterns called orbitals.

There's an old dad-style joke:

You know why you can never trust an atom? Because atoms make up everything. Yes, my friends, trust me, or trust the last few centuries of science: Atoms are what everything is made of, and atoms are made up of protons, neutrons, and electrons.

Nucleus

Protons

These bits of matter are part of an atom's nucleus. The prefix, or beginning, of the word "proton" reminds us that they carry a "positive" electric "charge." You've felt electric charges, if you've ever rubbed a balloon on your hair (or a sweater) and brought it near the back of your hand. The hairs on your skin are pulled toward the balloon by the invisible force of electric charges.

Neutrons

While these little particles are in the nucleus, too, and they weigh almost exactly as much as protons, they don't have any electric charge. We say they are "neutral." That's the "neu" in neutron. You have probably seen the letter "N" on the instrument panel of a car. It stands for neutral; the motor will not push the car forward or backward—neutral.

>> Each atom has a certain number of protons. Over the last couple hundred years, we have figured out ways to count the number of protons in any type of atom. We call any atom, with its specific (countable) number of protons, a chemical element.

Oxygen is a chemical element (8 protons). So are hydrogen (1 proton), carbon (6 protons), and gold (79 protons—show-off). They're all elements.

Everything in nature is made of or from one or more of just 92 of these chemical elements. As of this writing, scientists have created another 26 not-found-in-nature elements for a total of 118. But the human-made elements don't hang around very long; they change with time and break apart. If they existed billions of years ago when the Sun was formed, they've all changed into the ones we find today. The first 92, what we call the natural elements, are the ones we mostly need to think about. It's a very small number, really. Action figures, bridges, cupcakes, stars, planets, people, trees, fish, giraffes, crosswalk paint, and that sippy cup—all from just 92 elements!

All the elements are organized into something called the periodic table of elements. It was proposed and discovered by Dmitri Mendeleev in Russia in 1869. This table is among the greatest discoveries in human history. It doesn't just list all the elements; the periodic table tells you which elements will hook up or bond with which other elements. Mendeleev even used it to predict the existence of elements that had not yet been discovered back then, as well as their melting points. And then scientists dug around and found these elements; they melt at the very temperatures Mendeleev predicted. Amazing!

The table tells us that some chemicals will bond like two best friends when they meet. Others will explode. And still more just won't mix at all. By understanding the periodic table, we've created materials never before found in nature. We've harnessed the energy that makes farming our food, taking pictures from space, and printing books like this possible. Yet the periodic table turns out to be organized in a remarkably simple way.

Each element has an atomic mass, too, measured in grams. It's the mass of 6.022 hundred-billion-trillion atoms. This huge number, used to measure the mass of tiny atoms, is based on a whole lot of experiments. I hope someday you'll want to learn more about the scientist named Amedeo Avogadro and what came to be called Avogadro's number. Tables like this can carry a lot of info. Let's get started by meeting a few of these amazing elements.

HYDROGEN
Most common element in the cosmos.

| 1 |
| H |
| Hydrogen |
| 1.01 |

number of protons

element's symbol

element's name

mass: protons + neutrons (other tiny particles add nearly nothing)

3 Li Lithium 6.94	4 Be Beryllium 9.01				
11 Na Sodium 22.99	12 Mg Magnesium 24.31				
19 K Potassium 39.10	20 Ca Calcium 40.08	21 Sc Scandium 45.00	22 Ti Titanium 47.87	23 V Vanadium 50.94	24 Cr Chromium 52.00
37 Rb Rubidium 85.47	38 Sr Strontium 87.62	39 Y Yttrium 88.91	40 Zr Zirconium 91.22	41 Nb Niobium 92.91	42 Mo Molybdenum 95.94
55 Cs Cesium 132.91	56 Ba Barium 137.33		72 Hf Hafnium 178.49	73 Ta Tantalum 180.95	74 W Tungsten 183.84
87 Fr Francium (223)	88 Ra Radium (226)		104 Rf Rutherfordium (261)	105 Db Dubnium (262)	106 Sg Seaborgium (266)

Masses in parentheses can transmute.

| 57 La Lanthanum 138.91 | 58 Ce Cerium 140.12 | 59 Pr Praseodymium 140.91 |
| 89 Ac Actinium (227) | 90 Th Thorium 232.04 | 91 Pa Protactinium 231.04 |

Elemental All-Stars

H Hydrogen

Hydrogen is the first element in the table because it has one proton. Hydrogen is the most common element in the universe. It's kinda special, because of the way it hooks up with so many other elements. Without hydrogen, we wouldn't have water, or sunshine, or sugar, or paper, or even people.

He Helium

After hydrogen, helium, with just two protons, comes next, and it's a totally different kind of element. Helium behaves in a completely different way because of that one extra proton. Unlike hydrogen, it doesn't connect with anything. There's no "helium water." There's no "helium sugar" or "helium plastic." It's what we call a noble gas, which means it normally doesn't bond with any other element. (I guess we think if someone is "noble," they won't get involved with crooks. They don't bond with bad guys, or something. Anyway, in chemistry, the word "noble" has stuck with us for centuries.)

C Carbon

Let's skip ahead a little. At atomic number six, we find carbon with its six protons. You may have heard of carbon dioxide, carbon emissions, and carbon footprints. Carbon's importance has to do with how easily carbon bonds with other elements. This element bonds with itself, too. That's how you get graphite in your pencil and perfectly clear diamonds—it's all carbon. I like to think of trees as great big columns of carbon (which gets pulled not up through their roots, but right out of the air).

Bill's Periodic Table of Science

	2 **He** Helium 4.00

solids	metalloids, almost metal
liquids	natural, radioactive
gasses	human-made & radioactive
	solid/gas, same time

5 **B** Boron 10.81	6 **C** Carbon 12.01	7 **N** Nitrogen 14.01	8 **O** Oxygen 16.00	9 **F** Fluorine 19.00	10 **Ne** Neon 20.18
13 **Al** Aluminum 26.98	14 **Si** Silicon 28.09	15 **P** Phosphorus 30.97	16 **S** Sulfur 32.07	17 **Cl** Chlorine 35.45	18 **Ar** Argon 39.95

25 **Mn** Manganese 54.94	26 **Fe** Iron 55.85	27 **Co** Cobalt 58.93	28 **Ni** Nickel 58.69	29 **Cu** Copper 63.55	30 **Zn** Zinc 65.41	31 **Ga** Gallium 69.72	32 **Ge** Germanium 72.64	33 **As** Arsenic 74.92	34 **Se** Selenium 78.96	35 **Br** Bromine 79.90	36 **Kr** Krypton 83.80
43 **Tc** Technetium (98)	44 **Ru** Ruthenium 101.07	45 **Rh** Rhodium 102.91	46 **Pd** Palladium 106.42	47 **Ag** Silver 107.87	48 **Cd** Cadmium 112.41	49 **In** Indium 114.82	50 **Sn** Tin 118.71	51 **Sb** Antimony 121.76	52 **Te** Tellurium 127.60	53 **I** Iodine 126.90	54 **Xe** Xenon 131.29
75 **Re** Rhenium 186.21	76 **Os** Osmium 190.23	77 **Ir** Iridium 192.22	78 **Pt** Platinum 195.08	79 **Au** Gold 196.97	80 **Hg** Mercury 200.59	81 **Tl** Thallium 204.38	82 **Pb** Lead 207.21	83 **Bi** Bismuth 208.98	84 **Po** Polonium (209)	85 **At** Astatine (210)	86 **Rn** Radon (222)
107 **Bh** Bohrium (264)	108 **Hs** Hassium (277)	109 **Mt** Meitnerium (268)	110 **Ds** Darmstadtium (281)	111 **Rg** Roentgenium (272)	112 **Cn** Copernicium (285)	113 **Nh** Nihonium (286)	114 **Fl** Flerovium (289)	115 **Mc** Moscovium (288)	116 **Lv** Livermorium (293)	117 **Ts** Tennessine (294)	118 **Og** Oganesson (294)

60 **Nd** Neodymium 144.24	61 **Pm** Promethium (145)	62 **Sm** Samarium 150.36	63 **Eu** Europium 151.96	64 **Gd** Gadolinium 157.25	65 **Tb** Terbium 158.93	66 **Dy** Dysprosium 162.50	67 **Ho** Holmium 164.93	68 **Er** Erbium 167.26	69 **Tm** Thulium 168.93	70 **Yb** Ytterbium 173.04	71 **Lu** Lutetium 174.97
92 **U** Uranium 238.03	93 **Np** Neptunium (237)	94 **Pu** Plutonium (244)	95 **Am** Americium (243)	96 **Cm** Curium (247)	97 **Bk** Berkelium (247)	98 **Cf** Californium (251)	99 **Es** Einsteinium (252)	100 **Fm** Fermium (257)	101 **Md** Mendelevium (258)	102 **No** Nobelium (259)	103 **Lr** Lawrencium (262)

Li Lithium

Moving back now, we have lithium, which has three protons. These days, lithium is kind of critical, too. Many of the batteries that power our smartphones, computers, and electric cars need lithium. Humans discovered it, separated it from all the other elements, and then understood how we could use it. Amazing.

O Oxygen

At atomic number eight we find oxygen. About one-fifth of our atmosphere is oxygen. It makes up almost half the Earth's crust, or the rocks on Earth's surface. Oxygen really, really reacts with other elements. It makes iron and steel rust. Oxygen makes your blood turn red. We use it to get energy out of the food we eat.

>> We could keep going along the periodic table. We could discover silver (number 47) and iridium (77). We could talk about aluminum (13), which we use to make airplanes, bicycles, and popcorn popping pots. I have a bicycle called a "6-13" because it's made of both carbon (6) and aluminum (13). These days, we can count and study all the way up to element 118, oganesson, which has . . . that's right—118 protons. As much as I would love for us to visit every single element in the table, I have to leave most of that work to you, chemist-in-training. This is a big book. We have a lot to cover between these covers.

Massively Important Point About:
Why Chemicals Bond

What if you teased helium? What if you said, "Hey, helium—you got a problem with this chemistry?" Well, helium wouldn't care—it doesn't react (ha, ha, ha . . . sorry).

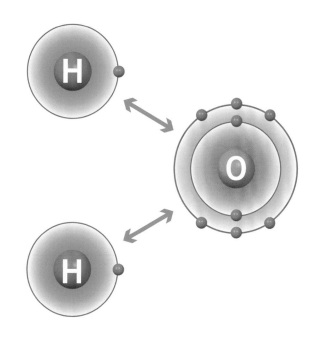

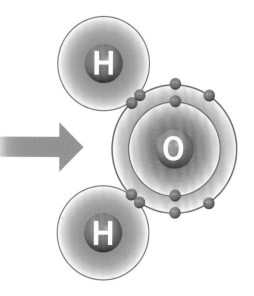

Why do any of these chemicals stick together in the first place? Great question. Even if I'm the one who asked. The answer: electrons. Chemical reactions are all about when, how, and how strongly elements share or exchange their electrons. These little particles have been around since the very beginning of the universe, and while they're attracted to the positively charged nucleus at the center of atoms, they never get too close.

Scientists have discovered that electrons organize around the outside of the nucleus into different energy levels—called orbitals or shells. Different orbitals can hold different numbers of electrons. As we go up in atomic number—I mean as we add protons—the orbitals or shells fill up. Electrons occupy higher and higher levels. If an atom has one or more openings or spaces available on one of those outer shells or orbitals, then it might share or exchange an electron with another atom, and form a bond. And if its outermost energy level is full, then it doesn't react at all.

The word **"HYDROGEN"** comes from the Greek words that mean "making water." You've probably heard of H_2O.

The first chemical element in our glorious table, **HYDROGEN,*** has one proton and only one electron in its orbital. For every atom you'll ever meet, this first energy level can hold two electrons. So hydrogen atoms everywhere have room for another electron. That's why hydrogen is ready to react with another chemical that has an electron to share or spare—including itself. At a science center, or on the Internet, you may see a demonstration involving a balloon filled with hydrogen gas. It's made of molecules of two hydrogen atoms. It bonds with itself that easily. It also bonds with oxygen easily. When I worked at the Pacific Science Center in Seattle, I reacted hydrogen and oxygen every weekend. When they combine fast, they explode! Oh, it's big fun. After the explosion, the hydrogen and oxygen bond together to make . . . water, a tiny bit that ends up as moisture in the air.

Helium, on the other hand, has two electrons. Its first and only orbital is always full, and it stays full. Helium normally doesn't form a bond with any other element. It's noble, and it's pretty much always just He.

THANKS, CARBON, FOR LIFE

Carbon is especially important because of its electron situation. Like any atom, carbon has electrons in those cloudy shells around its nucleus. Check your table and you'll see that carbon has six electrons in all, to match the six protons packed into its nucleus. But it has room for 10 electrons. That leaves four spots available for a chemical bond. And that is why carbon is such an important element. Because it's reactive! If carbon had feelings like, say, a puppy, carbon would be very happy to cuddle up with other elements to fill those empty spots, the way a puppy nuzzles up against your ankle while you're watching an episode of *Bill Nye the Science Guy*. One of the stronger bonds you'll ever encounter (after you and your puppy) is when one carbon bonds with another. It's one of the absolutely essential ingredients in life. You and I and everyone you know are all carbon-based life-forms.

>> Could you make life out of something else? Science fiction writers have invented stories about silicon-based life-forms. And silicon isn't a bad choice. It's right below carbon on the table, so it has a few electron holes to fill. But you'd probably need a world with a different temperature, and a thicker atmosphere. Here on Earth, where we're from, carbon is ideal.

TRY THIS!

Chemically Ballooning Yeast

WHAT YOU NEED:

Warm water (120 milliliters, or ½ cup)
Plastic bottle, 1- or 2-liter
Sugar, 5 milliliters (1 teaspoon)
Packet of yeast
Balloon

WHAT YOU DO:

1. Pour the warm water into the bottle.

2. Add the sugar.

3. Swirl or shake the water to dissolve the sugar.

4. Add the yeast.

5. Stretch the balloon over the top of the bottle.

6. Watch for bubbles and the balloon inflating. It takes just a few minutes.

Results: The yeast is carrying out a chemical reaction. It takes in sugar chemicals, and gives off molecules of carbon dioxide, or CO_2. By the way, that's just what animals like you do, too. Guess what else: You could take this water-yeast mixture, add about 350 milliliters of flour, 5 milliliters of salt, 15 ml of olive oil, knead or stretch the mixture till it's evenly gooey, roll it out thin, and make a pizza crust. Just sayin'.

Rates of Reaction

Who wants to wait around for something when you can make it happen faster? Chemists use various tricks and techniques to increase what we call the rate of reaction, or how fast a chemical reaction happens. Even though chemists are usually handling samples of stuff that are plenty big enough to see, a chemical reaction happens between the invisibly tiny, tiny atoms and molecules that make up that sample. In a reaction, you're trying to get these tiny bits to collide or bump into each other. When you increase the rate of reaction in a chemical experiment, you're hurrying things up. My chemist friend Victoria Brennan suggested an easy way to think about increasing rates of reaction.

Gedanken*: *Kids as Molecules*

Imagine a bunch of other students in a classroom. Pretend your goal is to get all of them to bump into each other, like human molecules. Now, think about the three tricks chemists use to boost reaction rates—to get those kids bumping into each other more:

1. INCREASE TEMPERATURE

If all the kids in our imaginary classroom are exhausted, or kind of moping around because it's Monday morning, those collisions aren't going to happen too quickly. But if we add a spark to the room and speed up all those kids—a few mice set loose on the floor, maybe?—then they're going to start running and jumping around, bumping into each other more often. They're going to collide with more energy, and more collisions mean more reactions. Increasing temperature has the same effect on chemical reactions.

2. BOOST PRESSURE

If you can't increase the temperature, or you can't find any mice, then another option would be to boost the pressure in the room. To do this, you could shrink the room itself, and reduce the space in which the kids can move around. Or you could get on the loudspeaker and call an all-school assembly in Mr. Nye's homeroom. Then you'd increase the pressure by boosting the number of kids in the same space. Jam a few hundred schoolmates into one room and they're definitely going to start bouncing off each other—and more collisions means a higher rate of reaction.

3. ADD A CATALYST

The idea behind a catalyst, which is a chemical you add to a reaction, is to quickly produce the same result without the effort of increasing temperature or pressure. A catalyst is kind of like a shortcut. Or in our classroom example, if we could make the floor super slippery, so that after one kid slips and bumps into another, that second kid bumps into a third, and on and on so that the kids could hardly stop from slipping and bumping into one another, well, that would be a good catalyst.

"I'm Only at 12%! How Will I Survive?"

The rechargeable batteries that power our beloved devices work because of chemistry. One part of the battery has atoms of cobalt, manganese, iron, or phosphorus holding quite a few extra electrons. The other part is packed with lithium atoms that are missing electrons. Because they're missing electrons, we call them lithium ions [EYE-ahnz], and they're positively charged. When you start using your phone, these lithium ions start hurrying over to the other side of the battery to get close to the electrons of the other materials. Electricity flows to your gadget. When enough of the lithium ions have moved, though, you start running out of juice. Your precious gaming, texting, and series-binging device goes from 20% to 11% to . . . shutdown mode! Recharging the battery is a way of pushing all those lithium ions back to the other side.

To-Do List: Find Better Catalysts!

You may have heard of what we call fuel cells. These are like batteries that combine hydrogen gas with oxygen right out of the air to make electricity. The exhaust, by the way, is just water. That's right, water vapor. But right now our fuel cells rely on expensive catalysts; the main one is platinum. It's used in jewelry. And it ain't cheap. Chemists are always looking for less expensive catalysts for all kinds of things, especially fuel cells. There's another assignment for you, young scientist. Go find us an excellent inexpensive catalyst or two.

Pocket Change

A nickel coin isn't made of very much nickel. Pennies are no longer made of very much copper, which is right next to nickel on the periodic table. Since we discovered how well copper conducts electricity, it's worth too much money to use for just money. In other words, making a penny with nothing but atoms of copper would cost more than a penny. Today, pennies are mostly zinc, which has 30 protons, and comes right after copper on the table. Changing one proton in an atomic number might not sound major, but it makes a huge difference in a metal's characteristics and, in this case especially, its cost.

Glove Boxes

Chemicals react, sometimes with explosive results. So how do you do chemistry without blowing up the lab? One of the instruments chemists use is called a glove box, which is actually a box with gloves. Go figure. The box is typically a see-through, sealed chamber. The gloves, which extend up to about your elbows, allow you to reach in and move stuff around—all while it's still in the box. The chemicals scientists work with are sometimes so reactive that they'll burst into flames when they come into contact with oxygen or even just the moisture in regular old air. So these glove boxes suck all the air out of the sealed chamber and replace it with pure argon or nitrogen—chemicals that hardly react with things. This way they can prevent nasty explosions. Then our chemist heroes can start breaking a few chemical bonds and forming some new bonds, which lead to whole new chemicals. How cool is that?

> " In a lot of scientific fields, you study nature. In chemistry we also get to create new things that have never existed before in the world. So it's a really amazing field because your only limit is your imagination."
>
> —CHEMIST RICHMOND SARPONG

THE SCIENCE OF SNACKING:
Why Apples Turn Brown

So, you bite a chunk out of an apple. Then you get distracted. Maybe you play a few rounds of an educational gaming app, or go outside and mow the lawn, or do a load of laundry for your family, without being asked. (I'm just thinking out loud.) Either way, when you're ready to snack again, and you return to your delicious fruit, you find the flesh has turned brown. The apple is fine, kids! But it has undergone a chemical reaction at the surface. Oxygen in the air has reacted with chemicals in the apple, including a complicated molecule that we call an enzyme. The reaction between the oxygen, the enzyme, and parts of the apple produces a brownish chemical. But it's still an apple. And you're still hungry. So, eat.

FASHION MOMENT:
THE COOLEST LAB COATS IN SCIENCE

Sure, one could argue that the best lab coats in all of science are those worn by the dedicated researchers at Nye Labs. But I might vote for the outerwear of chemists who work with chemicals that ignite when they come in contact with air or water. This is dangerous stuff! So many of them wear flame-resistant lab coats and capes. Yes, you read that right, capes. Well, why not? After all, chemists are a lot like superheroes anyway.

The Value of Horse Urine

WRONG!

> Some very, very smart people used to believe that you could turn many different materials into gold. These hopeful types were called alchemists, and Sir Isaac Newton himself was one of them. But they weren't all especially good about sticking with the scientific method. Back in the 17th century, a German alchemist named Hennig Brand thought he'd be able to pull gold out of an unlikely place: urine. He figured that if his pee was the color of gold, then it must have been hiding some of this valuable metal. (Or maybe he should have been drinking more water.) Brand collected a whole bunch of urine—from horses, beer drinkers, and others—then boiled it down to find his gold. Instead of discovering a new source of wealth, though, he ended up with a strange material that glowed in the dark. Today we know this stuff as the chemical element phosphorus, an atom with 15 protons and many uses. You can't live without it. It's in our DNA. It's great for storing energy in our cells, fertilizing crops, and glowing in the dark. So Brand might not have found his gold. But he did find fame, and his hard work with all that pee is proof that great science is often found in unexpected places.

NEED TO KNOW:

Acids and Bases

➤ You've probably heard of acids. They react with all sorts of things. They can pull one chemical out of another. When we think of acids, we often think of dissolving things. I put the acid vinegar, which dissolves salt easily, in my salad dressing almost every night. Really. Acids are one thing, but have you heard of bases? (Like in baseball, but without any balls or a field or players. Wait, chemical bases aren't much like baseball bases at all. Sorry.) Bases are like the opposites of acids. They can cause chemical reactions, too, but they work in what we might think of as the other direction.

WHAT YOU NEED:

Red cabbage

Water kettle

Oven mitt

Heat-resistant glass container or bottle that can hold boiling water

Second glass or heat-resistant bottle suitable for storing liquid

Sieve or strainer

Water, 1,000 milliliters (1 quart)

Two or more clear glasses or cups

Eyedropper or very small spoon

Vinegar

Baking soda (bicarbonate of soda)

Window cleaning spray

Lemon juice

TRY THIS!

Watching Protons in Acids and Bases

WHAT YOU DO:

1. Tear the red cabbage leaves into very small strips (use a blender or food processor, if you have one). Ask an adult to help you.

2. Boil the water.

3. Put the cabbage strips into the pot or glass container.

4. Pour the water over the cabbage strips.

5. Let it rest for 10 minutes.

6. Strain the liquid into the glass bottle.

You now have an indicator liquid. Because it's so versatile, we call this one a universal indicator. Red cabbage has a chemical called anthocyanin [Ann-tho-SIE-un-inn], which comes from the Greek and German words for "blue flower."

7. Pour some indicator liquid into a glass; add some vinegar: It changes color.

8. Pour some indicator into a second glass; add some baking soda: It changes to a different color.

9. Try the window cleaner. Then try lemon juice.

Results: When your indicator liquid turns red, that means the chemicals are acidic (contain some acid) and they are donating a proton to the indicator liquid. When it turns green or yellow, it means the indicator liquid is donating a proton to the chemical you added. It's what chemists like you call a base or a basic solution.

THANKS FOR THE FERTILIZER, NOT THE POISON

In the early 20th century, two German chemists, Fritz Haber and Carl Bosch, mastered a chemical reaction that keeps many of the people on our planet from starving. Haber found that combining a form of nitrogen with hydrogen molecules produces a chemical called ammonia. You may have smelled ammonia in glass and window spray cleaner. It's safe to get on your hands, but you can't drink it. Plants use a form of ammonia. Without it, they can't grow. And without plants, neither can we. As chemical reactions go, the Haber-Bosch process turns out to be a pretty easy way to make ammonia for fertilizer. My chemist friend Brandi Cossairt is pretty sure that our planet would not be able to grow enough crops to feed the more than 7.5 billion people living here right now, let alone the 9 or 10 billion that will be here by the year 2060, if not for the Haber-Bosch process.

The downside is that we humans are now so good at producing ammonia and fertilizer that it has become cheap (inexpensive). So farmers often put too much fertilizer on the soil their crops grow in, or suburban folks dump too much on their lovely green lawns. All that extra fertilizer seeps into the groundwater or is carried off by rains, eventually flowing into ponds, lakes, and the ocean. There it can overfeed algae and seaweeds. These life-forms bloom, sometimes sucking up the oxygen in the water, and fish can't get around or find food. It's a serious problem caused by serious waste. But it sure looks like a problem we can solve. Focus on that one, too, would you? Great. Thanks.

Oh, while we're at it, Haber also invented chemical warfare during World War I, so how much can we really thank him?

> 66 Chemistry is the science that explains everything. Physics tells you what's in an atom. But if you want to know why a tree grows or how your cell phone works, well, that's chemistry. Chemistry is everything!"
>
> —*CHEMIST BRANDI COSSAIRT*

Pho·to·syn·the·sis

We've already talked about photosynthesis in our chapter on plants. But let's speed through it one more time. Why? Because it's one of the most amazing chemical reactions on Earth! A plant gathers up water from the ocean it's floating in, or from the ground it's growing in, and combines the water with carbon dioxide that it sucks right out of the air or the sea. Then it uses the energy from sunlight to drive a chemical reaction between water and carbon dioxide, to make more of itself—more plant.

To make it all go, plants have come up with another compound, **CHLOROPHYLL**.* Through a complex reaction that it took scientists decades to decode, sunlight also helps a plant produce a sugar called glucose, which is the food fuel for living things—the plant itself, and for us animals, who eat plants. Just like you, photosynthesizing plants produce waste products. For a plant, the main waste is oxygen. Good thing for us! We need that stuff to breathe.

Think about what nature builds from this chemical reaction. Everything from bright green blades of grass to undersea forests of kelp plants, dozens of meters (hundreds of feet) long, to towering 100-meter (300-foot) tall redwood trees that live for over 1,000 years.

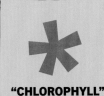

"CHLOROPHYLL" comes from the Greek words for "green leaf."

BEFORE WE MOVE ON...

Chemistry has changed the world, because everything is made of chemicals. Our ability to figure out how they react with each other and how they absorb, store, and release energy is a key to understanding the universe and a key to our future as a species here on Earth. Let's move on to a form of energy we see everywhere we look.

chapter 9

Light
Secrets of Sunlight, Starlight, and Our Friend Roy

➤ **Light doesn't weigh anything.** It has zero mass. You can't keep a bottle of it in the refrigerator. Most of the light in our world comes from outer space, from stars like our Sun. The light energy from the Sun helps plants produce leaves, fruits, and roots that animals like us can eat. Of course, we produce light, too, with electricity. But all the light we make around the world is a tiny, tiny fraction compared with the light that comes from the Sun. To understand the universe, we have to understand light. Let's go.

When you look around a room, or at a nearby cactus or tree, or even your grandmother's hippopotamus that's now wandering around your neighborhood, because you let her out of your yard (the hippopotamus, not your grandmother), you're not really seeing matter. You're seeing the light bouncing off all that stuff. Light shines from a source, like the Sun,* strikes an object, like that hippo's leathery skin, and then only brown and gray light, the color of the skin, manages to bounce back to your eyes. Once it does, your brain creates a picture, and you "see" the unusual neighborhood visitor. Got to say, hippos are seldom seen around my house in California—and I've kept a lookout. But enough about river animals. This is the science of light, people. Let's focus!

"RAYS": Light streams from the Sun, or a flashlight, or a torch in "rays." So we use the same word we used for heat: We say light "radiates."

Nothing travels faster than light. Oh, and believe me, scientists have looked and looked for something faster. In empty space, with no air, water, or anything around, light travels at nearly 300 million meters per second (just over 186,000 miles per second). How fast is that? Well, the Moon is about 380,000 kilometers (240,000 miles) from Earth. Astronauts need three days to get there. A beam of light makes the trip in a little more than a second!

NEED TO KNOW:
Light Bends

▶ When you look at the beam from a flashlight, you might think light travels in straight lines. And it pretty much does, through the air here on Earth, or in outer space, where there is no air. It turns out rays of light, microwaves, radar beams, and X-rays are all forms of light. And when they run into something, they can bend or change direction. One way is reflection. That's when light changes direction by bouncing off of something like a mirror or shiny spoon. But if you wear eyeglasses or contact lenses, or if you've ever used a magnifying glass, microscope, or telescope, you've seen light change direction in another way. Passing through the right material, light bends. We call this refraction. It turns out that light travels more slowly through denser materials like water, glass, and plastic than it does through air or in outer space.

I like to imagine a beam of light acting like the members of a marching band. If you're in a marching band, you know what I mean. A marching band can turn by having the band members on the inside of the turn take shorter steps than the members

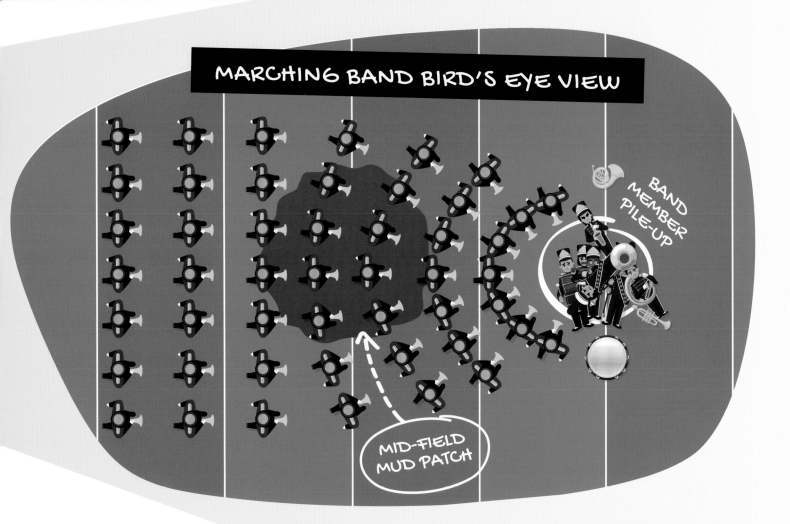

MARCHING BAND BIRD'S EYE VIEW

BAND MEMBER PILE-UP

MID-FIELD MUD PATCH

on the outside of the turn. Band members keep track of their place in the formation by keeping sharp corners-of-their-eyes on the band members next to them. They all march in step and keep time with the music, but the lengths of their strides change.

Now imagine a field with a great big patch of mud in the middle—a patch the size of the center circle on a soccer field. The band is stretched across the field, from one sideline to the other, marching and playing. As the band approaches this mud patch, the marchers in the middle have to march through the mud. Those middle marchers take shorter steps to avoid slipping. They slow down. Meanwhile, the other band members on the outer sides of the formation are marching on regular not-so-slippery grass. With all the musicians watching each other, and marching in proper formation, as they always do, the members taking shorter steps in the slow mud would make the ends of the rows of the

formation turn toward the middle. If everybody kept on going, the marchers on the outside of each row, who are standing shoulder to shoulder with their bandmates next to them, would be turned toward the middle of the formation. In a few more strides they'd have a pig-pile down field. And the music would stop and most of the people in the crowd would be disappointed, but some would laugh a little because, let's face it, the whole thing would be kind of funny.

The same thing happens to light as it passes through a pair of eyeglasses, a magnifying glass, telescope, or microscope. No joke—it slows down like those marchers in the mud. It changes direction. The beam of light even comes together in a pig-pile. Wait. It's not exactly a pile of light. But it does converge to a single spot, the focus or focal point of the lens. Sure, light is changing direction, as in reflection. But with refraction, light is passing through a substance, and changing speed, rather than bouncing off.

The Science of Eyeglasses

We can measure the speed of light as it goes through different clear substances. Through glass, it's about two-thirds as fast as it is in air. In water, light goes about three-quarters as fast as it does in air. In space there's no air at all. We say outer space is a vacuum. So is the inside of an old-fashioned lightbulb. Light goes just ever so slightly faster in a vacuum than in air. And the speed of light in a vacuum is as fast as light can go. The change in the speed of light is why images look funny when you look through a glass of water. Because people have been making eyeglasses for centuries, we have figured out just how to shape the glass or plastic lens of a pair of eyeglasses so the lenses bend the light just right. We can make it land on the perfect part of your eye so you can see well.

TRY THIS!

Bend a Little Light

WHAT YOU DO:

1. Find a clear glass drinking glass.

2. Fill it with water.

3. Look at something like your finger or a friend's face.

Results: The image is distorted because the light bouncing off your finger and passing through the water in the glass has slowed down and changed directions. The bent beams of light spread the image out, so your finger—or your friend's face—looks big.

MIND, BLOWN!

Galaxies as Telescopes

Even in empty space, a beam of light doesn't move in a perfectly straight line, because it can be bent a little by the pull of gravity. On Earth, the amount of bending is so small that you'll never notice it. But in space, there are massive galaxies, and even clusters of galaxies, with a lot of gravity. Astronomers call them gravitational lenses, because they act like nature's telescopes, magnifying whatever is behind them. Astronomers have learned to use these gravitational lenses to discover astonishing things about exploding stars, black holes, and the size of the cosmos.

How We See Things Large and Small

Understanding light has helped us understand the natural world around us and the amazing things way out in the universe, too. We use microscopes to see the tinier parts of our world, and telescopes to study the distant stars and galaxies. Both use lenses to bend light. A microscope takes a very small image and spreads it out so you can see the tiny world below. Since the lens is spreading light, we want as much light as possible coming up from the object we're magnifying. That's why microscopes often have a bright light source underneath. Going the other way, a telescope collects light from a patch of sky wider than your eye and narrows it down, so you see what is really only a small portion of the vast night sky magnified.

Split Light

WHOA, DUDE, IT'S ALL CONNECTED.

<u>WHAT YOU NEED:</u>

A prism, or something made of clear glass or plastic that has a sharp edge or two. The dangling parts of a chandelier are ideal. But don't take apart your parents' chandelier. Not without their permission, anyway . . .

<u>WHAT YOU DO:</u>

1. Let light shine through the glass or plastic.

2. Observe and think!

Results: You'll see that a light beam that looks white, or nearly white, is actually made up of all the colors of the rainbow.

Watching Waves

Light comes in many colors, just like my bowties. You've seen them—I mean all the colors, not all of my bowties (there are probably way too many). And if you're reading along here, and you can't see, for whatever reason, you still know that light comes in countless colors, because so many of us talk about colors all the time.

Through some wonderful experiments, scientists figured out that the colors of light can be described or understood by thinking of light as traveling in waves—just like the waves in the ocean, only different. For one thing, the peaks of waves in the ocean are usually a few meters or surfboard-lengths apart. The peaks of waves of light are much, much closer together—a few billionths of a meter apart, or even less. We call the distance from one peak to the next the wavelength.

Now picture ocean waves in your mind. Or if you're right by the ocean or a lake, don't imagine; just look at the waves (for cryin' out loud). Sometimes they're close together; sometimes they're a little farther apart. Their wavelength changes. Same with light. Only with light, the different wavelengths are what our eyes and brains see as different colors.

What's the Frequency, Bill?

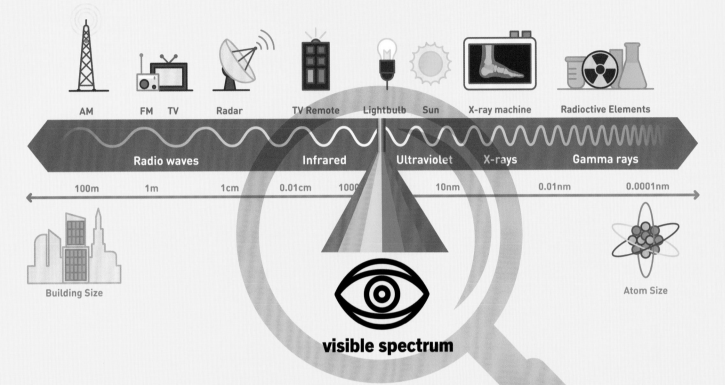

AM	FM TV	Radar	TV Remote	Lightbulb	Sun	X-ray machine	Radioctive Elements

Radio waves   **Infrared**   **Ultraviolet**   **X-rays**   **Gamma rays**

100m	1m	1cm	0.01cm	1000	10nm	0.01nm	0.0001nm

Building Size

Atom Size

visible spectrum

The colors of a regular in-the-sky rainbow are produced when sunlight passes through the front of raindrops, bounces off the back of the raindrops, and then back out through the front. It's exactly like light passing through a prism or one of those pieces of a chandelier. In that beam of white sunlight are all the colors we can name. And the different colors are produced by light waves with peaks that are different distances apart. They have different wavelengths.

If we're talking about one beam of light zipping through space, it travels at one speed. What scientists like you call the speed of light! So if you know the wavelength, and you know that light is going—well, it's going the speed of light—then you know how many waves will go past you in a given amount of time. The shorter the wavelength, the more waves will go by in any amount of time you choose: days, hours, seconds—or millionths or billionths of seconds. The number of waves that goes by in that amount of time is what we call its frequency [FREE-Kwen-see]. You may know the word "frequent." If you go to the mall often, we say you go there frequently. You might also hear someone say that you frequent that mall.

Once again, picture a ray of light as a long set of waves. Like any wave, it will have peaks, or high points, and troughs, or valleys. Now imagine that you have a super-accurate stopwatch and supernaturally fast fingers and really, really good eyesight, and you count the number of peaks that pass in front of your nose every second. That's the frequency of the light. Now pretend that you could measure the distance from one peak to the next in one of those light waves. You would have measured the wavelength.

When we compare one color of light to another, the light with the longer wavelength has a lower frequency. The color with the shorter-wavelength light has a higher frequency. Since there's less distance between each peak, the wave needs less time to pass.

The longer the wavelength, the lower the frequency. The shorter the wavelength, the higher the frequency. Now, let's meet our friend Roy.

NEED TO KNOW:
ROY G BIV

▶ Roy isn't a scientist. Or a kind of person at all. He's a memory trick. The "R" in his name represents the color red. And the color red has the lowest frequency of all the light we see, the visible light. That means its wavelength is . . . you know this . . . yes! Longer. Despite its angry reputation, red could be the most relaxed color, because its waves are the most stretched out (uh . . . sorry).

We call the collection of wavelengths of light the color spectrum. And, as we go left to right with ROY G BIV, each color of the spectrum has a slightly shorter wavelength than the previous one. We slide from red to orange, to yellow, to green, to blue, to **INDIGO**,* and then violet. ROY G BIV.

Besides the well-known hues of the rainbow, invisible light is hiding in every sunbeam. Invisible light? Yes! On either side of our color spectrum, there is light our eyes can't pick up. Just past red, for example, we find **INFRARED**,*

You may think you don't know the color **"INDIGO,"** but you probably do. For thousands of years, clothing, and eventually blue jeans, were dyed blue with a powder made from the indigo plant. It was originally grown as a crop in what is now the country of India. It's dark blue. We keep the color indigo in ROY G BIV's name so that there are three colors on either side of G, of green. It turns out, strange as it might seem to us humans, when we measure it, most of the light from the Sun is green. It's cool. Well, it's green. Plus, people seem to love the number seven. We have seven days in a week, etc. So we have seven colors of the rainbow. Am I right, Roy—or Mr. Biv?

or IR, light. On the far side of violet, we have ultraviolet. It has more waves going by per second, so you can think of it as having a little bit more energy than violet. That extra bit of energy can damage our skin and our eyes, so we wear sunscreen and sunglasses to protect us against this ultraviolet, or UV, light.

Just because infrared and ultraviolet are invisible doesn't mean we don't need to know and remember them. So I like to imagine a caveman version of Roy G. Biv introducing himself. He'd hold his club to one side, wipe his hand on his animal-skin coat, and say:

"I ROY G. BIV . . . U?"

I've met plenty of guys named Roy. And for a long time, I imagined I would someday meet a guy named "Iroy." I never have—not yet. Come to think of it, I've never met a Mr. or Ms. Biv, either. Furthermore, I've never met even one Dr. Bivu. I know, it's weird. Speaking of weird . . .

"INFRARED" is from the old Latin word "infra," which means "below." Nowadays, you've probably heard people talk about "infrastructure." That's the structure below floors, below the streets, and behind walls that we all depend on to get around and do things. As for ultraviolet, well, "ultra" is a Latin word that means "beyond." So, ultraviolet light is of a frequency higher or beyond violet.

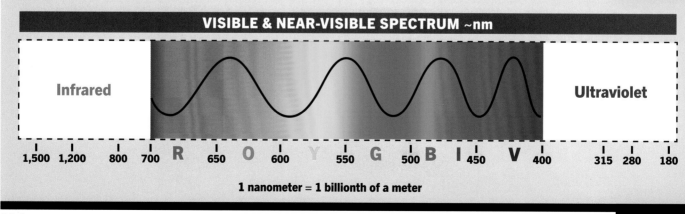

VISIBLE & NEAR-VISIBLE SPECTRUM ~nm

Infrared | R | O | Y | G | B | I | V | Ultraviolet

1,500 1,200 800 700 650 600 550 500 450 400 315 280 180

1 nanometer = 1 billionth of a meter

114 > Chapter 9: **LIGHT**

This collection of images from NASA's Solar Dynamics Observatory (SDO) shows how pictures of the Sun captured at different wavelengths give scientists information about the Sun's surface and its complex magnetic fields.

WEIRD! SCIENCE

Department of Light

1. You're always looking at the past.

You may want to hold your hands to the sides of your head as you read this, because your brain might explode. Ready? Light is fast. Really fast. But getting from one place to another still takes some amount of time. It cannot happen in an instant. So when you look at something—anything—you're really seeing that thing as it was in the past, when the light began its journey to your eyes. Over earthly distances, when you're staring at the ceiling or the goalposts at the other end of a soccer field, we're talking about ridiculously short blips of time. As you're reading these words, you're looking about one-billionth of a second into the past. When a radar wave beams from an airplane to the ground and back, the time is amazingly short, but quite measurable. That's how radar works. When we look at Alpha Centauri, the closest star system to our lovely blue planet, light has to travel four years to get to our telescopes. So we're really seeing Alpha Centauri as it was four years ago. Or are we? Maybe it's only logical, from an astronomer's point of view, to think of what happens on Alpha Centauri as not happening here, where we are, until the light gets here. Maybe time can only go as fast as light. Whoa . . . ! You can put your brain back together now.

2. Light is both a particle and a wave.

Light isn't just one thing. Neither am I. Sure, I'm the Science Guy, but I am also an engineer, once was a pretty good Ultimate Frisbee player, and still consider myself a decent dancer. Light is sort of the same way. Even though we talk about the different types and colors of light having different wavelengths, light doesn't always act like a wave. Sometimes it acts like it's made of particles, like grains of sand. It's like the ocean and the beach all at once. But still, something can't be a wave and a particle at the same time—can it? Well, when we do certain experiments, light behaves like waves. When we do other experiments, light acts like particles. It's always light. But it can act like two completely different things. If you could completely understand why light acts like both a particle and a wave, and explain it to scientists everywhere, you would change the world.

The Science of Lasers

I suspect you've seen laser light. Teachers use laser pointers, for example. You might see construction crews using a laser to line things up precisely. Lasers are very, very narrow beams of light, in which the crests and troughs, the peaks and valleys, of the waves are perfectly lined up with each other. We call it coherent [Koe-HEER-int] light. Since the waves of light in a laser are going up and down together, they're all the same frequency and only one color. You might see red laser pointers, green laser pointers, or blue lasers. Engineers get light waves to line up by bouncing them back and forth inside a tube of gas or a piece of precisely shaped silicon (glass has a lot of silicon). Coherent light like this seldom shows up in nature. We have to create it. And we do. Thanks to science!

TRY THIS!

Light Through the Hole of a Pin

WHAT YOU NEED:

- Push pin or thumb tack
- A round oatmeal box, empty
- Sharp pencil
- Scissors
- Wax paper
- Rubber band big enough to go around the box
- Bright lamp or light fixture

WHAT YOU DO:

1. With the pin, punch a small hole in the center of the bottom of the box.

2. With the pencil, make the hole a little bigger.

3. Cut a piece of wax paper big enough to cover the open end of the box with some room to spare.

4. Secure the wax paper in place with the rubber band.

5. Turn on a bright lightbulb.

Results: Look at the image of the bulb on the wax paper. (It's upside down, and you can change its focus by moving toward or away from the light.)

6. Try making the hole slightly, just slightly, larger with the pencil or pen.

Still upside down? Dimmer, brighter, or sharper?

BEFORE WE MOVE ON...

Light is fundamental, a basic feature of nature. Using light and the other wavelengths on the electromagnetic spectrum we can sense and measure so much about the world around us. But there is still a great deal about life, energy, atoms, and stars that we're trying to figure out. Right now, early in the 21st century, we've discovered that everything big and small is made of even smaller things— particles. So if we can understand the particles, we'll have a chance at understanding a great deal about the universe. Next we'll talk about what we know about these tiny particles— I mean, what we know so far.

chapter 10

Tiny Particles
What It's All Made Of

► Now we're going to talk about stuff.

Or, more specifically, matter. What is matter? Every . . . thing—everything. You are made of matter. So is every big and little thing that you can touch or see or feel. This book. The breaths of air you breathe. The water you drink. The stars in the night sky, and all those chemicals from chapter 8. How about the hippopotamus in your kitchen? (I'm kidding. How would your grandmother's hippopotamus get into the kitchen? Wait. You invited her? Maybe you're a zoologist. Hmmm . . .)

All of it is matter, and matter is anything that takes up space and has mass. It's all made of atoms and molecules. Look around in, say, the kitchen. You'll find all manner of solid objects: countertops, pots, spoons, one hippo, even the kitchen sink. But in the sink, you might be able to get some water, H_2O, two hydrogens and one oxygen. It's matter, too, only now it's liquid matter that flows from your kitchen faucet. In the freezer, that same water becomes a solid—ice. If you put that ice in a hot frying pan, the ice becomes liquid again, and then it disappears. The water didn't go off to some other science fiction dimension. No. It became what we call **WATER VAPOR.*** The molecules moved faster and faster, got farther and farther apart, and then left the pan for the air around it.

Water in all three forms is still matter. So is a tree, a concrete street, the air we breathe, the ocean we sail upon, and that hippopotamus. The three forms, or phases [FAYZ-iz], of matter in our everyday world are: solids, liquids, and gases.

You can see the root word **"VAPOR"** in the word **"evaporate."**

I hope you remember in chapter 7 about heat, we talked about Democritus, who came up with the word "atom" to describe something too small to divide; something "uncuttable." Then in chapter 8, on chemistry, we found that atoms are actually pretty cuttable. They have positive protons and neutral neutrons that make up an atom's nucleus. They also have negative electrons, which are quite cool, buzzing around the outside of the nucleus.

But we didn't talk about what those tiny particles actually are, or how they work. It turns out they are just the beginning of an amazingly big, amazingly small, story of how the universe is built.

> When we ask how does something work, we have to look inside. If you want to know how a car works, you have to look at the engine, and then you have to figure out how the pieces of the engine work. What we're trying to do by looking at tiny particles is to understand what everything is made of and what are the rules by which the different pieces fit together to form all the things we see."
>
> —PARTICLE PHYSICIST HELEN QUINN

ELECTRONS

The electron is what's known as a fundamental particle. Near as we can tell, electrons were among the first particles to appear in the universe. We say they're fundamental because we can't break an electron into anything smaller—as far as we know. The word "fundamental" comes from the Latin and French words "to found" or "begin." Electrons had a role in the beginning of everything.

PLASMA

Under the right conditions, electrons come completely loose from their atoms and protons. The atoms and electrons become a separate, fourth phase of matter called a plasma [Plaz-muh]. When atoms become plasmas, they behave differently from the way they do as solids, liquids, or gases. Plasmas form in air—way, way up in the atmosphere near outer space, and in certain types of lamp bulbs. Plasmas like these glow when they're charged up with electricity.

QUARKS

These particles are what we call subatomic, which just means smaller than an atom. And things get really small. Protons and neutrons are made of even tinier bits of matter called quarks, which are not even a thousandth the size of a proton. Quarks come in different flavors, but not the kind of flavors you'd find in an ice cream shop. The main types are up, down, charm, strange, top, and bottom quarks. Seriously, these are the words physicists use.

An artist's impression of the mayhem of particles inside the proton.

> "We thought the atom was it. For hundreds of years, we thought an atom was the smallest thing. Then we found that it has a nucleus with protons and neutrons. Then we looked inside the protons and found quarks. So how are we so sure the quarks are it? We don't know. Everything we've seen so far indicates that quarks are it, but we will continue to look for something smaller."

—PARTICLE PHYSICIST STEVEN GOLDFARB

In a plasma, electrons can jump from one energy level to another and emit rays of light.

PUDDING, GOLD, AND PARTICLES

IN THE LATE 19TH CENTURY, scientist J. J. Thomson demonstrated that electrons exist, and that they're part of these larger things called atoms. (J. J. was not William Thomson—not Lord Kelvin, either, not even distant relatives.) But J. J. Thomson and the scientists of his day weren't quite sure what atoms looked like—I mean if you could see them. He suggested they were probably a bit like British-style plum pudding, which is more like a dense cake or muffin—with some raisins and other bits of fruit baked in (hardly ever plums anymore), and it's typically eaten at dinner, sometimes with gravy. Mmm . . . oh, wait. Here's my point: Thomson imagined an atom would have electrons suspended in some kind of fluffy soft stuff. That might make a nice pudding, but researchers realized that Thomson's picture with electrons mixed in pretty evenly couldn't be quite right.

IN 1909, BUILDING ON THIS WORK, an earnest scientist named Ernest Rutherford set up a famous, famous experiment. He got a very, very thin piece of gold foil. He and his student Ernest Marsden, who was also earnest, beamed a stream of particles at the gold foil. When the particles passed through the foil, they hit a screen that would flash like a flickering old TV. Most of the particles went through the foil and hit the screen. But every now and then, a few would get deflected almost straight back.

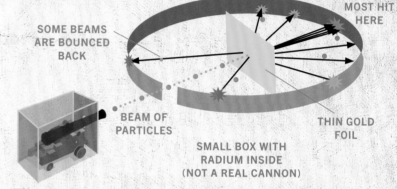

SOME BEAMS ARE BOUNCED BACK

MOST HIT HERE

BEAM OF PARTICLES

THIN GOLD FOIL

SMALL BOX WITH RADIUM INSIDE (NOT A REAL CANNON)

The experiment showed that atoms are mostly, mostly empty, empty space. That's why the beam of particles usually zipped right through the gold foil. Every once in a while, though, the beam would hit something very, very dense, so dense that the particles would bounce right back. Rutherford said, "It was almost as incredible as if you fired a 15-inch shell [like a huge cannonball] at a piece of tissue paper, and it came back and hit you." He was amazed. We all should be. He realized that the gold atoms were mostly empty space with a tightly packed nucleus in the center. That's the blueprint for all atoms, the building blocks of all the stuff we see in our world, including you and me.

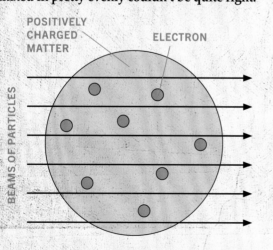

POSITIVELY CHARGED MATTER

ELECTRON

BEAMS OF PARTICLES

J. J. THOMSON ATOMIC MODEL (1904)

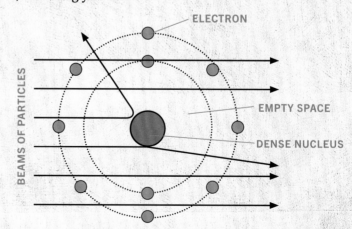

ELECTRON

EMPTY SPACE

DENSE NUCLEUS

BEAMS OF PARTICLES

RUTHERFORD ATOMIC MODEL (1911)

MIND, BLOWN!

Electrons and Uncertainty

When scientists first started working out their model of the atom, they dropped the plum pudding idea. The atom was shown with electrons orbiting the nucleus like tiny planets whipping around a sun. But there was a problem with this idea, too. Researchers discovered later that electrons don't seem to act like particles at all. They're something else entirely. When we conduct different types of experiments, electrons act differently. Sometimes they act like tiny particles, and sometimes they act like they're only waves of energy. Remind you of anything we talked about in chapter 9? That's right: light! In the subatomic world, our categories get blurry. Particles? Waves? It's like a beach out of focus down there.

Nowadays scientists think of electrons as being part of a kind of cloud. It's as though each tiny particle exists in many different places at nearly, but not exactly, the same time . . . or times. They're in one area, but never in one place. When we analyze them mathematically, we picture them in graceful hourglass patterns. So if we were to show you a picture of an atom with a nucleus in the middle and some electrons flying around the outside, we'd be wrong, wrong, wrong. Not to mention that they're both too tiny. Even if we were to expand an atom so that it could fit on this page, the nucleus would be too small to see. Our diagram of the atom would be mostly empty space. This is our long way of saying when you look at a picture of an atom, it's not quite right, because a real atom is kind of impossible to picture.

ELECTRON CLOUD

→ NUCLEUS

TRY THIS!

How Empty Is an Atom?

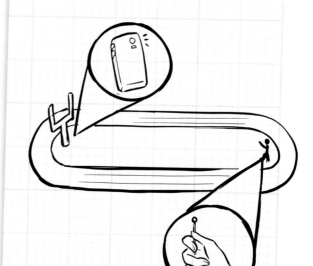

WHAT YOU NEED:

A phone with a light

A running track, like the one around a football field

A pin, like a sewing pin

WHAT YOU DO:

1. Turn on the light on your phone and set it upright at the edge of the track, or at a goalpost.

2. Go to the other end of the field or other end of the track.

3. Hold the pin in your hand . . . now imagine. I mean it. Take a few moments and look at all that emptiness. The head of the pin is like the nucleus of an atom. The light is like the nearest electron. Matter, all matter, is nearly empty space. Our universe is a strange and surprising place.

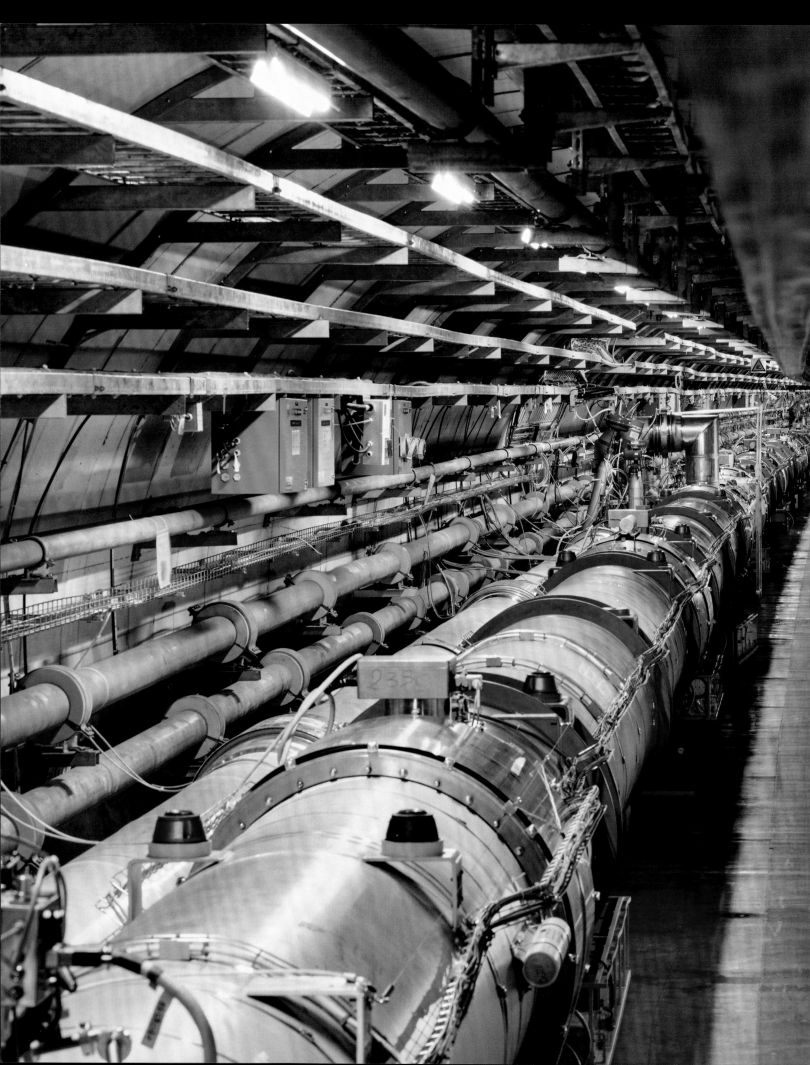

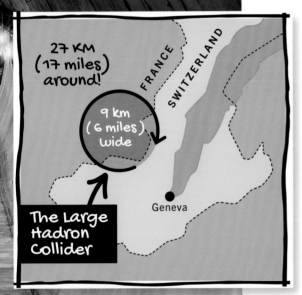

View of the LHC accelerator in 2018 (Image: Maximilien Brice, Julien Ordan/CERN); bottom: artist's conception of Higgs boson discovery.

27 KM (17 miles) around!

9 km (6 miles) wide

FRANCE

SWITZERLAND

Geneva

The Large Hadron Collider

The Large Hadron Collider

So far, you've taken my word for this tiny particle business. I hope you're wondering how we know all these tiny particles exist, when we can't see them. Well, how about this: What if you were walking through a room in the dark, and you kicked the leg of a chair (oooouch!)? You would know the chair is there, even though you couldn't see it. Same with subatomic particles. But we don't kick them in the dark. We smash them into each other and then watch what happens. No, really.

The Large **HADRON*** Collider, or LHC, is currently the world's most powerful particle accelerator, which you can also call an atom smasher. The LHC is huge. Really. It's like a racetrack for subatomic particles almost 9 kilometers (6 miles) across and 27 kilometers (17 miles) around. Inside huge hollow tubes, tiny particles race faster and faster until they smash into each other with so much energy that showers of completely different stuff pop out. Around the huge underground collision zones, technicians and engineers have mounted very specialized detectors. They produce amazing electronic snapshots of what happens to particles far too small to see when those particles collide at nearly the speed of light. In one of the great scientific experiments of the new century, the LHC helped physicists prove the existence of another, very special particle we call the Higgs boson (named for physicist Peter Higgs). It may be the tiny particle that gives everything its mass and inertia (its weight and everything) in the first place. Quite a discovery. And all thanks to an amazingly huge machine designed and built by thousands of scientists and engineers to prove the existence of the smallest thing we can imagine. Science!

A **"HADRON"** is a big tiny particle made of quarks. Protons and neutrons are hadrons, for example.

Artist's conception of a stream of high-energy neutrinos released by a supermassive black hole in a distant galaxy.

WEIRD ! SCIENCE

Neutrinos and Darkons

Well, if this part of this book hasn't gotten strange enough for you yet, try this: Every second of every day, 100 billion tiny particles are passing through every square centimeter of your body. One hundred billion! Every second! Every day! Through every square centimeter of you—areas smaller than the stamp on a letter from the post office. These amazingly tiny ghostly particles are called neutrinos [New-TREEN-ohz]. They barely have any mass. And as you might guess, they're neutral—neither positive nor negative. You can't possibly even feel the slightest nudge from them. Most of them zip straight through planet Earth and keep on going back out into space.

These days, researchers detect neutrinos in huge labs deep underground. The detectors can be way down below Earth's surface, because the particles pass right through all of matter's empty spaces all the time. By the way, neutrinos are not the only particles flying through your body at this very second. Scientists suspect that mysterious dark matter particles, which I like to call "darkons," constantly cruise through our bodies, too. (We'll talk about them in chapter 18.) It's a little rude, really. These neutrinos and darkons have no respect for our personal space, or even Earth itself. They fly right through you, me, rocks, and seas.

TRY THIS!

Stir Sugar into Space

WHAT YOU NEED:

Cup of warm water

Spoon

Powdered sugar

WHAT YOU DO:

1. Fill the cup to the brim with warm water.

2. Gently drop a spoonful of powdered sugar into the water.

3. Drop another spoonful.

RESULTS: The sugar dissolves. Its molecules end up in the spaces between the water molecules. It's wild.

Matter and Energy

Energy and matter are twins. Yes, under the right conditions, like under the crush of gravity inside a star like our Sun, matter turns into pure energy. And under other conditions—at the beginning of the universe, for example, or inside the LHC—energy turns into matter. I admit it's a little hard to believe. Imagine a thumbtack suddenly becoming an intense, blinding beam of light. That would be weird, right? And yet it's a really real feature of the universe.

When I saw a museum exhibit about the work of Albert Einstein, they had one of Einstein's famous papers displayed page by page in a long hallway. I could have read it all, if I could read German well. You get to the last page, and there it is, the equation that sums up the whole science of the matter-to-energy and energy-to-matter idea: $E/m=c^2$. With algebra, we can rearrange this so it's $E=mc^2$. This might be the most famous equation in science. "E" is for energy. The small letter "m" is for mass (things that could have weight, like protons or the Moon). The small letter "c" is for the speed of light. We use "c" to remind us that, as far as we can tell, the speed of light is constant—the value doesn't change. This equation is amazing. Einstein showed the relationship between mass and energy exactly. In a star, or in a nuclear reactor in a submarine or power station, we can know exactly what will happen to neutrons and protons, and how much mass will be converted to some neutrinos and pure energy in the form of heat and light. I hope you get the chance someday to learn more about this relationship; it is astonishing.

BEFORE WE MOVE ON...

Some scientists believe that quarks themselves exist because they're made of even smaller wiggling bits of energy and matter we currently call strings. The thing is, scientists like to test our ideas, and this one has proven tricky to prove. As we currently understand nature, it seems as though we might have to build a machine the size of our galaxy to detect some of these mysterious strings. That would be quite . . . er, uh, challenging. Are you up for it? I hope so. Particle physicists are always on the lookout for inspired, curious young minds. But start your thinking soon. Or at least after you read the next chapter. You're going to need to understand some forces to build a particle smasher that big.

chapter 11

The Four Fundamental **Forces of Nature**

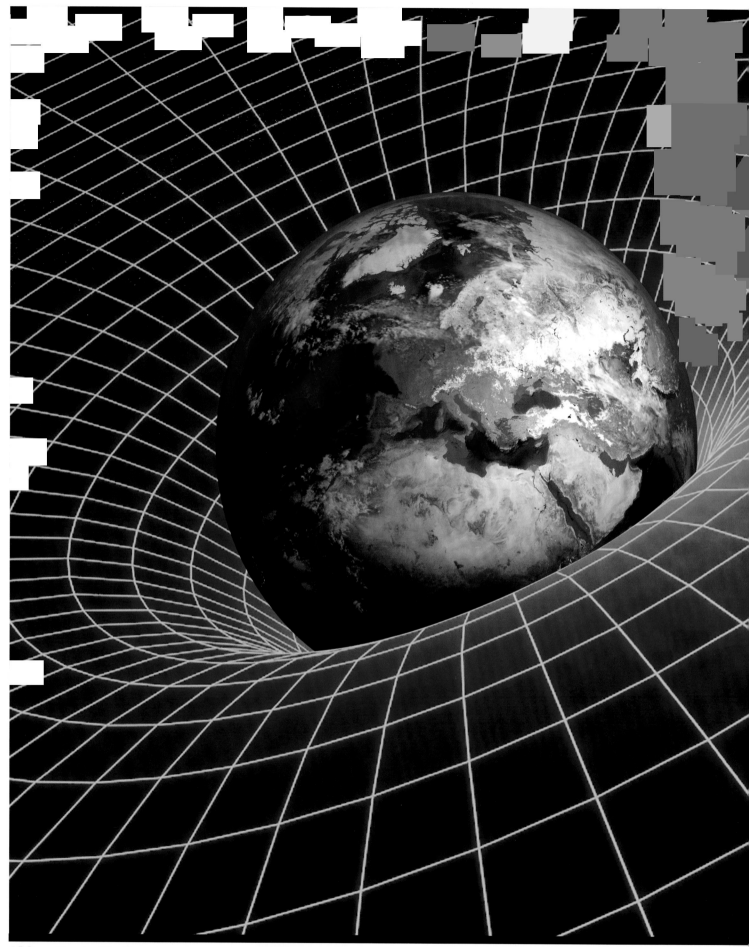

> ► **We've covered a lot of science so far:**
millions of species, billions of years, and trillions of cells, just
for starters. But I hope you've noticed that as big and complex
as our world and the cosmos seem to be, scientists are always
looking for patterns and basic ideas to simplify things. It's like
the old saying about machines. You want any machine to have
all the parts it needs but no extra ones—no parts that wouldn't
make the machine work better or do anything it doesn't need to
do. You could put roller skates on a can opener, but it probably
wouldn't open cans any better. Might not fit in a kitchen drawer
too well, either.

Since we realized that all the trillions of different types
of matter are made of combinations of just the same few
subatomic particles, scientists have tried to come up with
the simplest theory possible that would explain and make
successful predictions about, well . . . about everything. We
know that nothing moves or happens without energy, light,
heat, or chemical energy, for example, and that generally means
that something is getting pushed, pulled, or twisted by some
kind of force.

So get this: As far as we can tell today, early in the 21st century,
all the matter in the universe, every particle, every bit of
everything, big and small, gets acted upon by just four forces.
Not millions or trillions of forces, just four. We call them the
four fundamental forces, which has a nice ring to it in English,
three "f" sounds in a row. Let's meet them. I mean the forces,
not every bit of matter in the universe. Meeting all the matter in
the universe could make this part of the book really long. And
we've got a lot to cover.

I know, I know. We didn't meet all 25.
You can look 'em up if you like, and
I hope someday you do. But we have
talked about the main ones, so unless (or
until) you're applying for a job at an atom
smasher, you can get by very well with
the key few we've already covered.

66 When you look around the world it seems so
terribly complex. You have cars driving around on the
streets, people talking to each other, dogs peeing on
lampposts. Then you learn that all of this, everything
you see, really comes from just 25 particles* and four
forces! I still find this super fascinating. There's no
reason for nature to be this way. It just happens to be
the case. And what's even more amazing is that we
seem to be able to understand it!"

—PHYSICIST SABINE HOSSENFELDER

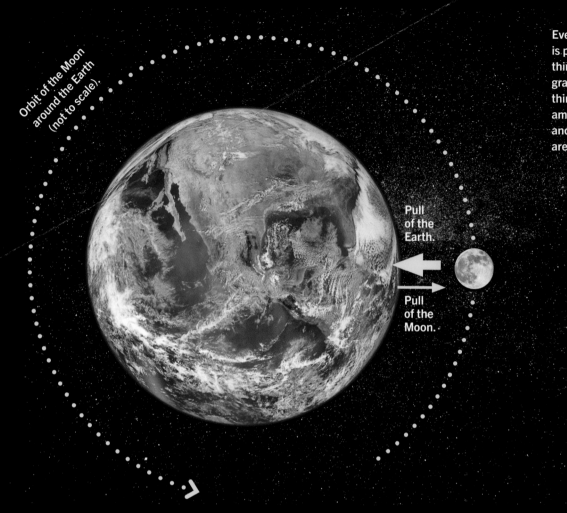

Orbit of the Moon around the Earth (not to scale).

Everything in the universe is pulling on every other thing, and the amount of gravitational pull between things is based on the amount of matter involved and how far apart things are from each other.

Pull of the Earth.

Pull of the Moon.

FUNDAMENTAL FORCE #1

GRAVITY

"GRAVITY" comes from the Latin and French words for "weight." Gravity is why anything weighs something.

> All the matter that we've ever seen (or lifted) has gravity. And gravity always pulls.* As far as we know, gravity never pushes on anything. Right now, we know of no such thing as antigravity or a "repelatron" that would push things around with an invisible magical beam of energy (like in a Tom Swift Jr. science fiction book). Gravity works on rocks, bowling balls, feathers, fish, water, whales, ants, aunts and uncles, even the atoms of air. It's the reason your grandmother's hippo is having so much trouble jumping over the hurdles you set up in your backyard. (Or one of the reasons, anyway.) All of this stuff is made of matter, and all that matter produces a pull of gravity. The Moon and Earth are held in their orbits by gravity. So are all the other planets and the rocky and icy objects that orbit the Sun. Gravity even keeps galaxies hurtling around each other.

Massively Important Point About: Gravity

As the story goes, Sir Isaac Newton was sitting under an apple tree one summer. Like anyone else, he noticed that every once in a while, an apple falls from a branch to the ground. That may be pretty obvious. But this next part isn't. As far as we know, he was the first guy to figure that not only is Earth somehow pulling a falling apple down, but a falling apple must be ever so slightly pulling Earth up!

Think about that for a moment.

Ready to move on? Good. He also wondered if the same force that pulls apples and the ground closer to each other also pulls the Moon toward the ground—I mean toward Earth—and keeps it from flying off into space.

Newton figured out that gravity is universal. It doesn't just keep our feet stuck in the vicinity of the ground. It's everywhere. Everything in the universe is pulling on every other thing, and the amount of gravitational pull between things is based on the amount of matter involved and how far apart things are from each other. There is only a tiny bit of gravity pulling you and your friend toward each other, but a tremendous amount of gravity is keeping you and the oceans stuck to the Earth. Simply put: the more matter, the more gravity. Our planet is enormous, and quite a bit bigger than your friend.

Everywhere there is matter, there is gravity. Try thinking about the tiny flecks of dust floating around your room. Earth's gravity is pulling the dust down, so that they eventually come to rest on your desk or bookshelf. But the dust has its own gravity, and it's ever so slightly pulling on Earth.

Why Is Gravity So Weak?

Gravity has a long reach, an extraordinarily long reach. It holds galaxies together! But gravity is the weakest of all of the fundamental forces. I know, it's weird, because we feel the force of gravity pulling us, and everything around us, down—nonstop, day and night— everywhere we go. But now, notice how easy it is to pick up a paper clip with a small magnet (maybe one from the refrigerator). The gravity of the whole planet Earth is pulling the paper clip down, while one itty-bitty magnet is pulling the paper clip up—and the magnet wins. So yes, the fundamental force of gravity is weirdly, weakly, weakly weak, compared to the other forces we'll meet in this chapter. How can that be? Are we missing something? Have we got gravity wrong? That's your next assignment, young scientist: Find out why gravity is weak. Then, change the course of human history. . . .

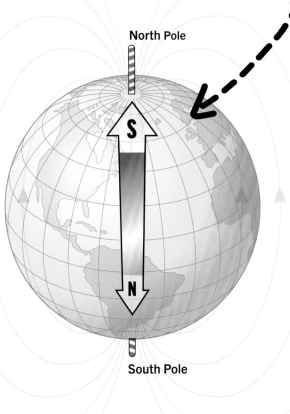

North Pole

S

N

South Pole

Earth Is a Magnet

The needle of a magnetic compass, like one you may have around for finding your way in the woods or out on the ocean, points north and south.

It works because the churning, very hot molten iron deep inside our spinning planet creates a huge magetic field. For centuries, we've called the end of the compass that points toward the North Pole we see on a globe or map the magnet's "north pole." The end that points toward a map's South Pole, we call the magnet's "south pole." On some magnets, you may see N for north and S for south. Hope that's kinda obvious. Now, think about this: The N or north end of a compass must be attracted to the magnetic south side of the Earth's magnetic field. It's as though Earth has a big magnet inside with its south end at Earth's North Pole and its north end at Earth's South Pole. It's tricky. Maybe it's surprising. But the universe is a surprising place, my friends . . .

Feel the Force (Field)

Ever since we started using the word "electromagnetism," scientists (maybe like you) have also imagined and measured electromagnetic fields. Since magnets and electricity can push or pull, we say these are "force fields." You already know about another kind of force field—one that only pulls: gravity. When you're near Earth, you're in its gravity force field. If you're on the Moon, you'll feel the Moon's gravity force field. Well, when it comes to the areas or regions around a wire or magnet, we can detect and use electromagnetic force fields.

Every magnet you'll ever find always, always has two ends or poles, just like Earth's North and South poles. If you cut or break a magnet in half, you don't end up with a north half and a south half. You end up with two half-as-long magnets that each have north and south poles of their own.

THE SCIENCE OF EVERYDAY GADGETS AND APPLIANCES

Electromagnetism is the key to our modern world, because we can use a moving magnet and its moving magnetic field to generate electricity. That's how electric power plants work, and that's where the electricity in your wall outlets comes from. We can work the other way, too, and use electricity to create magnetic fields. It's amazing. Almost everything we use to live relies on our ability to generate electricity with magnetism. Lights, air-conditioning, medical scanners, video games, mobile phones, and text messages all depend on electricity that we can generate because we understand this fundamental force of electromagnetism.

TRY THIS!

Comb a Flow of Water

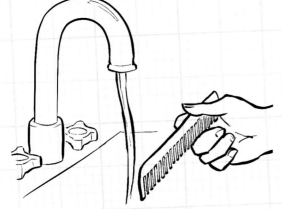

WHAT YOU NEED:

A sink where water can flow from a spigot or tap

A plastic hair comb

WHAT YOU DO:

1. Turn the water on so it's flowing smoothly, without bubbles.

2. Stroke the comb through your hair a few times.

3. Hold it near the flow of water. If the comb doesn't deflect the flow, try rubbing a rubber balloon on your hair and holding the balloon near the flow.

RESULTS: Electrical charges build up in the moving water, and in the comb moved through your hair. But the charges don't build up evenly. They become oppositely charged. So the water stream is pulled toward the comb.

DEPARTMENT OF ELECTROMAGNETISM

IN THE EARLY 19TH CENTURY, a Danish scientist named Hans Ørsted (spelled Oersted in English) was preparing a demonstration for his students when something unexpected happened. Or maybe it was slightly expected. We don't really know, because Oersted died more than 150 years ago. So he's not available.

Anyway, Oersted had used chemicals and metals to build a battery in his laboratory. On a nearby table, he also happened to have a compass, the kind that ships had already been using for hundreds of years. When he connected a single wire to the two ends of the battery, the compass needle moved. Back then, everybody thought a compass needle only responded to another magnet or to Earth's magnetic field. Oersted saw that electricity and magnetism were somehow connected.

At almost the same time, a British scientist named Michael Faraday showed that it works the other way, too. A moving magnet or a changing magnetic field can also create an electric current—a stream of flowing electric charges. In other words, either one of these forces can create or become the other force. Faraday started using the word "electromagnetism." A few years after all this, another brilliant physicist named James Clerk Maxwell figured out how electricity and magnetism are precisely mathematically related. He wrote what we now call Maxwell's equations. I very much hope you get interested enough in physics to learn about them someday. These equations—and electromagnetic fields—are amazing. Or let me put all this in more drastic terms: Without the work of Faraday, Oersted, and Maxwell, you wouldn't have a smartphone. No texts, no pics, no apps, no Science Guy show—arrggghh!

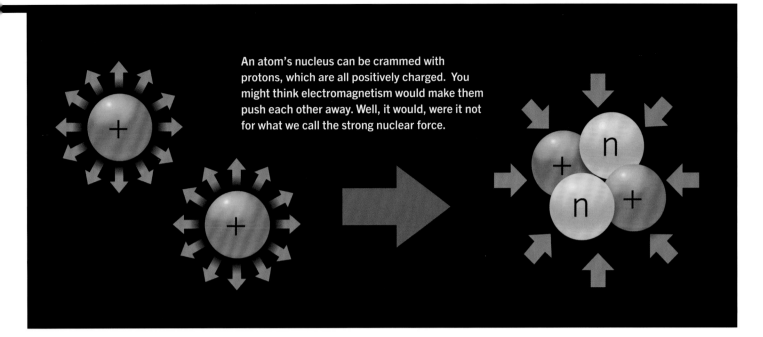

An atom's nucleus can be crammed with protons, which are all positively charged. You might think electromagnetism would make them push each other away. Well, it would, were it not for what we call the strong nuclear force.

STRONG NUCLEAR FORCE

As we talked (read) about protons, I hope you wondered about the middle of atoms, the nuclei [NEW-klee-Eye] (more than one nucleus). An atom's nucleus can be crammed with protons, which are all positively charged. (Here are a few: Boron has just 5 protons. Iridium has 77. I was just hoping you'd want to go back and check your periodic table from chapter 8.) With all those positively charged particles in the middle of an atom, you might think electromagnetism would make them push each other away. Well, it would, were it not for what we call the strong nuclear force. Sometimes nowadays, physicists just call it the strong force. This invisible but hugely important force holds these particles tightly together. Physicists in the 1930s realized the strong nuclear force was real, but it took another 40 years to figure out how it works.

It is an astonishing discovery. And the strong force really is strong! About 100 times stronger than the electromagnetic force. But it only works over short distances. We're talkin' really, really short distances, like the distances between protons—quadrillionths of a meter.*

In a star, there's so much matter that its gravity overcomes the electromagnetic force and the nuclei of hydrogen atoms (could also call 'em individual protons) are crushed together. Then the much more powerful short-range strong force takes over and pulls the protons together so forcefully that they become the two-proton nuclei of helium atoms—and a tremendously, hugely huge amount of energy is released. It's why stars shine, and it's how humans created the so-called hydrogen bomb more than 60 years ago. The process is called nuclear fusion [FYOO-zhun].

How short is that exactly?
A meter is about the distance from the kitchen floor to the rim of a glass holding a cold banana milkshake sitting on the counter. (I guess that would be the same distance even if the glass held a chocolate milkshake. Not sure. You should check.) Anyway, a quadrillionth of a meter is another way of saying a millionth of a billionth of a meter—of that floor-to-milkshake distance. That's really, really, really small. Studying something that tiny, and proving that the strong force is real, required experiments in huge particle accelerator machines, early versions of the LHC. But it's over these tiny distances that the strong force rules!

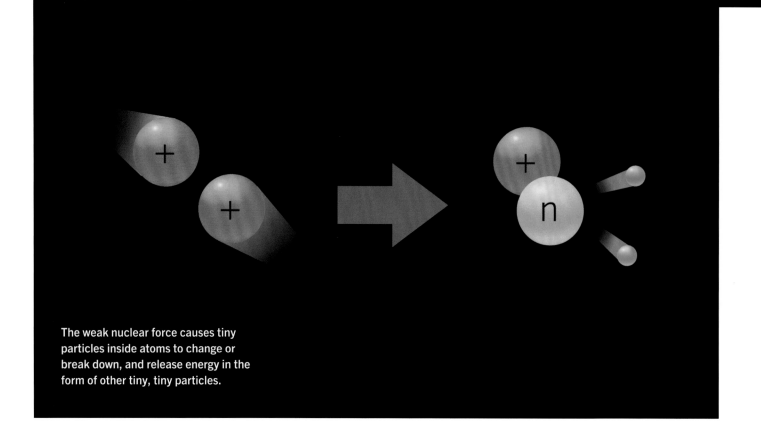

The weak nuclear force causes tiny particles inside atoms to change or break down, and release energy in the form of other tiny, tiny particles.

FUNDAMENTAL FORCE #4

WEAK NUCLEAR FORCE

▶ While everyone was going wild over the strong force in the 1930s (particle physicists were, anyway), Italian physicist Enrico Fermi realized there must be another force operating inside the nuclei, the middles of atoms. He figured this mysterious force would have to be about as strong as the electromagnetic force, but that it would only act over very, very, very short distances, even shorter distances than the strong force. So it got a wimpy name. Physicists (like you) call it the weak nuclear force, or just the weak force. It's the force that causes tiny particles inside atoms to change or break down, and release energy in the form of other tiny, tiny particles, some of which we measure as what's called radioactivity. Oh and by the way, radioactivity has nothing at all to do with what happens when a good song plays on my car radio. That would be seat-dance activity.

The weak force can turn one element into another. When uranium, with 92 protons, breaks down, or transmutes [Tranz-MYOOTs], it eventually turns into the element lead, with its 82 protons. That's the weak force in action. When hydrogen turns into helium in stars (like our Sun), it's not the work of the strong force alone. For one element to change into another, the process needs some help from the weak force as well. Big atoms breaking apart is what has kept Earth warm all these billions of years. It's how a nuclear reactor works. Splitting atoms that way is called fission [FIZH-unn]. Without the weak force, our nuclear reactors wouldn't be able to produce electricity. Without it, volcanos wouldn't ooze hot lava from deep below Earth's crust. The Sun wouldn't shine, and we'd all be dead. Or actually, none of us would have come into existence in the first place. So the weak force may not be very strong, but it is important—strongly important.

One Great Big Force?

The idea that we need four different forces to describe nature bothers a lot of physicists. Many of them are trying to find a way to combine the four into just one force. They think perhaps there was just one force when our universe was formed, and nature somehow spread it out into four. Sometimes they call this idea the Theory of Everything (the TOE) or the Grand Unified Theory (the GUT). They've been looking for this big idea for decades, and still haven't been able to figure it out, so this could be your chance to stand up and unlock the next secret of the universe. Speaking of us humans learning about the universe, do you think we're the only living things out there among all those galaxies who are working to understand it all? Read on . . .

BEFORE WE MOVE ON...

Life as we know or can imagine it wouldn't exist without any of the four fundamental forces. I guess it's another way of saying: If things were any other way—things would be different. If any of this seems strange or even hard to believe, don't worry. You are not alone. No, really. I'm standing right behind you. See? Ha, made you look.

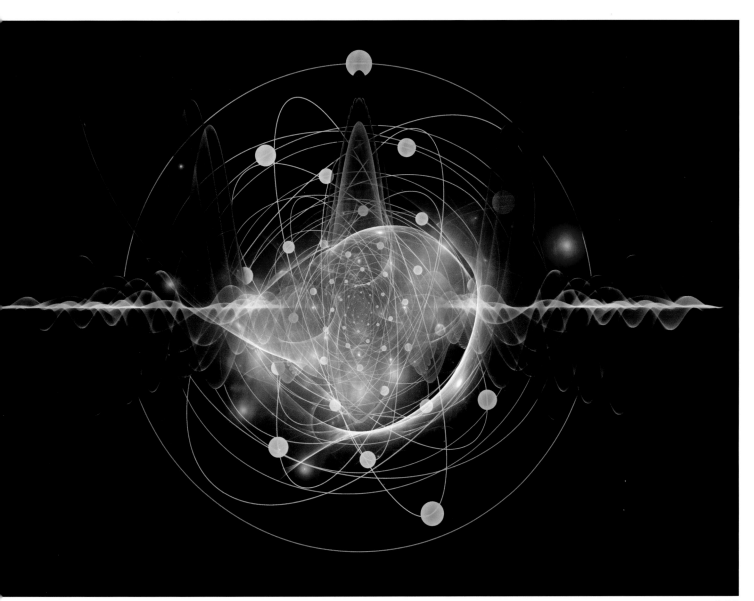

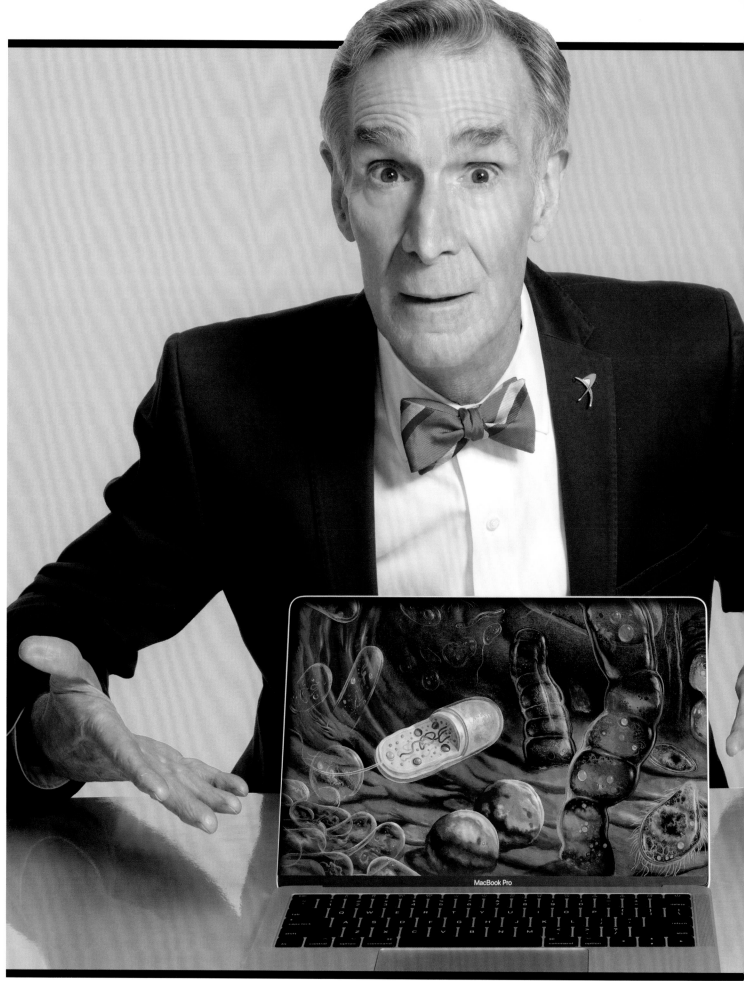

chapter 12

Astrobiologists
The Alien Hunters

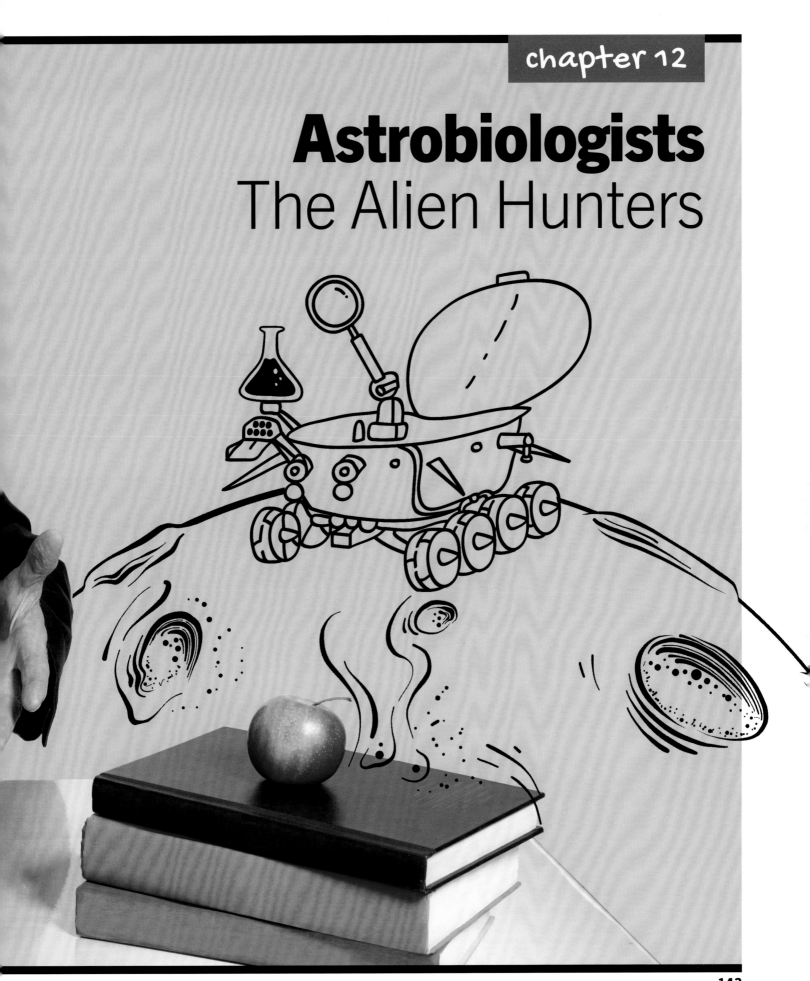

> **First, the good news.** Scientists are searching for aliens. They're searching for answers to one of the big questions we all ask: Are we alone here in the universe? Now the bad news. We're probably not going to find little green men or women. Or little green cats, or dogs, or hippopotamuses. Not right away, at least. If life exists on another planet or moon in our solar system, or far off around another star, these aliens are probably not going to be walking and talking and making strange noises. They're probably going to be simple. Closer to the kind of life that floated in our planet's oceans billions of years ago than to the hairy guy floating in the polka dot inner tube at the neighborhood pool. Sure, there's a chance they'll be complex and intelligent and maybe even hairy like our floating friend. Maybe they'll be a little like the restless (pink and gray) hippo that's now swimming next to him in the pool.

But simple is more likely.

Don't be disappointed. The search for alien life is not just the stuff of science fiction. This is real, and really exciting, science. Plus, the researchers who are trying to find alien life are going to need some help. They are going to need curious young people to aid in their search. That's you, I hope.

The official name of this field is astrobiology—the study of whether life exists on other worlds, and how

"ASTRO" means "stars," and "biology" means . . . well, it means biology, or the study of life.

> 66 I'm pretty sure we're not alone in our entire universe. It's a big universe. We're not that special, and astrobiologists are hopeful that we're going to find something out there. In terms of little green people, we're unlikely to find those in our solar system. We've taken enough pictures of the other planets to be fairly confident in our theory there. But elsewhere in the universe—who knows? The chance of intelligent life in some form is possible."
>
> —ASTROBIOLOGIST JENNIFER GLASS

MANY ASTROBIOLOGISTS started out as geologists or oceanographers. Some were thinking about becoming medical doctors or biologists first. Only later did they start to think about studying aliens. Solving the puzzle of whether alien life exists requires help from all kinds of scientists, including:

ASTRONOMERS to search for and study alien planets and moons from far away.

ASTROPHYSICISTS to figure out how those stars and planets handle the energy that strikes them and the energy they radiate back into space.

GEOLOGISTS to apply what they know about the way weather wears rocks out, the way continents ever so slowly move around, and the way life influences the chemistry of an atmosphere and an ocean to decide whether a distant world could be home to some form of life.

BIOLOGISTS to figure out what resources, which chemicals, might be available to some type of life that might be able to not only survive, but thrive, in one of these far-off places.

COMPUTER SCIENTISTS to write programs that help scientists sift through interesting evidence hidden away in all the information our telescopes gather.

ENGINEERS to build the telescopes, spaceships, rovers, and robots capable of studying, traveling to, and exploring these distant worlds.

it might have developed and evolved. All of the stars we see are suns, and each one of those suns could be shining its heat and light energy toward a planet, or even a few planets and moons, teeming with life.

Anyway, if you're interested in the stars and planets, rocks, life, or building stuff, you just might have what it takes to help us find alien life one day. To get you ready, let's go through some of what we know so far about astrobiology and the search for life beyond Earth.

Right now, astrobiologists figure we need four things for life to get started somewhere in the universe: water, warmth, carbon, and time, lots and lots of time. Now let's go looking for something alive out there.

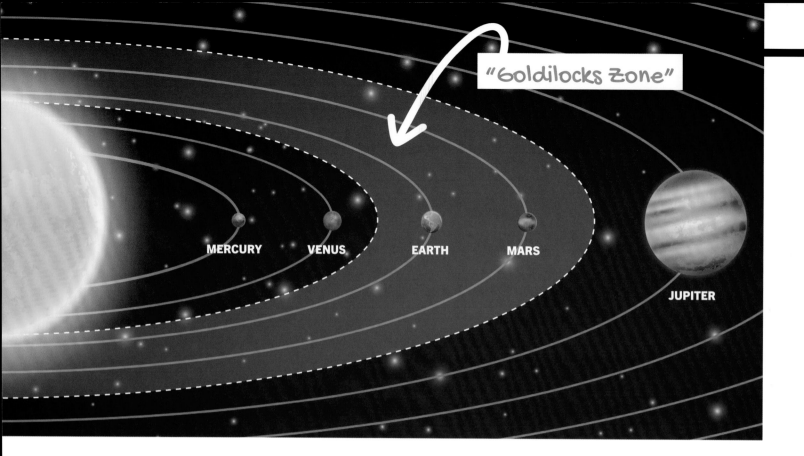

"Goldilocks Zone"

MERCURY VENUS EARTH MARS JUPITER

The Three Bears and the Search for Life

➤ You've heard the story of Goldilocks and the three bears, I'm sure. Little girl (with blond hair) gets lost in the woods, trespasses in the home of some intelligent bears, who can talk quite well, samples their porridge, and picks the bowl that's neither too hot nor too cold. Then the bears eat her, right? Or was it a wolf? Was it her grandmother's oatmeal, and the house blew down? I can't remember exactly. Anyway, when astronomers are looking for a planet that might host alien life, they look for the same qualities Goldilocks wanted in her breakfast mush—not too hot and not too cold. For a long time, scientists have figured life needs a liquid, something that can let chemicals move around and react easily. They've looked into all kinds of solvents—chemicals that dissolve other chemicals. Turns out, liquid water is fantastic for the job. On Earth, water is the key ingredient in the recipe for life. If another planet is like ours, it has to have water, and that water has to remain liquid. The planet needs to be just the right distance from its sun to keep its water liquid, and probably have enough of an atmosphere to hold in some heat.

If Earth were too close to the Sun, our oceans might boil off. If our planet were too far away, the surface would be too cold, and all our water might freeze. Luckily, Earth orbits our star (the Sun) in what scientists like to call the "Goldilocks zone." Since our planet is just the right distance from the Sun, Earth is kind of like that porridge: not too hot and not too cold. Since life seems to be doing pretty well here on Earth, in spite of all the things we seem to do to make life hard for other creatures and ourselves, astronomers are looking for other planets in this Goldilocks zone around other stars. These distant worlds, which orbit faraway suns, are called exoplanets ("exo" means "outside"). If we find one that's not too far from its sun, and not too close, then it just might have liquid water. And where there's water sloshing around, there's a chance for life.

The Planet Hunter

Now, how do we find these alien homes? Telescopes! Really, really, really big telescopes with giant mirrors and very clear lenses that capture and focus as much starlight as possible. Then, to make sure no dust or clouds or water moisture fog up our view, we station some of our telescopes in outer space. There they orbit Earth and the Sun to capture clear and stunning pictures of distant planets and stars. In 2009, scientists launched the Kepler Space Telescope. The spacecraft, named after the astronomer Johannes Kepler, spent nine years capturing images of distant stars. When it was finally retired in 2018, Kepler had helped scientists find more than 2,600 planets outside our solar system. That's 2,600 planets we didn't even know were out there! It's reasonable to think that a few or even a great many of those worlds could harbor life.

Aliens on Earth

When it comes to climate, Mars isn't much like Earth. It's cold and very dry. Mercury is cold or hot depending which side you're on. Venus is way, way hotter than anywhere else, and Europa, a moon that orbits Jupiter, is frigid. We'll get into more details about these worlds in chapter 17. For now, the important thing to remember is that the planets and moons in our solar system are very different from Earth. So if alien life were to survive on these worlds, it would probably be very different from the kind of life that survives here. Monkeys on Mars? Not likely.

One of the biggest breakthroughs in our search for alien life came because we looked down instead of up. In 1976, using a set of instruments towed behind a research ship, marine geologist Kathy Crane found something strange on the seafloor off the Galápagos Islands. Hot spots. Well, not that hot, areas just 0.1 degree Celsius warmer than anyone expected. The next year, a team of scientists returned to the area, and piloting a deep-sea sub, found spots where superhot minerals were spurting out of the seafloor, forming what scientists now call hydrothermal vents. The really strange part? Life was thriving down there, too. Tiny bacteria were feeding on the minerals. (Well, they still are.) Small creatures eat up the bacteria, which enables giant clams, seven-foot-long worms, and other oddities to live in an otherworldly ecosystem down there. Meanwhile, up here on the surface, creatures like us humans—elephants, trees, and bees—get our energy from the Sun. For centuries, we figured life couldn't exist without sunlight. But it's completely dark down at the seafloor. Seawater soaks up all the light before it can get down that deep. What these amazing creatures down at the hydrothermal vents taught us is that life doesn't need sunlight to thrive—hot rock and seawater can do the trick, too.

Nowadays, we call these creatures extremophiles [eks-STREEM-uh-Fialz]—because they survive in what to us are extreme environments.

Here's where we get back to aliens. If life can survive in these strange, extreme, out-of-the-way spots here on Earth, then maybe there are extremophiles hiding away on another planet. If scientists are going to find this alien life, they're going to need to learn everything they possibly can about how life survives in extreme places on our own planet—from the frigid, ice-covered South Pole to the warm, salty waters of the Dead Sea.

You have to figure that extremophiles don't think much about being extreme. They might just be thinking that you and I are the extremophiles, or at least pretty weird, living on dry land, under that bright star, and all.

Water bears, or TARDIGRADES (Tarr-du-Graidz), are found throughout the world, including regions of extreme temperature, such as hot springs, and extreme pressure, such as deep underwater. They can also survive high levels of radiation and the vacuum of space.

LUNAR ANIMALS
AND OTHER
OBJECTS,
Discovered by Sir John Herschel in his Observatory at the Cape of Good Hope and copied from sketches
in the Edinburgh Journal of Science.

For Description, See Pamphlet Published at the Sun Office.

The Great Moon Hoax

> In 1835, a New York newspaper called *The Sun* printed a series of articles describing how a scientist named John Herschel had discovered life on the Moon. Not just little bugs, either. The article claimed that John had found evidence of goats, beavers, four-foot-tall men with wings, and even unicorns. (Which would have to be called "moonicorns," don't you think?) It told of lakes and oceans and magnificent buildings. And yet it was all a giant joke. John Herschel was a real scientist, a successful astronomer. His father, William Herschel, had discovered Uranus [YER-inn-iss] and named its moons. Yet poor John had no idea the newspaper had used his name until he returned from an expedition.

What We're Looking for When We're Looking for Life

▶ Once scientists learned that life doesn't need direct sunlight, the number of places where life might exist in the solar system, or even the larger universe, suddenly grew. Today, when searching for spots where life might thrive, astrobiologists look for a few different things.

1. WATER

Life thrives when there's water around, so astrobiologists search for water on other worlds. That's one of the reasons we get so excited when scientists find hints of water on Mars. We're not just thinking about ways for astronauts to fill their water bottles. If water was present, or is still there today, then life could have been there, too. Maybe you'll be the one who finds evidence of microbes (Marscrobes?).

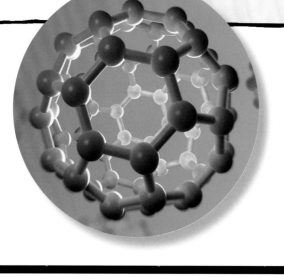

2. CARBON

We're carbon-based life-forms. All the life we've studied here on Earth is built from carbon and needs carbon to grow and thrive. Carbon has those six protons and four ways to bond with other chemicals, and even itself. Here on Earth, life grabs energy from carbon-packed chemicals, too. If all the life we know about needs carbon, then it kinda makes sense, when we're looking for aliens, to look for signs of carbon, right? Yep.

> This very complex molecule is made of 60 carbon atoms. Don't you kinda want to kick it?

3. TIME (AND MORE TIME)

Our solar system and our Earth are over 4.5 billion years old. That's old enough for planets like ours and Mars to cool off and have an atmosphere and an ocean. Mars had a huge ocean four billion years ago. But it doesn't have enough mass to keep a strong magnetic field like we have on Earth. Particles streaming from the Sun dragged most of its ocean and air off into space. It may be that life started there and thrived. But now if there's anything still alive on Mars, it's under the sand somewhere.

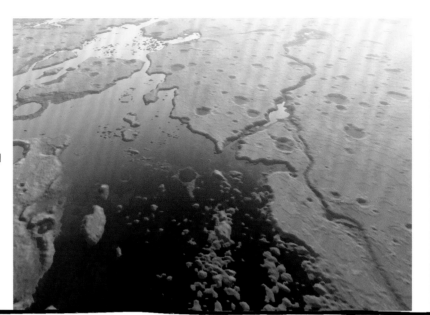

> An artist's version of the watery past of Mars. Maybe some early Martian life was hiding below.

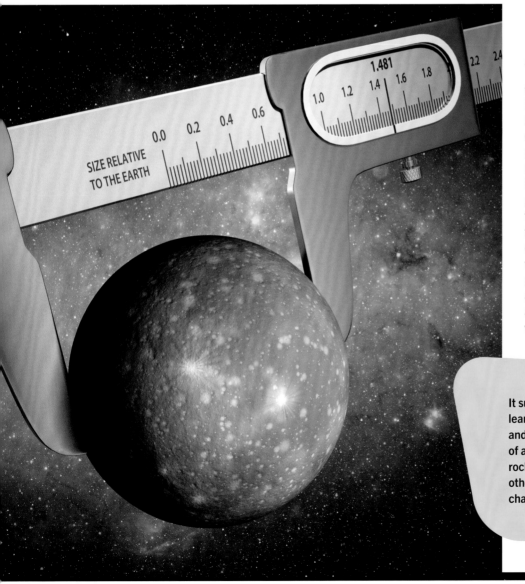

4. WARMTH AND A PLANET'S SIZE

If a planet is too small, it won't be massive enough for its gravity to hold onto an ocean or an atmosphere. It'll probably be cold. No liquid water means no solvent for the chemistry of living things and nothing to breathe or protect the surface. When a planet is too large, it may have so much gravity that hydrogen becomes a liquid and complex molecules wouldn't form very well, which would probably prevent life from developing. So astrobiologists look for planets that are right around Earth's size, and are warm but not too hot or too cold.

It surprises a lot of people I've met to learn that it's gravity that holds the ocean and atmosphere in place. Every particle of air and water, and every particle of rock and soil are pulling toward each other. We just talked about this in our last chapter. But still . . . whoa . . .

5. OXYGEN

Most of the life here on Earth needs oxygen to live. Thanks to photosynthesis, our air has enough oxygen to support organisms like houseflies and you, and me. So if we were to discover a planet with enough oxygen in its air, then maybe that world could be hiding alien life-forms, too. But oxygen may not be a requirement. We've also discovered plenty of life-forms in extreme environments here on Earth—such as those deep-sea hydrothermal vents—that don't need oxygen to live. Instead of breathing air, and oxygen, they basically breathe rock. You shouldn't try this yourself, though. Not even with a small rock.

6. METHANE

This chemical is an important one because scientists think it is mostly produced by life—microbes in swamps and in animal tummies like ours. Methane (also called natural gas) is a great source of carbon, too, which is key for life as we know it. Here on Earth, some of the methane that makes its way up into the atmosphere is produced by cow burps. Not their farts; their burps. Really. If we see traces of methane in the air surrounding a far-off world, that doesn't mean it has belching bovines, but it might host some living things.

7. GREENHOUSE GASES

Most greenhouses aren't green houses, until there are plenty of plants growing inside. A farmer's or gardener's greenhouse is usually made of glass. Sunlight passes through the glass—hey, who just passed glass?—and energizes the plants inside. The heat they give off keeps a greenhouse warm. On a planet like ours, sunlight passes through the atmosphere, strikes solid ground and ocean, and is given off (see chapter 7) as heat. Molecules of different gases in the atmosphere hold in a great deal of that heat, and Earth stays warm enough for living things like us. All these particles in the atmosphere work a little bit like a greenhouse, so we call them greenhouse gases. If a distant planet has enough greenhouse gas to trap heat and keep the planet warm, then it could be a good spot for aliens.

8. FAT

The scientific term for what I'm talking about here is lipids [LIPP-idz]. They have certain kinds of molecules that have oxygen and a combo of oxygen and hydrogen hanging off to the side. Scientists call these fatty acids, but we can just call them fat. All living things make fat. We'd need a very close-up view—a robot on the surface, for example—to find evidence of these fats, but if we found them, wow, they'd be a strong clue that life existed there now or at some point in the past.

TRY THIS!

There's Nothing like Ice

WHAT YOU NEED:

Two drinking glasses

Rubbing alcohol (70% is fine, but 91% gives you even more dramatic results)

Two ice cubes

An adult to make sure you're very careful with the rubbing alcohol (Good on skin. Do not drink.)

WHAT YOU DO:

1. Fill a glass nearly full with water.

2. Fill another glass nearly full with rubbing alcohol.

3. Gently drop an ice cube in each glass.

RESULTS: What do you see? At temperatures we find on our planet's surface, water is the only substance we know whose solid phase is not as dense or heavy as its liquid phase. Some solid metals float on their liquid phases, but only at very hot metal-melting temperatures. Look at what the ice cube does in the water, then compare that with the ice cube in the glass full of rubbing alcohol.

Is water the key to life on another world? It sure seems to be. There is nothing like it that we've been able to find anywhere in the universe, and you and I are made of it. Perhaps every alien in the cosmos needs water, too. So let's keep looking for signs of water everywhere out there and report to NASA. Okay?

WEIRD! SCIENCE

Sanitizer in Space

You think your teachers use a lot of hand sanitizer? Astrobiologists are way more obsessed with cleanliness. Since the early days of astrobiology, thanks to a scientist named Joshua Lederberg, researchers have been worried about accidentally introducing tiny life-forms like bacteria to other worlds. You cover your mouth when you cough or sneeze to avoid covering your friends or family members with germs. Scientists have to think the same way about aliens. Every spacecraft or planet-exploring robot has to be free of any Earth microbe. Otherwise we could contaminate that world forever. And keep in mind, we'd really mess up the scientific process, too. Imagine if we discovered some miniature bacteria crawling around on Mars, and then found out we actually brought the tiny things to the Red Planet by accident. Ouch. So we sterilize spacecraft with strong chemicals and by baking them in very hot ovens. The spacecraft have to be able to take a serious wipe-down and stand some high heat. In the search for life on other worlds, you've got to keep it clean. Really, really clean.

> 66 To me being a scientist was such a distant dream when I was young. I didn't think there was room for me in science because no scientists looked like me. It can be pretty overwhelming if no one else looks like you or talks like you. It makes you feel out of place. But original ideas always come from unusual places. You don't need to fit in. Great ideas come from people who don't fit in, and in astrobiology we need everyone's help. As long as you are bold and brave and you think big. There's room for everybody."
>
> —ASTROBIOLOGIST BETÜL KAÇAR

THE CANALS OF MARS

IN THE LATE 19th and early 20th centuries, a clever and very wealthy amateur astronomer named Percival Lowell wrote a number of books suggesting there were aliens on Mars. Lowell believed that these Martians were so advanced that they built a series of canals that could carry water down from the poles of the planet to distant cities. He made sketches of what he observed with his telescopes. His drawings included the canals. He wrote wonderful books and gave very popular talks to the public about his Martian canal idea. But as telescopes improved, and scientists enjoyed a closer look at the Red Planet's surface, it became clear that there were no Martian-built canals—and no evidence of advanced Martians, either. Turns out, there really are streambeds and lake beds all over the place on Mars. There's overwhelming evidence of water flowing there a long, long time ago. But there are no artificial canals like the ones Lowell claimed to see. I often wonder if Lowell wasn't looking at the reflection of the pattern of blood vessels in the back of his eyeball in the eyepiece of his telescope, and somehow believed he was spotting a pattern of waterways on Mars. Hey, it could happen. Any way you look at it (uh . . . sorry), Lowell contributed to astronomy in his own way, building public enthusiasm and a fantastic observatory in Arizona that is still in use today.

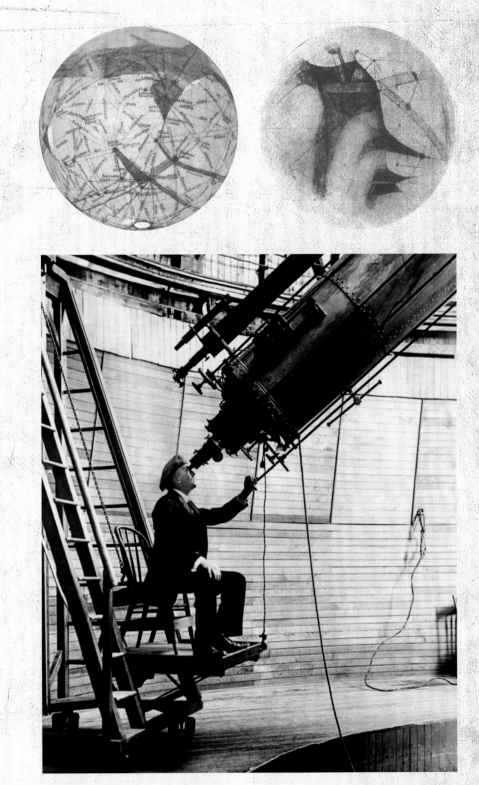

Percival Lowell observing Venus from the Lowell Observatory in 1914.

To-Do List:
Where to Look for Alien Life

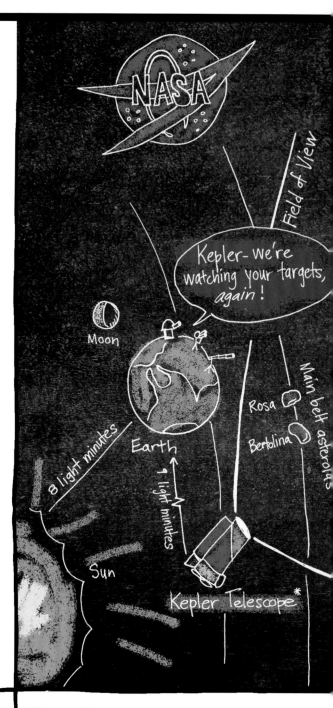

Kepler- we're watching your targets, again!

Field of View

Moon

Earth

Rosa

Bertolina

Main belt asteroids

8 light minutes

9 light minutes

Sun

Kepler Telescope *

☐ Mars

Evidence of water has been detected on Mars, and scientists have also found clues that the Red Planet might have once had hydrothermal vents like the ones in our deep ocean. Most scientists are searching for signs of life that existed there long ago—they're not exactly optimistic about something crawling or hopping in front of one of our rover spacecraft camera lenses anytime soon. But some astrobiologists believe there could be life hiding deep, deep beneath the Martian surface today. They'd be like the microbes we find in our own Earth's soil.

☐ Europa

This moon of the planet Jupiter is covered in ice, but below that frozen crust, Europa has an ocean with twice as much seawater as we have here on Earth. Water below the ice is liquid, because the moon itself is constantly being squeezed and unsqueezed by Jupiter's gravity as it orbits the huge planet. This squeezing isn't as dramatic as a scrunched squishy toy, but the regular motion generates heat. Could that warm, hidden ocean be home to some kind of life?

☐ Enceladus

Enceladus [Enn-SELL-uh-duss] is an icy moon that orbits the planet Saturn. It has a frozen surface, and it's far outside the Goldilocks zone. You wouldn't want to hang out on the surface. You'd suffocate, for one thing. But scientists have discovered jets of water- and chemical-rich plumes shooting out of huge cracks in that ice. This means that this moon is harboring an ocean under its icy shell. Where there's water, there may be life.

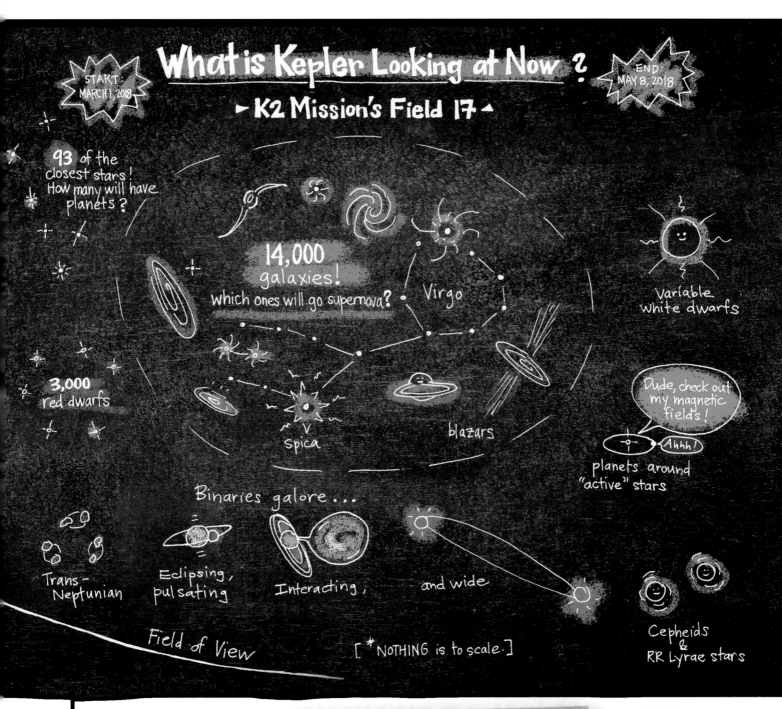

What is Kepler Looking at Now?

► K2 Mission's Field 17 ◄

START: MARCH 1, 2018

END: MAY 8, 2018

93 of the closest stars! How many will have planets?

14,000 galaxies! Which ones will go supernova?

Virgo

Variable white dwarfs

3,000 red dwarfs

Spica

blazars

Dude, check out my magnetic fields!

Ahhh!

planets around "active" stars

Binaries galore...

Trans-Neptunian

Eclipsing, pulsating

Interacting,

and wide

Cepheids & RR Lyrae stars

Field of View

[*NOTHING is to scale.]

☐ Exoplanets

Now that astronomers have discovered so many Earth-like planets beyond our own solar system, orbiting distant suns, astrobiologists would love to explore them. The only catch? They're kind of far away. The closest exoplanet is still more than four light-years from Earth. That means it would take a beam of light over four years to get here from there. And light travels way, way faster than the fastest spacecraft. With our fastest rocket, we'd need more than 15,000 years! For now, at least, we'll have to explore these planets with telescopes, from a distance.

This NASA cartoon illustrates some of the objects that Kepler observed in 2018. See some words you don't know? Well, look 'em up.

1.
Is There Life on Other Worlds?

We've found Earth-sized exoplanets. We have a pretty good idea of what life needs to develop and survive. But we still don't know if life actually exists anywhere else. When it comes to unsolved mysteries, this is the first one. It's kind of a big question. It would change our world.

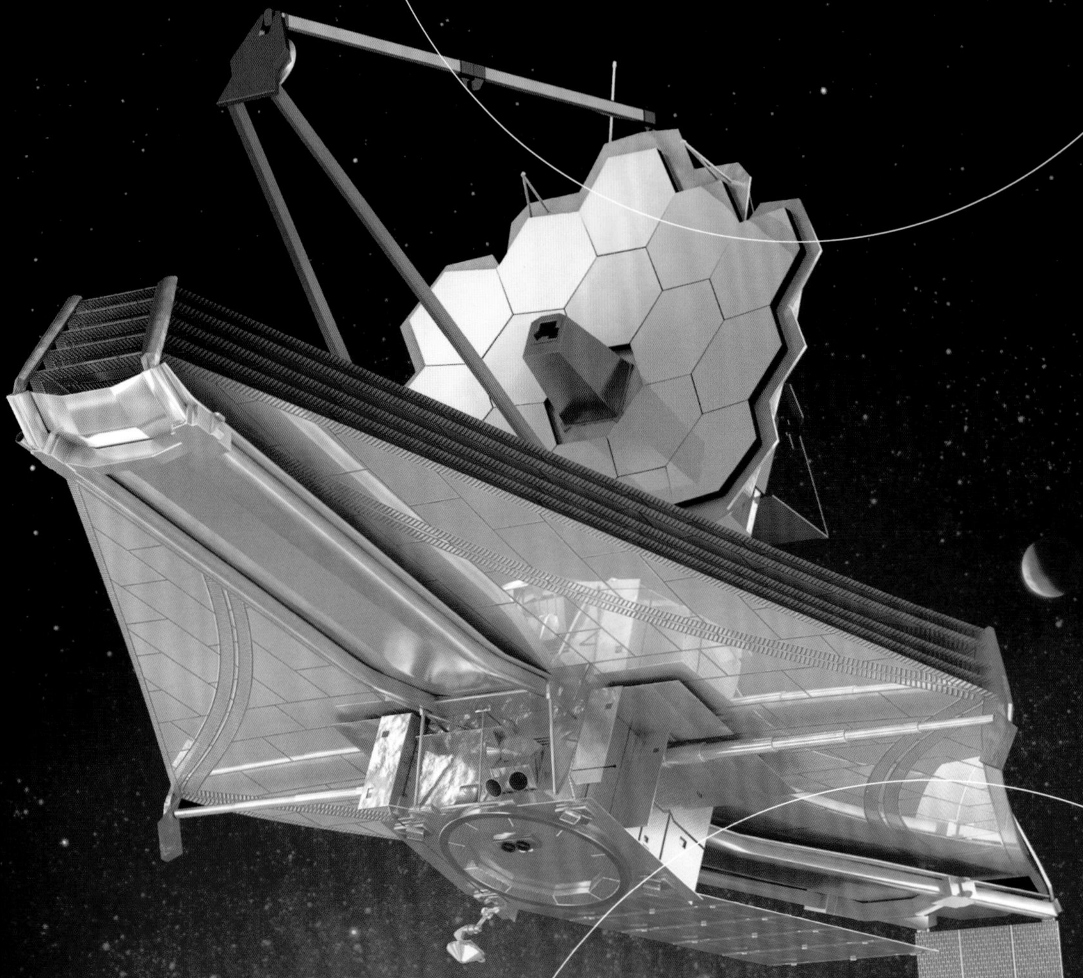

Scientists picked up signs of water vapor in the atmosphere of the exoplanet K2-18b (which might look like the picture on the right), which also orbits within its local star's Goldilocks zone. Could this exoplanet be hiding life? The James Webb Space Telescope (above) could help us find out.

"The search for life is far from over. We're really just getting started. The more questions that we're starting to answer in astrobiology, the more new questions we're coming up with. We need people to work on these questions. And if we did end up finding life on another planet, it would change our whole understanding of life and evolution and our position in the universe!"

—ASTROBIOLOGIST CAITLIN CASAR

2.
Where and How Did Life Begin?

Life could have begun here on Earth at one of our deep-sea hydrothermal vents. It could have evolved separately on another planet, or many other worlds, independent of what happened here. Or maybe life originated on Mars, then hitched a ride to our planet on a meteorite. We don't know. You should find out. It would mean designing cool new spacecraft equipment with just the right instruments to look for some of these signs of life, and then getting one or more space agencies to help pay for it. Please get this done, okay?

3.
Are There Intelligent Aliens?

"As far as intelligent alien life, we should not close our minds and eyes and ears to that possibility, but most of the work being done now is searching for the slimy, sludgy stuff that dominated Earth for most of its history."

—ASTROBIOLOGIST MICHAEL KIPP

BEFORE WE MOVE ON...

This search for life, and places in the universe that could host some form of life, makes me think a little more about our own home. It's a big universe out there. It can be a dangerous one, too. (Just ask an ancient dinosaur. . . . Wait. You can't; an asteroid wiped them out.) And yes, we've discovered all kinds of interesting exoplanets. But you have to wonder, if any intelligent aliens are out there looking back our way, if they're a little jealous. After all, Earth is a pretty special place.

➤ In case you haven't realized,

Earth is amazing. And not just because you're here. There are so, so many other reasons. Our planet isn't too hot or too cold. We have gravity, which holds the ocean and the atmosphere tightly to Earth's surface. Heat from massive atoms fissioning in its core causes Earth's insides to stay warm and churn. The Earth has been spinning since it was formed, which causes its hot metal insides (Earth's core) to spin, too. The spinning hot almost-liquid metal creates a magnetic field, which directs charged particles from the Sun to mostly zoom around our planet instead of just zapping us and tearing our DNA apart. We call this protective region the magnetosphere [Mag-NEET-uh-sfeer]. It's like a giant force field. I mean . . . really? We even have our own protective force field? What a planet!

Earth's amazing force field in action.

Two Massively Important Points About: The Earth's Crust

The outer layer of Earth, called the crust, is made of rocks. If you're outside, you're standing on the crust. Your house or apartment is built on the crust. Your secret laboratory cave or evil lair? Still on, or barely in, the crust. Mountains, deserts, all the water that makes up our lakes and seas and oceans, all the air we breathe—all of it is sitting or sloshing around on top of the crust. And there are two really important things you need to know about the crust.

Ever heard of **GEOLOGY?** It's not just about rocks. **"GEO"** comes from a Greek word meaning "Earth." So geology started out as the study of Earth. But some geologists end up studying other planets, too.

1. THE CRUST IS THIN.

Earth's crust compared with the whole planet is thinner than the shell of an egg compared with the whole egg. It's much thinner than the crust of a slice of bread compared with the bread. Earth's crust is thin.

2. THE CRUST IS ALWAYS MOVING.

The layer of rock that surrounds our planet is broken into about ten major pieces—or seven, or maybe a dozen, depending on which scientist you ask—and plenty of small ones (plates, not scientists). We call these pieces tectonic [Tek-TAHN-ik] plates.

Some tectonic plates grind against each other, sliding in one direction or another. Others slide into head-on collisions, forcing one plate to slip down, under another one, into the hot, gooey part of Earth's insides. At still other places on the planet, the plates are slowly, slowly sliding away from each other, and some of Earth's hot insides ooze up to the surface.

What's Inside the Earth?

▶ If we were to slice our planet right down the middle, it would look a little like what you see over there on the right. The first layer is the crust, which is 70 kilometers (40 miles) thick in some places and only 10 kilometers (6 miles) thick in others (along the bottom of the ocean). Next we have the very hot mantle. It flows like goo or slime, but it's ridiculously hot, almost-but-not-quite solid rock. Beneath the mantle, Earth is really hot liquid—liquid metal. That's the outer core. Underneath that, Earth has a solid inner core. It's mostly made of iron and nickel, mixed with some other dense metals.

Geologists like to say the mantle is "plastic." The mantle bends and oh so slowly oozes just a few centimeters a year. Even your hair grows faster than that. Go ahead, stand up in front of a mirror and watch your hair grow—or your fingernails. No, don't come back just yet. Give it a few more days . . . okay, great. That's perfect. Now do you see what I mean? It's slow going, but it's flowing.

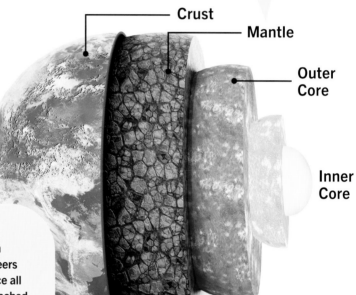

Crust

Mantle

Outer Core

Inner Core

ADVENTURES IN GEOLOGY

No one has ever been to the core. We can't even get close. A team of Soviet scientists and engineers once tried to drill from up here on Earth's surface all the way through the crust to the mantle. They reached 12 kilometers (7.5 miles) down. They couldn't get any farther. At 12 kilometers, the temperature was 180 degrees Celsius (just over 350 degrees Fahrenheit). Hot enough to bake cookies!

MIND, BLOWN!

Geological Time

The plates that make up Earth's crust move slowly, barely two or three centimeters per year. But geologists don't think in years. They think in hundreds of thousands, and millions, and billions of years. On that time scale, the crust starts to look busy. Earth's plates move and stretch and snap. They create new land, and new crust, when they spread apart. They make brand-new rocks and bury old rocks when they ride over or under each other. All this slow, steady movement gives us mountains, valleys, undersea peaks, earthquakes, and volcanos. It takes time, time, time, and more time. Did I mention time? Lots of it?

THIS ROCK FROM CANADA IS **4.03 BILLION YEARS OLD.** →

Acasta Gneiss (shiny rock near the Acasta River).

Proof!
Rocks as Clocks

Geologists figure Earth is about 4.54 billion years old. They got to this number because a lot of rocks have a natural clock built right in. Take a look at your periodic table again. Along with the number of protons (an element's atomic number), there's another number written below the letters of its atomic symbol. That's an element's atomic mass or weight. It's bigger than the atomic number because of the mass or weight of a few or a whole lot of neutrons.

Atoms being the way they are, and nature being the way it is, now and then, subatomic particles will fly out of the nucleus of an atom. Energy from the beginning of the cosmos is stored in these atoms, and it gets released. As we mentioned in chapter 11, certain atoms will change from one atomic number to another. Uranium can become lead (92 becomes 82). Potassium can become argon (19 becomes 18). Rubidium can have one of its neutrons become a proton and turn into strontium (37 becomes 38), and so on. With the right tools, geologists can tell when a rock cooled and changed from liquid, or nearly liquid, to solid. It's amazing. From that, they

can work back, back, back into time. It's like a detective story, in which our hero figures out who did what by studying clues at the crime scene. Except in geology, we're not talking about crimes that happened in the last year; we're talking about events over the last few million or billion years.

These tricks have helped geologists piece together the entire history of Earth. Many people think we humans are the start and the stars of this story. But if the history of Earth were shown as an hour-long television special, we'd only appear in about the last three-quarters of a second! I mean—whoa . . . ! Looking at it this way, we are hardly part of Earth's story at all. We're just the storytellers. Weird (in a way).

> 66 Studying Earth's history is as close to visiting a foreign planet as you can get because you're looking at an Earth without land or a world without life as we know it. You can paint a picture of what the early Earth looked like based on what a rock is made of and what it looks like."
>
> —*GEOLOGIST NOAH PLANAVSKY*

Four Massively Important Points About: The Earth's Plates

Pangaea

1. Earth is making new crust all the time. In the rift zones, where tectonic plates are spreading apart, hot rock squeezes up to form new crust.

2. North America is moving away from Europe at about 2.5 centimeters (about an inch) every year.

3. The continents we know today were once joined together as part of one big supercontinent we call Pangaea [Pann-JEE-uh] ("all earth").

4. This wasn't the only supercontinent. Earth has gone through several of these supercontinent cycles in its history.

BUT, GOOD!

⬖ REALLY OLD SCIENCE ⬖

CRUST DEPARTMENT

WHEN ALFRED WEGENER DIED IN 1930, most scientists thought his theory about how the Earth worked was nutty. He studied maps and globes and noticed that it sure looks like South America could nestle right up next to Africa. They might fit together like puzzle pieces. He found the same layers of rock bearing the same type of fossils on both sides of the ocean. He figured the major land masses must have moved apart, and they were probably still moving. But he didn't quite figure out just how these continents could drift or move. So very few of the geologists of his day believed him. And you can't blame them, really. The idea is wild—but true!

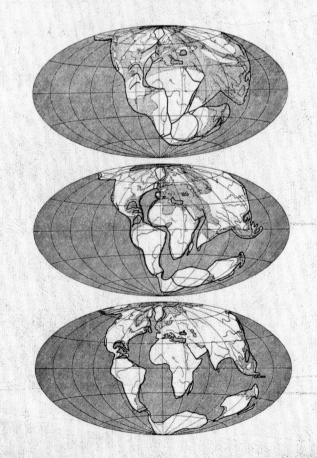

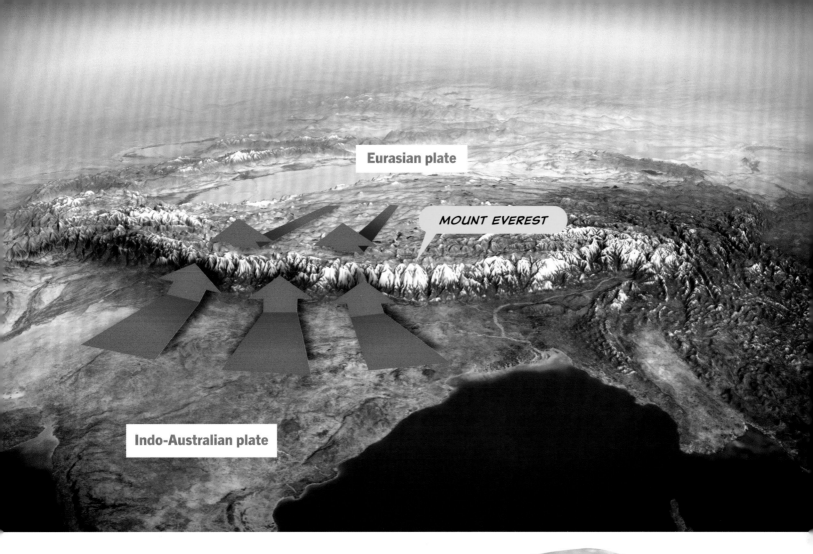

Eurasian plate

MOUNT EVEREST

Indo-Australian plate

The Science of Building Mountains

➤ What is now India used to be an island. But that island wasn't floating on the ocean. It was riding on the plastic (bendable), hot rock of the mantle. As the world churned, the plate moved, and the island moved north toward another continental plate—one that's carrying what is now Europe and Asia. After creeping northward for about 150 million years, what we now call the Indo-Australian plate began to crash into the Eurasian plate. The slow but powerful collision forced the plates to buckle and lift upward. An enormous wrinkle in the rocky crust got pushed up higher and higher for tens of millions of years, until Earth had its tallest mountain range, the Himalayas, and our tallest peak, Mount Everest.

WEIRD ! SCIENCE

A World Built on Candy

" The ground we're standing on feels rigid and solid. But over millions of years, it acts more like a piece of toffee or candy. It stretches when you pull, but if you pull it hard enough, eventually it will snap. That's what we call rifting, where two plates end up moving apart from one another, and that's how Earth makes new land. Then we add new toffee from below as the magma rises up and turns into new land. This way, you never run out of candy."

—GEOSCIENTIST CHRISTOPHER JACKSON

Sure, they've scorched cities, buried people, shaken buildings into rubble, and created all kinds of problems in modern times, but without volcanos, our planet might not be a good place for humans. Or any other kind of complex life. In the early years of Earth, volcanos were belching and spewing their insides all over our rocky planet. But all that magma carried some extremely important chemicals to the surface. Without volcanos we wouldn't have an atmosphere or oceans. And without an atmosphere or oceans we wouldn't have life at all.

Uh-Oh:
Volcanic Eruptions

▶ The mantle—the part of Earth below the crust—is hot, not-quite-solid rock. But in some places that rock melts more completely, and pools of hot liquid rock called magma [MAGG-muh] collect within the crust. Cracks and vents form, and the magma burbles up to the surface. When magma spews up out of the crust, by long tradition, we call it lava [LAH-vuh] instead, and blam! We have a volcano. And you should run. Or walk. It depends. If it's an oozing, shaped-like-a-gladiator-shield volcano, like in Hawaii, you can walk. There's less risk of pent-up volcanic energy exploding. But if it's erupting because of moving magma and the edge of a tectonic plate soaked in ancient water from the sea, I'd say you should be ready to sprint—then maybe zoom off in a jet airplane. The water turns to steam, and the volcano can blow its top. The amount of energy in a volcano is astonishing. We're talking about red-hot rocks that set fire to everything in their path. There's no stopping them. We're talking about mountainsides sliding downhill at the speed of a fighter plane. Can't stop them, either. It's ancient heat energy stored just below Earth's crust making its way to the surface. **KA-BOOM!**

Eruption of Anak Krakatau Volcano in indonesia, July 2018.

❝ When I was 13 years old, my science teacher wrote 'volcanologist' on the board and I thought, 'Oh, that's me. That's what I am.' I grew up fascinated by volcanos and I remember thinking the idea of studying them for a living was way too cool to be a real job. But that's what I do. Today I study them for two reasons. One is that I love them. The other is that I want to help people get out of the way when they're about to erupt."

—VOLCANOLOGIST JANINE KRIPPNER

SCIENTISTS SAVING THE WORLD

DEPARTMENT OF VOLCANOLOGY

Mount St. Helens

When Mount Saint Helens erupted on May 18, 1980, in the great state of Washington, rocks and other debris rushed down the side of the mountain at 50 meters (or more than 160 feet) per second. Some rocks got up to 80 meters (or about 260 feet) per second, according to my volcanologist friends Janine Krippner and Alison Graettinger. That's faster than a jet taking off. I've climbed to the rim and I've hiked in the crater of Mount Saint Helens. It's wild. It looks like some giant person took a bite out of a piece of Earth's Crust Candy to see if it was caramel or chocolate cream. I mean, you can see the many layers of rock formed by many other eruptions long in the past.

Scientists cannot predict exactly when a volcano will erupt, but these clues let them know if an eruption might happen soon. I say "might," because these signs still aren't a guarantee. The gas, for example, might be just the volcano's way of relieving some pressure. It might actually prevent an eruption, not encourage one. Kind of like when you've eaten certain . . . never mind. This is a science book. We're trying to explore the mysteries of life, the universe, and everything in between. We need to stay focused, people.

Luckily, most of us don't have volcanos in our backyards. We know where the big ones are located, and scientists are watching them for signs of activity. My volcanologist friends say there are a few different signs they monitor.

1. Small Earthquakes
These rumblings of Earth's crust can be a clue that a volcano might be getting ready to burp.

2. Rising Temperatures
Why in the world would the temperature of spring water or groundwater rise before an eruption? That's right! Because scorching hot magma is working its way up from Earth's scorching hot interior.

3. Escaping Gas
Not every volcano will create an ash cloud as large as the 1980 Mount Saint Helens event—that one spread to the middle of the United States, all the way from the West Coast—but rising gases can be a hint that something serious is happening beneath the surface. When I've hiked and climbed Mount Saint Helens, I've seen plenty of steam still rising out of huge cracks in the mountain.

4. Rising Ground
Before a volcanic eruption, the surrounding ground might actually lift up a few millimeters or even a couple of meters—the height of a tall human.

5. Stinky Water
As magma rises up from below, the chemistry of water near the volcano can start to change, too. It might start to smell like a rotten egg.

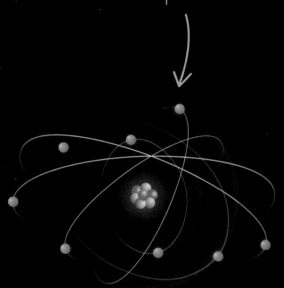

I know, I know. This is not what atoms really look like. We went over that. But we needed to see the particles here.

Protons and electrons attract each other like crazy. That's the electromagnetic force at work. Left on their own, particles carrying the same charge—proton and proton, or electron and electron—push each other away.

FUNDAMENTAL FORCE #2

ELECTROMAGNETISM

> This is what we call the invisible force, the one that makes electricity flow and magnets stick to your refrigerator . . . or stick to paper clips. I don't know about you, but the word "electromagnetism" looks to me like two words, electricity and magnetism, smashed together. And it is . . . or they are. It turns out that electricity and magnetism are separate effects produced by the same basic force. You may have heard the expression "opposites attract." Remember our tiny particles from the last chapter—the protons and electrons? One has a positive charge. The other has a negative charge. The electromagnetic force holds electrons and protons together inside atoms. It's the reason opposites attract. On the atomic level, anyway.

So electrons and protons attract each other like crazy. But particles carrying the same charge, electron and electron, or proton and proton, push each other away.

Close-up of a fault line or fracture in the Earth in the Flaming Gorge area, Utah.

WRONG!

Animals Can Predict Earthquakes

> No scientist has ever predicted a major earthquake with useful accuracy. People who claim to have psychic powers never guess correctly, either. How about animals? The electronic Internet, that great protector of unproven ideas, will tell you that elephants, rats, cats, and all other manner of creatures have the ability to predict earthquakes. You'll find stories about animals running away or behaving strangely before a major crust-shaker. But these claims have never been proven. And a claim that cannot be proven is not much use in science.

TRY THIS!

Earth's Rocky Wrinkles

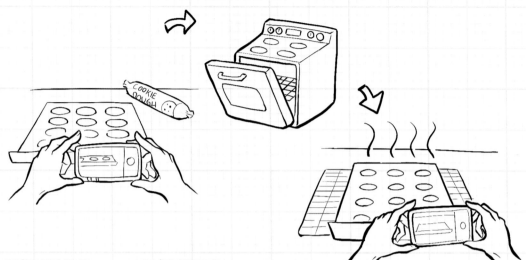

WHAT YOU NEED:

Oven

Cookie dough
(a slice-and-bake
version is ideal)

Cookie sheet

Adult to oversee
oven operation

WHAT YOU DO:

1. Preheat the oven according to your preferred cookie recipe.

2. Drop the cookie dough onto the cookie sheet; or slice and place them.

3. Take a picture of the uncooked dough.

4. Start to bake the cookies, per the recipe instructions.

5. Halfway through the suggested cooking time, take the cookies out of the oven and take another picture.

6. Put 'em back and finish baking the cookies.

7. Move them to a rack or plate and let them cool; I mean really cool.

8. Take another picture.

9. Compare your photos of the cookie surfaces, hot to cold.

10. Eat the cookies as you contemplate the science.

RESULTS: The surface of the dough changed from smooth to cracked because the dough shrinks a little bit as it cools. Same thing happened on Earth as it cooled! See, Earth started out hot. Gravity slammed a whole mess of space dust together with enough force to make it get very, very hot—hotter than an oven, hot enough to melt solid rock . . . er, uh, dust. Eventually our planet started to cool. As the surface cooled, it shrank and cracked, just like your cookies.

BEFORE WE MOVE ON...

Do you kind of appreciate this planet of ours a little more? I'm telling you, it's a special place. A wild spot in a wild universe. You just need to think about it on a different scale. Not by the minute or even the year. Consider how our home changes over millions or even hundreds of millions of years. This place builds mountains from scratch! It belches fiery rocks! Now, if you agree with me that Earth is pretty special, I have another question for you . . .

chapter 14

What You Need to Know About **Climate Change** and Why

February 15, 2019: Protestors at a Youth Strike for Climate march in central London.

▶ This planet of ours is a pretty interesting place.

Go ahead and try to find another giant rock swarming with life, covered with warm salty oceans and fresh (nonsalty) water, green landscapes, and breathable air. It'll need to be surrounded by a huge force field protecting its inhabitants from dangerous cosmic rays, too. There really aren't many planets like this in our cosmic neighborhood. Astronomers have searched. So now here's the big important question.

Why aren't we taking care of our rock?

Humans are changing our planet's climate. The science is undeniable. Our factories, vehicles, ships, airplanes, and power plants are pumping carbon dioxide and other gases into the air, trapping heat and forcing our planet to warm.

Because of the extra heat in the air and ocean, our planet's climate has already begun to change. More heat in the atmosphere means more wild weather—more droughts, floods, and extreme weather events. And it will continue to change as you grow older. The world is going to be a very different place when you're as old as your parents and teachers. And possibly not as nice a place.

Two Massively Important Points About: Climate

Psst: My coauthor, Greg, walks his dog, Toby, every morning. Greg heads in one direction, but Toby races forward, back, and all around. Toby is like the weather. He's all over the place. Greg keeps moving straight ahead, so he's more like the climate. But they have similar hairstyles. Some days, I can hardly tell them apart. The dog and the coauthor, I mean. Not weather and climate.

1. Weather and Climate Are Different.

Are you reading closely here? Good. Here we go. Weather happens day to day or week to week. If it's cold out tomorrow, or rainy—that's the weather. Climate is different. It's the big picture, what happens with moisture and temperature over many years and decades. So if it snows one day in the late spring, that doesn't mean our planet isn't warming. It means there's a spell of strange weather. When scientists talk about climate change, they're not talking about weather. They're talking about what's happening on Earth over many years.

2. Our Climate Is Changing.

You may have heard people talk about the greenhouse effect. In a greenhouse, light streams in through the windows and warms up the room. Plants use this sunlight to carry out photosynthesis and release heat. The warm air gets squeezed up by cooler air (recall natural convection and heat in chapter 7), but the windows trap most of the heat inside. This way, the greenhouse room stays warm even in winter.

Now imagine our planet as one big greenhouse. Earth doesn't have windows. But we do have layers of air, the atmosphere, that act a bit like the windows of a greenhouse.

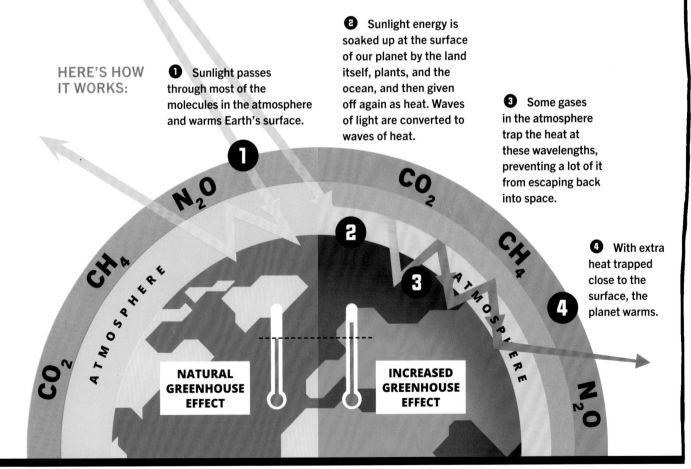

HERE'S HOW IT WORKS:

1 Sunlight passes through most of the molecules in the atmosphere and warms Earth's surface.

2 Sunlight energy is soaked up at the surface of our planet by the land itself, plants, and the ocean, and then given off again as heat. Waves of light are converted to waves of heat.

3 Some gases in the atmosphere trap the heat at these wavelengths, preventing a lot of it from escaping back into space.

4 With extra heat trapped close to the surface, the planet warms.

N_2O CO_2 CH_4 ATMOSPHERE CO_2 CH_4 ATMOSPHERE N_2O

NATURAL GREENHOUSE EFFECT

INCREASED GREENHOUSE EFFECT

Invisible Gas, Infinite Power

So what is this carbon dioxide gas? And why is it so powerful that a boost of 130 parts per million makes such a difference? It's clear and invisible. You breathe it out every few seconds, and it comes with some interesting chemistry. Imagine a carbon atom in the middle holding an oxygen on either side. The three link up in a line. Up in the atmosphere, these straight-line molecules let sunlight pass through to the surface, but they block the longer wavelength heat that bounces back up. Windows in a greenhouse let sunlight in, but prevent warm air from escaping. Greenhouse gases do almost the same thing.

As I type this book, we are pumping more than 100 million tons of carbon dioxide into the atmosphere every day. It's more than 37 billion tons a year. The amount of carbon dioxide in the atmosphere has increased almost by half since the 18th century. With every day, and every passing year, we're turning our planet into a more powerful greenhouse. This is not good.

NEED TO KNOW:

The Link Between CO$_2$ and Climate Change

➤ There's overwhelming evidence showing that we're already changing the planet, especially when we're talking about carbon dioxide. It's not the strongest greenhouse gas, but since we're adding so much carbon dioxide to the air every second, it's the most important one.

Let's say you could break the atmosphere down into a million equal parts. Before humans built factories and cars and power plants that churn out greenhouse gases, 280 parts out of that million were carbon dioxide. Today, more than 410 parts out of that million are carbon dioxide. (If you like math, 410 parts per million is the same as 0.0410%.) Sure, it seems like a small number, but it's a huge jump in carbon dioxide, young scientist. As we add more greenhouse gases to our air, our atmosphere traps more heat. And when our atmosphere traps more heat, the temperature rises, and our climate changes.

SOURCES OF CARBON DIOXIDE IN THE ATMOSPHERE IN 2017

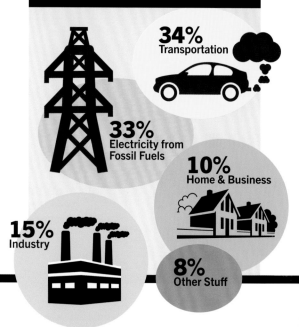

34% Transportation

33% Electricity from Fossil Fuels

10% Home & Business

15% Industry

8% Other Stuff

To-Do List:
RIDE YOUR BIKE

We're not going to stop global warming and climate change right away. But we can slow the rate of change and reverse it eventually. The longest journey starts with a single step, so let's get rolling. What I mean is: Don't stop riding your bike.

Unless you're heading for a wall. Or a cliff. You shouldn't stop riding your bike as you grow older. I still ride my bicycle as often as possible. Yes, I have an electric car, but if I need to pick up some groceries, or grab a coffee, or even jump in the ocean, I use my bicycle. And you should, too, if you want to slow the pace of climate change. Why? Your bicycle does not pump out carbon dioxide! Oh sure, some carbon dioxide was produced in manufacturing your machine, but that is a teeny tiny fraction of how much carbon dioxide would be made by driving everywhere you can ride. And one of my bikes is 45 years old. Still rides like new, maybe better.

Of course, you can't ride a bike everywhere. We can't use bicycles to carry all the things and food we move around in trucks and trains. But if we have all-electric cars, trains, and trucks, we can slowly (or pretty quickly) convert our transportation systems to be all electric all the time.

Today, the same car that runs on electricity generated by a natural gas—fired power plant can tomorrow run on a completely clean renewable source of energy. A wind turbine, for example. You know, those towering towers whose blades slowly turn as the wind flows past. That slow, majestic turning generates electricity we can use to power our cars and our homes and our robots . . . without burning fossil fuels and pumping carbon dioxide into the atmosphere!

Think about what you use, what you eat, how you travel, and whether any of your behavior or choices have an impact on the climate. We can change the kind of cars we drive and the way we produce electricity all at the same time. We can get this done. In the meantime, though, keep pedaling. Bicycles are fantastic for the air and for your heart. Learn to ride safely, and you can change your part of the world.

> " Climate change is one of the biggest issues if not the biggest issue that's going to affect the future of our world. Understanding it will help you contribute more to the world. You don't have to be a climate expert. You could also think about other processes that affect our planet— glaciers, oceans, forests. Thinking about how the world around us works and what drives changes in it is so, so important."
>
> —*GLACIOLOGIST ALLEN POPE*

ANOTHER CHANGE-THE-WORLD CLIMATE TIP:
Turn out the lights when you leave the room. I'm not kidding. It makes a difference.

Uh-Oh:
Extreme Weather Is Extremely Likely

➤ Storms thrive on energy. As the climate changes and we trap more heat near the surface, we're also trapping more energy there. Storms are going to swallow up that energy, leading to more intense hurricanes, rains, and snowfalls. Here are a few of the things we might be looking forward to:

Rising Seas

The warming world is also expanding the ocean. Melting ice sheets and glaciers dump more water into the sea, and the added heat from increasing global temperatures causes the ocean itself to balloon, to expand— we call the process thermal expansion. As the sea level rises, the ocean climbs higher and higher on the beaches and seawalls with each passing year. What's going to happen to the 600 million people who live near the coast? How are they going to manage in this new world of higher waters?

More Floods

Increasing global temperatures pump more energy into the atmosphere, which leads to more warm air getting squeezed up by cool air, which means powerful storms. Warmer air also holds more moisture, so these storms carry more water, and they dump that water onto cities and landscapes that just aren't ready for it, leading to more extreme floods.

More Dry Spells

While it will rain more in some places as the climate changes, other areas will receive less rain. Warmer air can hold more moisture, so we end up with more water moving up into the atmosphere in places. Higher temperatures in some areas force even more water to evaporate from the ground, leading to dry spells, or droughts. And then there's less water for people to drink, cook with, or use to clean themselves and their dishes.

One More Massively Important Point About: Climate Change

Earth Doesn't Care About Climate Change

Keep in mind: The Earth doesn't care about us or what we do. Really. I mean, it's a mostly superhot rock, so it probably doesn't have feelings, but even if it did, our planet would shrug off all this change. Earth's climate has changed many, many times in the past. Change is nothing new to it. Our planet will go on spinning. It has been here for 4.5 billion years. We humans appeared less than 2 million years ago. The Earth is all set. However, when it comes to us and our well-being, and all the many, many life-forms and ecosystems thriving on our planet today, well, that's a different story. We should be worried.

TRY THIS!
Rising Temperatures and Rising Seas

WHAT YOU NEED:

Glass jar with a top

Drill, plus an adult to use it

Food coloring

Reusable straw

Modeling clay

Bowl large enough to hold the jar

WHAT YOU DO:

1. Drill a straw-sized hole in the jar's lid.

2. Fill the jar to the very top with cold water.

3. Stir in some food coloring.

4. Insert the straw, screw on the lid, and check the water level. Seal the straw to the lid with some modeling clay

5. Fill the bowl with hot water.

6. Submerge the jar in the hot water.

RESULTS: What do you notice? Does the water level change once the jar is exposed to the warm water? This is thermal expansion on a small scale. Now imagine it happening across an entire planet! That's what climate change is doing to our oceans.

Four Common Arguments Against Climate Change

For a number of frustrating reasons that really frustrate me, because they're so silly and frustrating, some people insist that climate change is either not real, or somehow nothing to worry about. Sure. Okay. But what about nearly every climate scientist out there who thinks otherwise? Shouldn't we pay attention to the experts? Apparently not, or not for everyone. So what do we do? We engage. We talk. We discuss. That's what I do, anyway. And I have found that climate change deniers often use one or more of the following arguments.

WRONG!

1. The Unexpectedly Cold Day

Maybe it snows one day in the spring or a blanket of cold air settles down for a while in the summer. Every time something like this happens, you'll hear people shout that climate change isn't real. "Where's your global warming now, Science Guy?" But remember: What we're experiencing when this happens is a change in the weather. The day-to-day happenings in a specific area. Climate effects happen over years and decades. It's about the whole planet. A snowfall in spring doesn't mean the greenhouse effect isn't real. Keep in mind that without the greenhouse effect, none of us would be alive. But when we pump too many greenhouse gases into the atmosphere, then we trap too much heat, and our climate changes.

WRONG!

WRONG!

2. Earth Has Warmed Before

In the good ol' ancient dinosaur days, our world had a great deal more carbon dioxide in the air, and it was much, much warmer. Much, much more recently, some areas of Earth, where people were keeping records, warmed from around the year 950 to about the year 1250. We didn't have any factories then. Or trucks or cars. So unless a race of highly advanced aliens settled here briefly, this change in climate was entirely natural. Some people will use this story to argue that if the planet warmed before from natural causes, maybe that's what is happening now. Maybe all of our cars and trucks and factories and power plants don't really matter. No. No, no, no. The problem for us is the speed—the rate at which our world is warming. Scientists have found no evidence of the world ever warming this quickly (except after asteroid hits). We're changing the planet faster than ever before, and those 35 billion tons of carbon dioxide a year are the reason why.

3. Carbon Dioxide Is Great!

We exhale carbon dioxide. Plants take in carbon dioxide. That's one of the reasons I talk to my plants every morning, after I walk my hippo around the block a few times, and tell them about my schedule for the day, the experiments I hope to run, things like that. So some people will argue that more carbon dioxide should be good for the planet, because plants love the stuff. And it has been good for us humans, generally. But now we're adding way, way too much of it, way, way too fast. Milk is generally good for you, too. (Unless you're lactose intolerant, of course. We talked about that in chapter 5, about evolution.) But not if you drink a whole gallon in 30 minutes. One of Greg's friends tried that once. Not pretty, kids. The cleanup was horrific. And so it goes with carbon dioxide. Too much of a good thing leads to floods, extreme weather, droughts, and more.

WRONG!

WRONG!

4. The Dinosaurs Dealt with It

Around 175 million years ago, there was about three times as much carbon dioxide in the atmosphere as there is today. At the time, Earth was swarming with dinosaurs. So some people will argue that if the dinosaurs could deal with high levels of carbon dioxide, then so can we. Yeah, okay, but . . . they were dinosaurs! They came into existence when Earth's climate was very different. For millions of years, they did not have to deal with rapid change. They adapted to survive and thrive in that kind of climate. We have not. We're built for the climate Earth has enjoyed for the last few million years. Our cities and towns are designed for this climate. Our farms ended up where they are for the same reason. As the climate changes, all that's going to change, too. And it will be an awful drag, unless we get to work.

Ancient air is trapped in this stunning ice core.

How Scientists Measure Climate Change

▶ Right, right, so how do scientists know what the climate was like a few hundred years ago, or even a few hundred thousand years ago? We're collecting information. Data! There are two main ways scientists find clues about old and even ancient climates.

∧ Drilling Ice

Scientists can study what the atmosphere was like going back hundreds of thousands of years because ancient air gets trapped between the snowflakes of fallen snow. I've been to the middle of an ice sheet in Greenland and seen the layers of snow that form each winter. As the years go by, the weight of the snow above crushes the flakes below into clear ice. But even then, the ice is still 10% air. Not just any air, though: old air. Go down far enough and you'll find ancient air that was trapped in that ice hundreds of thousands of years ago. When those ice samples are brought to the surface, scientists can measure the makeup of the ancient atmosphere. There's no faking these facts. They've proven that hundreds of thousands of years ago, the world used to have less carbon dioxide than it does now. And more important: They can show that the world is warming faster now than it probably ever has. Scientists have drilled down about 3,000 meters (around two miles) in Greenland, Antarctica, and Siberia to pull up samples of this ancient ice and ancient air.

< Reading Rocks

As any librarian will tell you, be it in a book or on a screen, reading does rock; it's how you can learn about almost anything. Well, while you and I normally read words on pages, or listen to someone else reading them, geologists can read rocks. They can study really old rocks and compare them with relatively young rocks to learn how the chemistry of the atmosphere reacts with minerals of Earth's crust. As rain falls through the air it becomes mildly acidic, and slightly corrosive, which means it can break things down. The more carbon dioxide in the air, the more acidic or corrosive raindrops become. The surfaces of certain rocks get worn away faster today than they did in the past. So geologists and other scientists read the rocks and work their way back in time to see how the atmosphere has changed over the centuries.

Uh-Oh: **Killing Nemo**

➤ Every important question about the way the world works forces you to learn about different scientific fields. So yes, this is a chapter on climate, but it's also about oceanography, and chemistry, too. One of the many things chemists test is whether a liquid is acidic or basic. Orange juice is acidic. Spit, too. Seawater is basic, but it's becoming more and more acidic. If you haven't already, try the acid and base demo back in chapter 8.

The oceans cover almost three-quarters of the surface of our planet, and they also pull down most of the carbon dioxide. Almost one-third of the carbon dioxide we pump into the atmosphere swirls around the world and is quickly dissolved in the world's oceans. Twenty-two million tons of carbon dioxide, or the weight of about 10 million cars, drop into the ocean each day! Over time, our seas will pull even more of this gas out of the air. The more carbon dioxide, the more acidic (check chapter 8) the ocean becomes—and that's a problem, too.

The oceans have changed like this in the past, but the change happened over thousands and thousands of years. We humans have changed the chemistry of the ocean in less than 250 years, and this is seriously hurting different marine life-forms. Sea creatures like crabs, oysters, and mussels need a really important molecule, carbonate (carbon with three oxygens), to grow their shells. When carbon dioxide reacts with seawater, it forms carbonic acid, and ties up lots of the carbonates that creatures—including phytoplankton—need to grow their shells. Phytoplankton are the super-important tiny creatures at the base of the food pyramid. They need their carbonates. And if the acidity goes up even a tiny bit, it can dissolve the shells of other complex sea creatures, including the zooxanthellae, the small animals that form coral reefs. That is bad, young scientists, because coral reefs support thousands of species of fish, among other things. Even poor, cute little Nemo is affected! Clownfish become confused in more acidic ocean water and fail to swim away from predators. So they get eaten.

Bubbles of methane gas frozen into clear ice, Lake Baikal, Russia.

Keep Siberia Cold!

Carbon dioxide isn't the only greenhouse gas. Another one, methane, also traps heat. Although there is less methane in the air than carbon dioxide right now, methane is a much more powerful greenhouse gas. It turns out that billions of tons of methane, from ancient swamps and prairies, are buried in the frozen ground in places like Siberia and at the bottom of the ocean. But if Siberia warms enough, and the ground thaws out, that methane will be released into the atmosphere. The same goes for the ocean—warmer water could allow the buried methane to bubble up. We don't know what's going to happen with all this trapped methane, but it's a problem that you future scientists need to keep your eyes on.

WHOA, DUDE, IT'S ALL CONNECTED.

Slowing the Conveyor Belt

A nice feature of bright white ice is that it reflects sunlight back into space. Since it reflects the light, it doesn't absorb very much of the Sun's energy, so it helps keep things cool on the surface of polar seas. As our climate has warmed, though, less of this ice forms in our northern seas each winter. When there's less ice, sunlight strikes the ocean surface directly. The dark ocean water soaks up the heat and becomes slightly warmer. That causes more ice to melt, and more sunlight warms the sea, and so it becomes warmer and warmer. A key part of the giant ocean current conveyor belt that moves heat around the planet (back in chapter 4) is that water cools in the North Atlantic Ocean and sinks. If that water is too warm, these water masses won't sink as quickly, and that will slow the global flow of the ocean current conveyor belt. And the Gulf Stream may slow which could mess with weather in Europe. Phew . . .

Thirty years ago, the Arctic ice pack contained significant areas of old, thick sea ice that had lasted through several years (white in the image). Now only a fraction of that ice remains frozen through the summer.

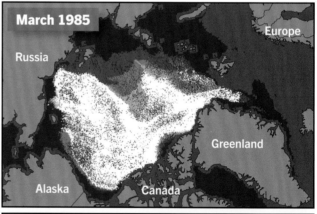

March 1985
Europe
Russia
Greenland
Alaska
Canada

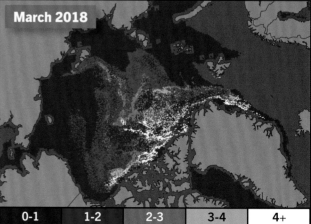

March 2018

0-1	1-2	2-3	3-4	4+

Sea ice age (years)

TRY THIS!

Coldly Predict Our Icy Future

WHAT YOU NEED:

Ice cube

Drinking glass

Water

Pencil and paper

WHAT YOU DO:

1. Place an ice cube in a glass.

2. Fill it to the brim (I mean the very brim) with water.

3. Wipe away any drips or spills.

4. Draw a picture of what you think the glass and the countertop will look like after the ice is completely melted.

5. Come back in an hour or so and see if you predicted correctly.

RESULTS: Most people get this one wrong. Because ice pushes away or "displaces" exactly the same amount of water as the ice weighs, the glass remains absolutely completely full to the brim (or brimmy whim bim, as my mother would say). Ice melting in the Arctic is not raising our sea levels. Ice streaming off of Greenland and Antarctica is raising sea levels, because that ice was resting on land (before it slid into the sea). Climate deniers or contrarians act like they can't understand this. I think they can. You can watch it work; it's science!

BEFORE WE MOVE ON...

I'll leave you with a hockey stick. Not an actual stick. It would be difficult to cram a real one into the pages of this book. This hockey stick is a chart originally developed by one of my friends, a climate scientist named Michael Mann.

Since he first published a version of the graph in 1998, critics have tried to attack Professor Mann and his work. But he's a scientist. So he responded by doing science: gathering more data and fine-tuning his research. Twenty years later, dozens of groups of scientists have studied all the clues and come to the same conclusion shown here on the graph. Our planet is warming, and it's warming fast.

Let's do something about it, young scientist! Let's change the world for the better. Ride your bike. Study renewable energy—the wind turbines and solar panels that generate electricity without using fossil fuels. Invent new batteries and power lines. Harness the strong nuclear force. Learn more about climate science. Whatever you do, remember this: Earth is our home. It's the only planet we've got. Let's take care of it.

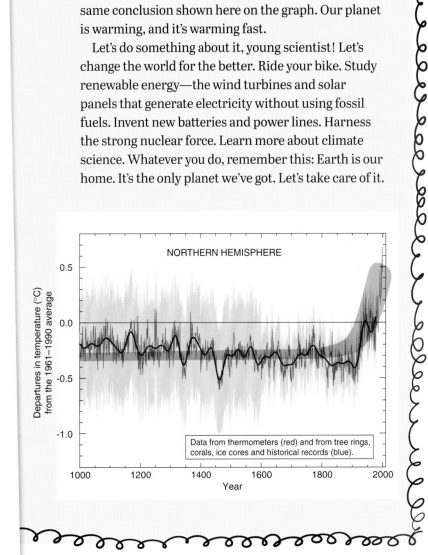

chapter 15

Water

Why It's Hard to Find on Our Very Wet World

> **Wait.** We already talked about water. It's all in the ocean. Right? Yes, almost. But now we're going to move on to the water we drink. The stuff we use to clean our dishes and water our tomato plants and shower. We call this stuff freshwater. That doesn't mean the water has not been sitting around for a while; it means it's not salty like water in the ocean. Hydrology is the science of moving freshwater—especially water that flows on and through land. Along with water wells and mudslides, hydrologists study water that has spent thousands or even millions of years in the soil and rocks below the surface. This field of science is becoming extremely important, because many parts of the world are running out of clean, reliable sources of freshwater. This might sound strange. We live on an ocean planet. A pale very blue dot. But most of that water is in our salty seas. We can't drink salt water. It would make the water that's naturally in our cells work its way out of our cells, right through our cell membranes. So drinking salt water wouldn't quench our thirst; it would dehydrate us. Land plants, like our farm crops, can't handle salt water, either.

Most of the freshwater on Earth's surface is locked up in snow and ice. Along with rain that falls from clouds and collects in lakes, streams, and reservoirs, much of the water we drink and use comes from that melting snow and ice. It flows down from snow-packed mountains. As water on the ocean surface evaporates, it leaves its salt behind, and those water-packed clouds drop fresh rain and snow on our forests and landscapes. Freshwater is also held deep underground in what we call aquifers [AHH-kwih-ferz]. That's from old words that mean carrying or bearing water. The water in aquifers is called? That's right: groundwater. Wow. You were able to come up with that? Amazing.

One of the big problems facing humans today is that many places are using up their groundwater. By the year 2025, experts predict that two out of every three people on our planet will be living in areas where water is hard to get. Water is going to become so important in the next few decades that countries will probably go to war because of water. So read on, young scientists, because the world needs to solve these problems. We need more hydrologists.

Where is Earth's water?
Nearly 70% of the world is covered in water.

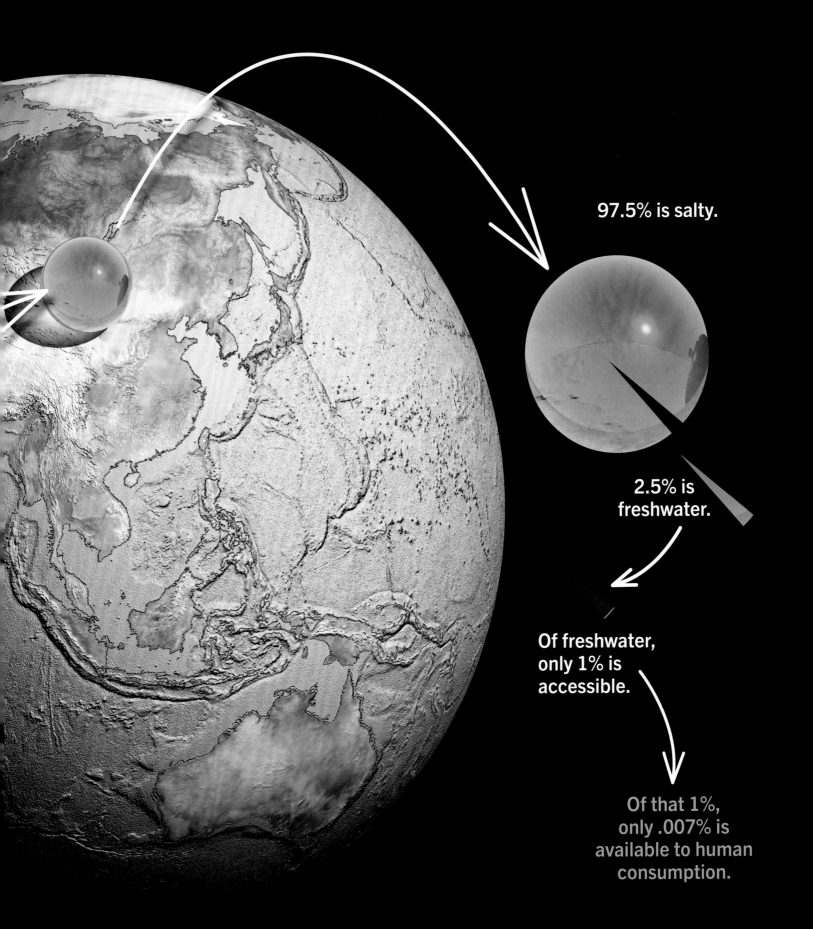

97.5% is salty.

2.5% is freshwater.

Of freshwater, only 1% is accessible.

Of that 1%, only .007% is available to human consumption.

The Water Cycle

▶ We already went over the water cycle. I know. That was on a global scale. Now let's look at the smaller version. Here are a few things that drive what we call the terrestrial water cycle:

Evaporation

The atmosphere picks up water from oceans and lakes, feeding clouds.

Transpiration

Plants release water vapor into the air.

Precipitation

Water falls from the sky as rain, snow, hail, or sleet.

Gravity

Once that water falls on trees, lakes, rivers, plants, soil, or your head, gravity pulls it downhill.

Simple, right? Uh no, not exactly. Water then has a few paths:

1. Out and Away

Some water that falls as precipitation moves across the surface or through the soil and eventually flows out into creeks, streams, rivers, and our oceans and seas.

2. Down

As water floods the earth, soil and even rocks can soak it up, storing it for days or decades. In some places, water takes weeks or even years to flow down through the soil. But like a sponge, soil can hold only so much water. If the soil is already full, the water runs off of the surface.

3. Up

Some of the water that falls to the surface will rise again through evaporation. (Think of a steaming street after a thunderstorm.) When animals like us exhale, we release some water vapor into the air. (That's respiration.) Plants do the same thing. They draw water from the soil up through their roots, and then release some into the air through their leaves. (That's transpiration).

4. Nowhere

Of course, water doesn't always rush off like you dashing out of school at the sound of the last bell. It can also collect on Earth's surface. For example, a lake is basically just a big bowl in the landscape that collects freshwater flowing through an area, storing it for a few weeks or even decades, before it makes its way to a cloud or to the sea.

> " When most of us think about water, we think about rivers, lakes, snow, reservoirs, and the water we can see. Most people don't really know about groundwater, but a third of the people in the world rely on groundwater stored in rocks and aquifers. Some of these aquifers took hundreds of millions of years to fill with water and we're burning through them. That water is gone and it's not coming back.
>
> —HYDROLOGIST JAY FAMIGLIETTI

> "One of the things we've taken for granted forever is that our soil is capable of absorbing rainfall we typically see. The question is whether the capacity of that soil to hold the water or absorb it is keeping pace with the changes we're seeing in rainfall. More water going from the landscape into the atmosphere results in more water going back to the landscape as rainfall. If the landscape can't hold the water in the soil or if it's coming in too fast, the water goes off as storm runoff. It's like a bucket overflowing."
>
> —HYDROLOGIST TODD WALTER

ABSURDLY PROFOUND DEMONSTRATION:

Hydrology Department

1. Find a small cup. A paper cup will do, but a compostable one is better.

2. Pack the cup almost to the top with soil. Place this outside on the ground.

3. Fill an eyedropper with water.

4. Squirt some water into the soil-filled cup. Observe.

5. Fill a pitcher with water.

6. Dump water into the soil-filled cup in one dramatic downpour. Observe. When there's enough water to completely surround every particle of soil, we call it hydric soil. Microscopic organisms in hydric soil get hardly any oxygen. That changes everything in a wetland ecosystem.

TOY DEPARTMENT

Measuring the World's Water

One of the questions scientists would like to answer is how much water moves into the oceans through rivers and streams, how much evaporates and from where—and then, how much water do rivers and lakes hold in the first place? Okay, so maybe that's more than one question. Anyway, a new NASA satellite is going to help study these questions by continually measuring the height of rivers and lakes around the world as they rise and fall with the water cycle. And it's going to do that by shooting radar waves at the water. But don't worry, the fish will be fine. The electromagnetic radar waves are fantastically weak. Imagine standing outside, looking up, and trying to see a burning match while it's orbiting Earth. You couldn't. The light would be way, way too dim. Same with the radar waves.

To-Do List:
Compost!

When soil is packed with stuff that many living things aren't using anymore, like dead leaves, what we call organic matter, or compost, it's healthier. There are bacteria and other organisms chomping away at it. And according to my hydrologist friend Todd Walter, it can hold more water. Those half-eaten vegetables from last night's dinner? The moldy bagel you found in your brother's shoe? Any and all food scraps can be composted and turned into healthy, rich soil. (Maybe stay away from meat and dairy, though, since those'll attract some pests.) You can certainly collect your compost and dispose of it at the nearest composting facility—more and more town waste-disposal places have them now. But why not set up a composting center yourself?

Uh-Oh:
Slow Down, Rain!

➤ Our warmer climate is increasing the rate of evaporation. More water is moving from the landscape into the atmosphere. That water has to come down as precipitation. So more water going up will somehow come back down as rain or snow. Scientists are saying, sure enough, that is what's happening. . . . The problem is that this water is not falling in steady rainfalls, a little one week and a little the next. Instead, it's coming in intense bursts. The soil below isn't always ready to hold onto all that rain. So rainwater runs off the land, causing more floods.

**HERE'S WHAT
YOU NEED:**

**A five-gallon bucket
with a lid**

A drill

Leftover food

**Some soil or dirt that
you want to make
better for plants**

Time

Nose clips

HERE'S WHAT YOU DO:

1. Drill a few small holes in the sides of the bucket, near the bottom; with an adult's help, of course.

2. Grab the rotten vegetables from the depths of the fridge drawers, any leftover scraps of food, any moldy bread on the counter, and stuff it all into the bucket.

3. Cover the food scraps with a little soil.

4. Seal the top on the bucket and leave it outside in the sunlight.

5. Fill the bucket every day until it's jam-packed with rotting food; add some more soil now and then, too.

6. Visit the bucket every few days or so to see and smell—unless you use the nose clips—what's happening inside.

7. The bugs and worms and pestering flies will help, but what you're doing here is making healthy, rich soil. After a few months, you'll want to dump the black, rich, stinking mess into a garden or donate it to a farm for them to use. I have a round composter bin in my yard. Every week, I spin it to mix the scraps and soil inside. It takes practice and trial and error to get the compost to form where you live with your local climate. If more of us with outdoor spaces composted, we'd not only have healthier soil that's able to hold more water, but we'd also reduce the amount of garbage we're sending to landfills and dumps.

To-Do List:
Four Freshwater Challenges

 ## 1. Prepare for Droughts

Scientists are finding that the dry areas of the world are getting drier, the wet areas wetter. In California, the water systems for farms and cities were built based on the reasonable idea that a lot of the water would fall as snow, and that this snow would cover beautiful mountain slopes, and as spring and summer came, the snow would melt and the water would gradually flow down to farms and towns. Lovely. It's not like that anymore. Nowadays, it's more likely to rain than snow, and rain doesn't come to rest on mountains and flow down slowly. It rushes down in bursts. And between the heavy rains, Californians experience long droughts, which are leading to horrible fires in some areas. Here's hoping some young hydrologists and engineers can help us design ways to store water and provide irrigation to the huge farms and cities in the region. We need solutions to this growing problem. We need you. So study hydrology, irrigation, and water resource engineering, then get on it, kids.

 ## 2. Fight Floods

More people lose their lives to sudden floodwaters each year than any other natural disaster. Hydrologists can help prevent and predict floods—a job that has become harder and more important as the climate changes, and some areas of the planet are getting pummeled with far more rainfall than ever before. We have to predict where these floods will go and build structures and systems to manage the flow of all that water. We can do it, but we need your help.

3. Reduce Plastic

Plastic water bottles tossed onto the sidewalk can roll into storm drains, then out into streams, rivers, and eventually the ocean. But much smaller pieces, which we call microplastics, also flow out to the sea through rivers. Right now, it looks like a bunch of it comes from cigarette filters. Another excellent reason not to smoke. What about the fleece jackets that keep us warm in winter? Their comfy threads are often made from recycled plastic—which is good, since it's recycled—but tiny pieces of plastic lint rub off in the wash, go down the drain, and with the flow, all the way to the ocean. And that's probably bad. But how bad? And how much plastic enters the ocean this way? That we do not know. So get on this one, too, kid.

4. Filter Salt Water

The vast majority of our planet's surface is water. Most of that water is too salty to drink or farm with. And many people are running out of precious freshwater. So let's get the salt out of some of that ocean water, okay? This process, called desalination, turns out to be a lot more difficult than you might think. Just think how much heat it takes to get water to boil, which is one way to collect nonsalty water. Another way is to push salt water through special filters and get freshwater on the other side, but that pumping requires a lot of energy. So does manufacturing the filters or membranes. And anything that requires lots of energy can cost lots of money. So what we need is an inexpensive way to filter salt out of water. Maybe tackle this one first, okay? The future of humanity might depend on it. No pressure. Wait, the right pressure at the right temperature might be the key. Please go get 'er done.

MOTHER GOOSE, LOUIS, AND PIERRE

DEPENDING ON WHOM YOU ASK, hydrology is either a really, really old science, or a pretty new one. Humans have been trying to figure out how water flows—and how to redirect it to farms—for thousands of years. Those folks had to be hydrologists. But one of the first scientists we know who really tried to measure the flow of freshwater, and how it related to rainfall, was a Frenchman who'd lost all his money.

Pierre Perrault lived in Paris in the 17th century. His brother wrote the famous Mother Goose stories, and he worked for this king named Louis the 14th (XIV). You know: Big hair? Lots of curls? Built himself a weird, absurd palace? You'll want to look him up sometime. Anyway, Pierre collected taxes for Louis. Which was a pretty good job until Louis decided to stop collecting taxes. Pierre owed some people money, but he didn't have a job anymore, and so . . . he became a scientist! Really.

Pierre decided to measure rain flow, then track the flow of water through a famous river called the Seine; it's the one that runs through Paris. Then he compared his measurements, finding a link between rainfall and river flow. He also began developing a model of the water cycle, including the role of evaporation and transpiration. Few people know much about Pierre, but everyone seems to know his brother Charles, who wrote those tales about Mother Goose.

Department of Trees and Rivers

TREES PREFER OLD WATER

Today hydrologists can track and trace water molecules to understand how long they've been in the soil. One of their strange discoveries: Trees prefer to drink older water, not recently fallen rain. This water that has lingered in the soil longer may have more nutrients.

RIVERS HIDE OLD WATER

Sure, rivers and streams rise with heavy rains. But that doesn't mean all the water flowing past comes from those downpours. Hydrologists have found that rainwater flowing in a river pulls older groundwater out of riverbanks like a conveyor belt running by. So in addition to newly fallen rainwater, a rushing river might be carrying some water that had been trapped underground for a very long time.

ABSURDLY PROFOUND DEMONSTRATION:
Department of Transpiration

1. Find a leafy potted plant that splits into at least two branches or sections. A young tomato plant, perhaps, or a fern.

2. Take a clear plastic bag—compostable, if possible—and gently place it around one section of the plant, then take a string and tie it around the stem, at the mouth of the plastic bag.

3. Water the soil until it's wet but not sludge.

4. Watch what happens to the inside of the plastic bag as the plant transpires. (Transpiration is like respiration for a plant.)

5. Quick, take off the bag! And carefully, too! Take care of this plant. It just helped you learn something. Then reuse and recycle the bag, please. The amount of moisture captured in the bag depends on time and weather. Try it a few times with different plants.

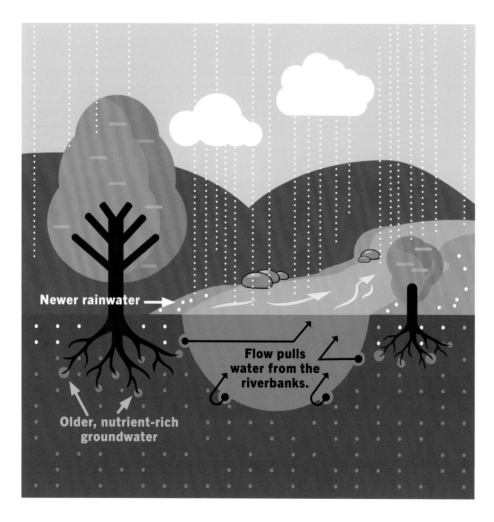

Newer rainwater →

Flow pulls water from the riverbanks.

Older, nutrient-rich groundwater

> "When you go somewhere like northern Ethiopia and you meet a group of women who are walking six hours a day—each and every day—to get water for their families, you realize that you could have a tremendous impact on people's lives as a hydrologist. You could find better options for them, maybe study that site and find a place to drill a well or identify a spring on higher ground and route the water down to a village. You could give them a stable source of water."
>
> —HYDROLOGIST JEFFREY MCDONNELL

TRY THIS!

Water We Drink Carries Chemicals of Many Kinds

WHAT YOU NEED:

Two clear glass dishes or bowls

Distilled water (from a store; it lacks the minerals in regular water)

Water from the kitchen sink

WHAT YOU DO:

1. Pour some distilled water in one dish.

2. Pour some tap water in the other dish.

3. Let them dry in the sun completely.

RESULTS: The tap water dish will have a film of minerals. You drink them every day. Water carries vital minerals all over the world.

BEFORE WE MOVE ON...

We're not losing water. Our planet is awash in the stuff. But as our climate changes, the water is moving. Some parts of the planet are going to have more water. Others are going to have much less. Hydrologist Jay Famiglietti has spent years studying how water is moving around the world, and the problems that result. He thinks we won't just need hydrologists to help, but inventors and engineers, too. We're going to need scientists to develop crops that can grow in drought conditions and crops that can survive floods. We're going to need to find better ways to recycle and reuse water. "Water is the stuff of life," Famiglietti says. "It could very well be the most important resource of the 21st and 22nd centuries."

So, young scientist, study water in all its forms and flows, and you just might help save the world.

chapter 16

How to Build and Shape a **Solar System**

► **Our planet,** Earth, resides in what we call the solar system. I like it here, and you should, too. This solar system of ours has a nice warm star in the center, a warm and watery planet that we call home, and zero options for a second home should we mess this one up. We're not ready to discuss all those planets and moons yet, though. That's in our next chapter. First, let's run through how this solar system of ours formed, and meet some of the fascinating leftovers from its early days.

OUR NEIGHBORHOOD BY THE NUMBERS

1 star.

8 (traditional) planets.

158 moons (more might be discovered by the time you read this).

More than **3,500** comets.

More than **800,000** asteroids.

GERARD KUIPER was an astronomer who predicted these things would be out there—way out there. Strangely, though, he didn't think the Kuiper Belt would be where we know it to be—he actually predicted nothing would be there, and that these objects would be much farther out. So in a way, he anti-predicted it. But it's still his belt.

Millions
of icy wanderers called
Kuiper Belt Objects,
or KBOs, including dwarf
planets like Pluto.

he Science of Earthquakes

> An earthquake happens when Earth's crust shakes. Really. It's that simple, or that complicated. What would make the crust shake? The tectonic plates are crunching and grinding and sliding against each other all the time. Sometimes they stick. Surprising as it might seem, what you and I might think of as solid rock can bend a little. The major plates are thousands of kilometers across. The flexing from all that pushing and pulling builds and builds. The edges of a plate can break free, or a crack can form suddenly somewhere, and all the energy of a moving slab of planet is quickly released. Earth's big plates are so long and flexible that they often bend in waves. The waves become earthquakes.

Earth shakes 500,000 times per year. That's more than 1,300 earthquakes every single day. Or one almost every minute. So how in the world are you still in your chair? Why haven't you been thrown to the floor two or three times already? We don't feel most of these earthquakes. They're tiny. But still, there are one or two major earthquakes every month. That's around 16 major ones around the world each year.

HOW PLATES MOVE

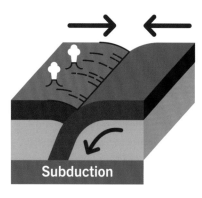

Subduction

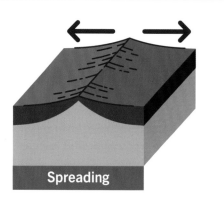

Spreading

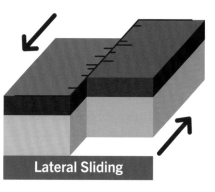

Lateral Sliding

A seismograph recording our planet's rumbles.

66 Unlike other sciences, geology is all around you. You can go outside and see it live. We're always reading the landscape and the processes we see around us. Our minds work on different time scales, too. If I look at a beach, I wonder if I were to come back 20 million years later, what would it look like?"

—*GEOSCIENTIST CHRISTOPHER JACKSON*

How the Solar System Was Born

▶ Scientists are pretty certain that our solar system formed about 4.6 billion years ago. So how did it happen? Here's the massively simplified version (massive— get it? Mass-ive . . . ha . . . uh, sorry):

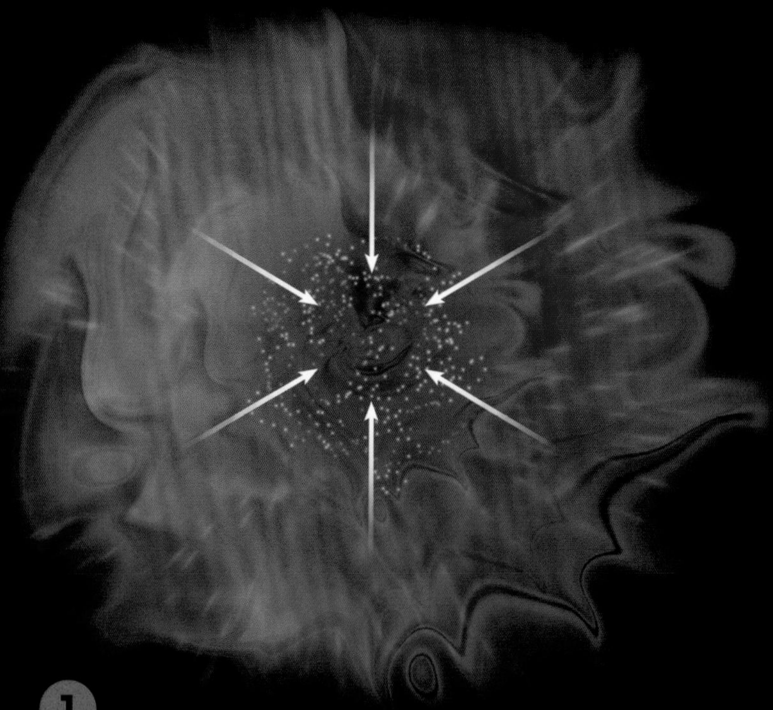

1 Gravity pulls together an enormous cloud of gas and dust loaded with elements like hydrogen, oxygen, carbon, and almost all the elements on the periodic table. You might ask, where did all that dust come from? That's coming up in the next chapter. Read on!

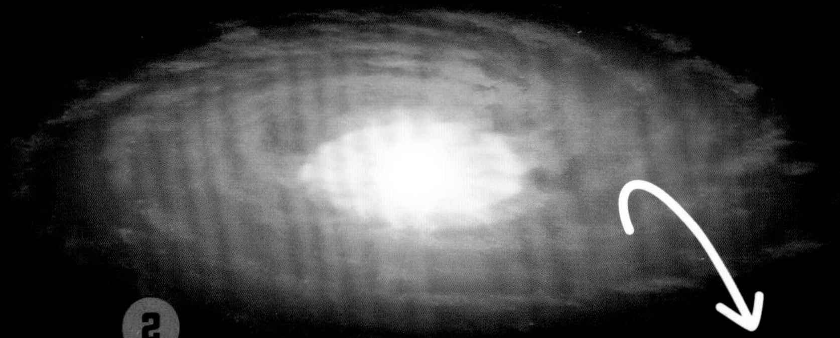

2 The cloud of gas gets smaller and smaller, and begins to spin faster and faster, as gravity pulls all those bits of dust and gas closer and closer together. As the little particles smash together, their energy of motion is converted to the energy of heat.

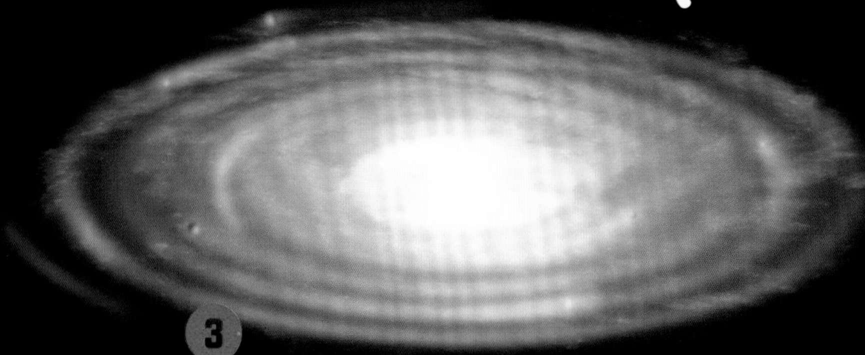

3 In the center of the swirling cloud, the atoms start to fuse. Some mass gets converted into energy. (Remember Einstein's most famous equation from chapter 10?) Light and heat burst outward. But gravity's still pulling everything in tight. The bursting heat and light, the crush of gravity, and the strong and weak nuclear forces get things cooking, and we've got a star.

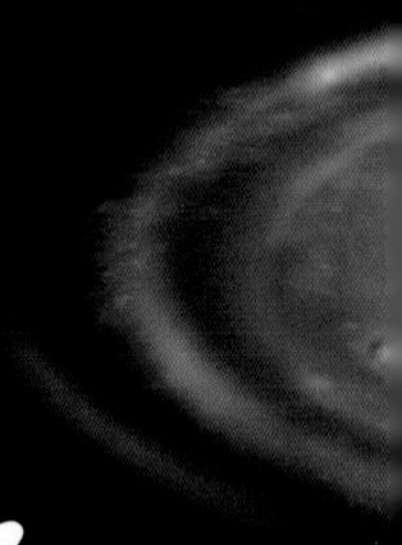

5

Ice forms in the outer and colder parts of the disk. Ice and dust particles collide, forming bigger and bigger chunks of stuff. Gravity holds it all together, and pulls more ice and dust into their little icy dust parties, forming whirlpools. Eventually gravity squeezes them down into small round planets.

6

The first planets form out of all these leftovers, close to the Sun. The inner planets, like Mercury, Venus, Earth, and Mars, are made of dense, rocky materials.

4

The leftover gas and dust that did not get swept up into the center swirl around the outside of the new star—in this case, our Sun. The combination of gravity and the spinning of the dust around the star causes this swirling mix to flatten out into a big disk. It's like shaping clay thrown on a potter's wheel. If you spin it long enough, it gets very even—a near perfect circle.

7

Solid ice lasts a lot longer farther away from the Sun than it does closer in, and there was a lot of it. Because all this stuff was not too hot, it could combine with hydrogen compounds, rocks, and metals to form the giants—Jupiter, Saturn, Uranus, and Neptune.

8

Meanwhile, still more of the leftover chemicals bunch up into what we now call asteroids and comets.

This whole process took a few hundred million years. A long time for you and me, but on a cosmic scale? That's barely a blink.

Comets and Asteroids

➤ If a comet and an asteroid fought in a dark alley, or maybe deep space, who would win? Hard to say. Probably neither, since they'd likely destroy the neighborhood surrounding the alley, or even the whole country, just getting to the fight at their typical speed of thousands of kilometers (or miles) per hour. But I digress. What are these cosmic wanderers? And what's the difference between them? And why should you care?

DUST TAIL

ION TAIL

SUN

Comets

A comet is a rocky mix of frozen water, gas, and dust. Scientists have counted upwards of 3,000 comets in our solar system, but there could be billions more that we haven't seen yet. What makes comets interesting to regular old stargazers like you and me are their fantastic tails. They almost always have two tails. When a comet passes close enough to the Sun, the warmth of our star vaporizes some of the ice. Dust is usually mixed in the ice, so it forms a "dust tail" behind the comet, pointing mostly away from the Sun. But since the dust is being let loose continuously as the comet moves in its orbit, the dust tail will often curve with the comet's path. At the same time, though, carbon, oxygen, nitrogen, and molecules of other stuff are outgassing, or vaporizing, from the icy body of the comet. As charged particles streaming off the Sun collide with these atoms, they lose electrons and form positively charged ions and a comet's ion, or gas, tail. These comet ion tails always point directly away from the Sun; they don't quite follow the orbit's curve the way the dust tails do. When conditions are just right, you can see both tails of a passing comet—the dust tail and the ion tail.

Comet tails can be millions of kilometers (or miles) long, and some comets may take tens of millions of years to complete a circuit around our star.

Asteroids

Asteroids are really, really interesting space rocks that come in all shapes and sizes. Many of them are gathered in the main asteroid belt, which is less like a belt than a giant, slightly squished space donut orbiting between the planets Mars and Jupiter. Some asteroids are larger than the state of Rhode Island. One is the size of New Mexico. Asteroids don't hold as much water as comets, so they lack those beautiful tails, but some of them are packed with minerals that would be quite valuable, if we could get to them.

Why don't asteroids hold as much water ice as comets? Because they formed closer to the Sun, where water doesn't easily freeze. Comets, on the other hand, formed much farther out; they spend lots of time in the cold, far reaches of the solar system, keeping their water ice chilly

Three Massively Important Points About:
Space Rocks

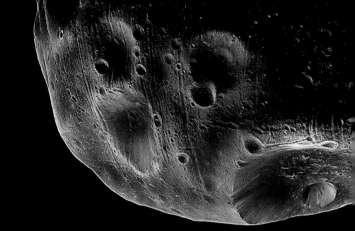

Tom Prettyman, a planetary scientist and asteroid/comet expert, points to three big reasons we should study comets and asteroids:

1. They're Time Capsules.

Asteroids have been orbiting our Sun in the icy blackness of space, without too many changes, since the solar system was formed. Studying them tells us what the universe was like back then.

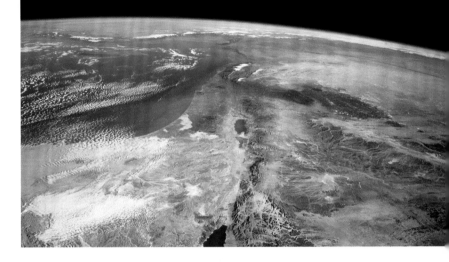

2. They're Rich.

Not in the sense of freshly scented, unwrinkled cash. Some asteroids are loaded with minerals like iron and platinum, which might be useful someday. Others have icy water packed in the rocks. If we start traveling farther and deeper into space, we're going to need a good source of rocket fuel to power our ships. We might be able to capture and turn some asteroid H_2O (that's water, people) into hydrogen and oxygen, which could be used to make rocket fuel out in space. Asteroids could be cosmic gas stations. It's a wild idea, but people are working pretty hard on it.

3. They Might Be Dangerous.

Space agencies around the world (NASA, ESA, JAXA, ISRO, and Roscosmos) track and study what we call Near-Earth Objects, or NEOs, to make sure we know about any of them that might be on a collision course with the planet. Right now, we're looking pretty good, so you can relax. But asteroids and Earth do have a little history. One space rock wiped out the ancient dinosaurs—and most other life on the planet. Another flattened a decent chunk of a Russian forest in 1908. (Now we celebrate "Asteroid Day" on its June 30 anniversary.) So we need to keep watching the skies to make sure another big one isn't heading our way. A majorly big asteroid impact—bigger than the 1908 forest flattener—has a very, very low probability of happening again soon. But if one big one did hit us, it would cause very, very, very serious damage. Very low probability. Very high consequence.

> 66 Comets and asteroids are the oldest things in the solar system, and because of that you can look at them and say this is what the solar system looked like when it was born."
>
> —ASTRONOMER ARIEL GRAYKOWSKI

ADVENTURES IN
Asteroid Mitigation

I remember well when an asteroid the size of a house hit Earth's atmosphere going so fast that it exploded over the skies of Chelyabinsk, Russia, in 2013. The shock wave blew out the windows of many buildings on the ground and injured more than 1,000 people. Luckily, no one was killed. But let's say we spot something larger on a direct collision course with Earth. How would we stop it? There are a few different ideas out there.

∧ The Bruce Willis

In the 1998 film *Armageddon*, NASA sends a team to set a nuclear bomb on an approaching asteroid and blow the threat to dust. Naturally the group succeeds, but real-life scientists aren't so fond of this approach. Asteroids can be porous, or filled with holes. So a bombing might not destroy it, but simply split the giant space rock into a few smaller but still threatening asteroids without changing their collision course enough to do any good.

The risk of a truly damaging space rock striking our planet again soon is pretty small, but that doesn't mean we shouldn't prepare. First, we have to find them all, and finding an asteroid is like looking for a piece of charcoal in the dark. But they are warm, compared to the rest of space, a very snuggly 200 Kelvins. So if we're good at designing instruments for spacecraft, we can use specialized infrared telescopes to spot them. Anyway, if you're not sold on the other scientific fields we've raced through in this book, how about becoming an asteroid expert? Someday you might have a chance to save the world. Or maybe just a large city or two.

∨ The Tractor

Another way to change the asteroid's course would be to fly a spacecraft or two alongside the rock. Gravity between the spacecraft and the asteroid could change its path just enough to prevent a collision. The gravity would be like a science fiction–style tractor beam. But this would require a massive spacecraft that carried with it tons and tons, and more tons of fuel. But it's a cool idea.

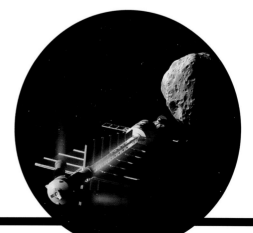

> Laser Bees

At The Planetary Society we did quite a bit of research on deflecting an asteroid by hitting it with laser beams. No kidding. Here's how it would work: We'd fire lasers at the rock from a spacecraft, or better yet, a swarm of spacecraft. The lasers would cause bits of the asteroid to vaporize. The jets of vaporized rock and ice would give the asteroid a push, a reaction to the vapor jets' action. (Chapter 6, young Newton.) The key would be to build several or maybe a few dozen of these laser spacecraft. They'd use solar panels to make electricity to drive their lasers, and we'd send them out in a swarm, like bees. So we decided to call them the "laser bees." It's ideas like this that made me want to take my job at The Planetary Society. I love using science to solve problems. That's engineering!

> The Nudge

Before an asteroid crashes into Earth, one strategy would be to crash a spacecraft or two into the rock while it was a long way off, like NASA's DART (Dual Asteroid Redirection Test) mission. On a bigger scale, the impact could nudge the asteroid and either speed it up or slow it down enough so it crosses Earth's orbit when we're not there: I mean, so we avoid a collision. Think of two cars heading for a crash at an intersection. If one of them brakes enough, or speeds up enough, they'll miss. Each car will drive through without an accident. This is the same idea. Only in space. And it involves a giant rock. Okay, so maybe it's not quite the same, the speeding-up idea especially.

Backyard Bombardment

WHAT YOU NEED:

A large mixing bowl, the bigger the better

Flour, a kilogram or two (a few pounds)

Ground pepper, a tablespoon or two

A small measuring cup or cereal bowl

A few milliliters (teaspoons) of water

WHAT YOU DO:

1. Fill the large bowl partway up with flour.

2. Mix equal parts of pepper and flour in the small cup or bowl with a small splash of water.

3. Make several balls from the flour-pepper mixture, each about the size of a pea (that's really big enough).

4. Take it all outside (seriously: do not do this inside!).

5. Drop (or throw) your flour-pepper ball into the bowl of flour.

6. Examine your flour-pepper crater.

7. What happened to the incoming space rock (the flour-pepper ball)?

8. What happened to the flour in the bowl? (It goes everywhere with a poof.)

9. What about the dark pepper?

Try dropping or throwing peppery asteroids from different heights and angles and distances. Then study the differences in the craters. I hope you're surprised at how far the flour flies. (And that is why you don't do this experiment inside.)

RESULTS:
When the asteroid that finished off the ancient dinosaurs hit off the coast of what is now Chicxulub, Mexico, the rocky materials blasted up and out from the crater, the ejecta, were ejected upward in a cone, with a diameter that was as big as Earth. Wow. Another discovery from the impact is that asteroids are made of about the same stuff as our nearby planets and the Moon, and they travel fast. Their shock waves (like thunderclaps) create craters that are usually round no matter what angle the asteroid (or flour-pepper ball) comes in at. Scientists spend lifetimes studying impact craters. It's a blast (uh . . . sorry). The more we know about asteroids, comets, and craters, the more we'll know about our past, which will help us plan for our future. The planets and moons across our solar system, our Earth included, have been getting smacked and dinged by space rocks for billions of years.

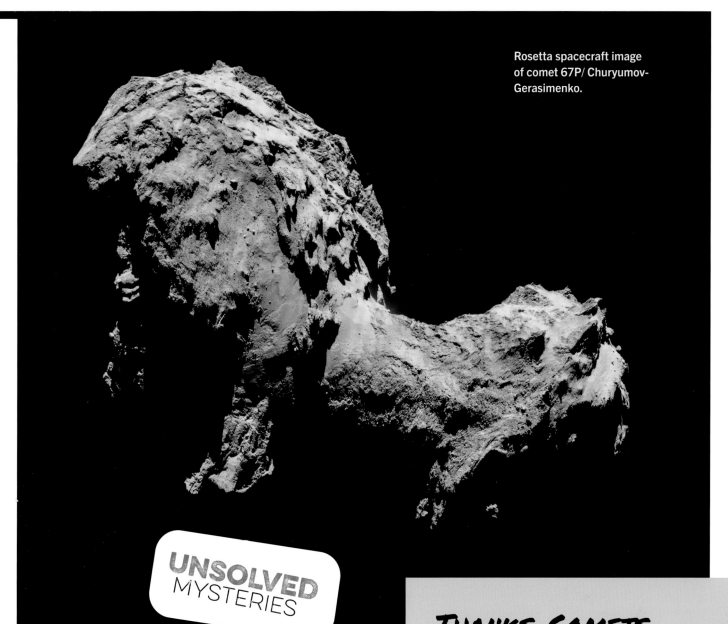

Rosetta spacecraft image of comet 67P/ Churyumov-Gerasimenko.

DID LIFE BEGIN ON COMETS?

Comets don't just carry water around. They also have organic materials—the carbon-based chemical ingredients for life. One space mission analyzed the dust coming off an icy rock called Comet 67P, and half of the dust was organic. The same comet contained distinctive chemicals called amino acids—key chemicals for living things. So if comets have water and the ingredients for life, does that mean it's possible that life actually started on one of these lonely space rocks and then crashed to Earth? Cue the spooky music. Or the funky music. Your call. Either way, get cosmic, young scientist. This is big stuff.

THANKS, COMETS, FOR THE WATER

Water is one of the reasons life has thrived here on Earth. But how did our planet get all of its water in the first place? Today scientists think that water might have been part of the first materials that gravity gathered to form Earth. But some of our water may have arrived via comets and asteroids, too. Like giant water balloons, these water-packed space rocks may have crashed into our surface and filled our seas. But even if the heat of the impact turned the water to steam and vapor, sooner or later it would all cool off and fall to Earth.

We Land Robots on Asteroids

Here's a wild idea: Landing a spacecraft on the surface of an asteroid is not impossible. We've already done it! Way, way back in 2001, the NEAR Shoemaker mission landed a spacecraft on the asteroid Eros. In 2014, Hayabusa 2 left Earth. It scooped up samples of asteroid Ryugu and headed back our way. Meanwhile in late 2018, the OSIRIS-REx spacecraft arrived at Bennu, an asteroid named for an Egyptian heron god. This particular rock, named by Michael Puzio when he was in third grade, has a slight shot of crashing into Earth in the late 22nd century. The rock was traveling at around 100,000 kilometers per hour (60,000 miles per hour) at the time, but we still caught up to it. If all goes well, you could be studying some of these samples when you become a scientist. Really. This kind of space mission takes years, but it never gets old: Scientists are still making amazing discoveries about the Moon based on rocks and other samples astronauts brought back to Earth more than 50 years ago.

Maria Mitchell

The astronomer Maria Mitchell was born in 1818 on Nantucket, an island off the coast of Massachusetts. Initially, Mitchell worked as a librarian, but she often spent her nights studying the stars and planets. One night, Mitchell had set up a telescope on the roof of the bank for which her father worked when she noticed something she suspected was a comet. Scientists eventually recognized the object as "Miss Mitchell's Comet" and the discovery earned her worldwide fame. She went on to map the heavens in more detail and became known as America's first female astronomer.

Shooting Stars Are Falling Rocks

MIND, BLOWN!

I hope this doesn't disappoint you. A shooting star looks like a star that suddenly decided to dash across the sky and show off its bright streak. But most of them are tiny asteroids, leftovers from the early days of the solar system. When they enter the atmosphere, we call them meteors. (If bits of them make it all the way down to the ground or ocean, we call them meteorites.) They may look as bright as an enormous star, but that's because they come so close to Earth. They streak through our atmosphere going so fast that friction with the air makes them burn up, creating a brief but brilliant display. If you see green in the streak, that's a short-lived plasma of oxygen. They're not stars, but they sure seem to shoot. You're witnessing the spectacular final seconds of a 4.6-billion-year-old rock. Kind of cool, yes?

BEFORE WE MOVE ON...

Why so much focus on the space rocks and ice balls? Well, one of them, even a small one, could be a big deal. Now I hope you're wondering about all the wonderful worlds orbiting our local star. Well, space cadets, that's where we're heading next.

Interesting Places to Visit

in the Solar System— If You Could

chapter 17

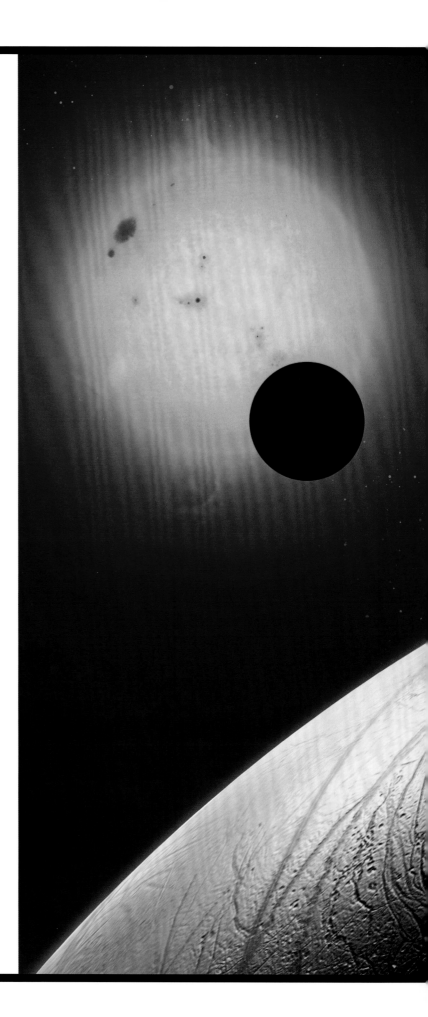

> ➤ **Hundreds of years ago,** before even your parents were born, people used to think Earth was pretty special. Until the 16th century, we assumed our planet was the center of the universe. Then we learned Earth actually orbits the Sun, and that seven other planets do as well. Not that long ago, in 1930, we discovered little old Pluto. (It really is little, smaller than our Moon, and it is very old.) As our telescopes became more powerful and scientists thought up clever new ways to search the skies, they started to find even more planets—orbiting other stars! The Kepler telescope alone discovered 2,600 exoplanets.

But here's the thing: We still have oh so much to learn about the fantastic worlds right here in our cosmic neighborhood. The planets, their amazing moons, Pluto, and the nearly uncountable objects orbiting the Sun at enormous distances will keep scientists like you busy for decades to come. Studying other worlds is how we know and appreciate our own.

Someday soon, I hope a few humans will visit Mars, for example, and have a look around. If there is a lot to see there, perhaps they'll establish a research base of the sort we have in Antarctica. Plus, as my college professor Carl Sagan put it in one of his books: "If our long-term survival is at stake, we have a basic responsibility to our species to venture to other worlds."

So let's take a tour of these worlds, shall we?

The Planets

What is a planet, exactly? Well, it has to orbit a star like the Sun. It has to have enough mass so that gravity squeezes it into a spherical, or ball-like, shape, and it has to dominate its orbit (nothing else is in its way). Unlike what we call planets, most asteroids don't become spheres. They're often just jagged old rocks. They don't have enough gravity to become round. Pluto's gravity makes it round, but it is also quite small, so it doesn't have enough gravity to push—wait, to pull—on other objects in its orbit very strongly. By comparison, the gravity of the traditional planets is strong enough to attract any nearby asteroids and space rocks. Over the last few hundred million years, their gravity made any asteroids and rocks in their orbits fall onto them. The rocky material became part of our traditional planets. These days, astronomers call objects like Pluto a "dwarf planet."

Mercury

The closest planet to the Sun is a strange one. A few hundred million years after this rocky planet formed, it shrank, leaving amazing long wrinkles on the surface. Only a little bigger than Earth's Moon, Mercury has more craters on the surface than any other planet in the solar system, and even though it's the closest to the Sun, it's not actually the hottest. It has no atmosphere to hold in heat. And since Mercury is so close to the Sun, it completes its orbit much faster than Earth. A Mercury year is only 88 Earth days long. You'd celebrate a birthday every three Earth months! But getting people to come to your parties might be pretty difficult, because of the challenging temperatures. Mercury rotates slowly, so the side of the planet that faces the Sun has plenty of time to heat up, and hits highs of more than 400 degrees Celsius (800 degrees Fahrenheit). The other side drops to almost 200 degrees below zero Celsius (-300 degrees Fahrenheit). Not great conditions for a party. Mercury is also the fastest planet, zipping through space at an average speed of around 47 kilometers (29 miles) per second. Compare that with Neptune going a little over 5 kilometers (a bit more than 3 miles) per second. And thanks to the MESSENGER spacecraft mission, we discovered that the planet Mercury is still cooling off and shrinking.

Venus

The second planet from the Sun is about the same size as Earth. It spins very slowly, and in the opposite direction from most other planets. Venus has volcanos, mountains, and a very thick atmosphere. When I say thick, I mean 90 times thicker than Earth. The crushing pressure would feel like you were a mile deep underwater in the ocean here on Earth. Venus even has tides in its atmosphere (not its ocean—its "air"). The Venusian air is almost entirely carbon dioxide, so the greenhouse effect is really strong. It's so strong that the surface of Venus is around 500 degrees C (more than 900°F). That's hot enough to melt a lead fishing weight. It would kill you or me in an instant. We know all this because more than 40 spacecraft have explored this fiery world. All but five of these missions happened before the year 2000, but still. Forty missions! Even with the heat, Venus has a mysterious superwind that swirls around the planet at over 310 kilometers per hour (almost 200 miles per hour)! Some scientists think Venus might have been the first planet with a liquid ocean on its surface, but the heat-holding atmosphere cooked it all into the Venusian sky. And the air up there is now filled with—no kidding—sulfuric acid. That's right, future planetary explorers: On Venus, it rains deadly acid. What a world!

"It's so hot that if you looked at the surface using your own eyes, the rocks would be glowing like the heating elements on a stove. It's so hot that the lava flows longer and farther than anywhere else in the solar system. There are lava flows on the surface of Venus that are longer than the Nile River."

—PLANETARY SCIENTIST DARBY DYAR

> "What makes Earth special and why are we on this planet is the driving question for me. My daily life is trying to answer that question, and I don't know if we'll ever have a detailed answer."
>
> —*PLANETARY SCIENTIST SARAH STEWART*

Earth

You know Earth. You're on it. Right now. And you should take care of it. But there are a few mysteries about exactly how our home developed within this group of planets and worlds.

How Did Earth Really Form?

I hope the answer to this question is easy for you now. Gravity and collisions pull gas and dust together so they form a roughly ball-shaped planetary body. Asteroids and comets strike the surface, and over time that mix of stuff transforms into our very round planet. Maybe. Or maybe not quite. The planetary scientist Sarah Stewart suspects that Earth was born of a collision between two other early planets. She thinks these two planets, each with land, oceans, and air, smashed together with enough energy to match the power of the Sun. In the process, they were completely destroyed. Smashed into a big, donut-shaped cloud! Then they cooled, and gravity pulled all the dusty motes of molecules back together, eventually forming Earth and the Moon.

Mars

The surface of our closest planetary neighbor is frigid and dry, and the atmosphere is thin and cold. If you were to participate in a track meet on Mars, you might break the world record in the long jump, since gravity is weaker, but you wouldn't be able to breathe. That of course would hold back everyone on the track. There's just not enough oxygen—actually, hardly any. Oh, and it might not be a new "world" record, because you'd be on another world. But anyway, it's not all bad. Scientists have found evidence of water under the sand in several places, so Mars could be the ideal place to set up a science base. One of the big questions we're still trying to answer is whether life ever developed—or still exists—on the Red Planet. Overwhelming evidence shows that Mars was once a warm, wet planet in the past. But was it warm long enough for, say, tiny life-forms to replicate? Did its oceans and lakes survive for enough time to support little creatures? This makes me (and I hope you) want to send some spacecraft there with the right instruments to look for life.

> "We've learned that in the past Mars had environments that could support life. We've sent rovers to places that have ancient lakes, where you could've drunk the water and it would have been fine. The question is how long was Mars like that?"
>
> —*PLANETARY SCIENTIST ALEXANDER HAYES*

MIND, BLOWN!

Are We Martians?

It's wild, but not entirely nuts, to suggest that life started on Mars. Then Mars was hit with an asteroid or comet. The impact launched a Mars rock into a long orbit all the way to Earth. The rock dropped off life, and you and I are descended from Martians. What a hypothesis to investigate! It would be world-changing, if it could be proven. Add this idea to your assignment list, and get back to me, young scientist.

"Jupiter gives us a very dramatic show of colors, and we have lots of images of Jupiter. I'm not sure everyone knows these images exist. Look on the NASA website and look for images of Jupiter!"

—*PLANETARY SCIENTIST THOMAS NAVARRO*

"If I could pick a destination for a new mission, I'd send a spacecraft to Uranus or Neptune because we know so little about them, and there's a lot left to be discovered. Most of the exoplanets we've discovered so far are like miniature Neptunes, so I think we'd also learn a lot about the exoplanets by studying the ice giants."

—PLANETARY SCIENTIST KRISTA SODERLUND

Uranus

In the clouds of Uranus [YER-inn-iss], scientists discovered a chemical called hydrogen sulfide, which smells like rotten eggs. Nope. I will not make a joke about any of that. Not even a little one. But it's something to think about, if you're ever out there 2.9 billion kilometers (1.8 billion miles) from the Sun. Uranus is known as one of the two ice giants. It has a source of heat inside, and it gives off about as much heat as it receives from the Sun. Uranus also spins a little differently than its other planetary buddies. Earth's spin axis is almost at a right angle to the Sun. But Uranus is tilted on what seems to us like its side, so sometimes the spin axis points almost right at the Sun. Scientists think the planet was struck by another huge object early on in its life, even before its moons had formed, and the collision knocked it over. Ah, but there's more! Uranus is about four times bigger in diameter than Earth, and it's made of a mix of water and other chemicals surrounding a small rocky core. It does have an atmosphere, but it's unlikely that this planet hosts life. The sunlight way out there is dim. I'm pretty sure I wouldn't want to visit, anyway. It's wildly windy and cold. And winter on Uranus is 21 Earth years long. Maybe I'll head to Hawaii instead. They have some great telescopes there.

"Please stop making jokes about our fascinating and unique planet."

—THE CITIZENS OF URANUS. THAT'S CITIZENS OF [YER-inn-iss].

Neptune

Speaking of windy, the windiest planet in the solar system is Neptune, the other ice giant. It, too, is really, really far away. Neptune is the only major planet you can't see with the naked eye. (Why is your eye naked anyway? At least put on some eye socks, or something.) Neptune wasn't discovered until 1846, and it needs 165 Earth years to complete an orbit around the Sun. That means you wouldn't even have one single birthday party if you lived on Neptune. And if you did have a party, maybe because you felt bad for yourself, you definitely wouldn't get to blow out the candles. The winds on Neptune travel at the speed of fighter jets. Oh, and there isn't enough oxygen in the air to feed the flame anyway—or let anyone breathe. But there is hydrogen, which might get you part of the way toward making yourself a glass of water. Then who knows what could happen?

Pluto

No, Pluto is not technically a planet anymore because it's so small, and doesn't have very much gravity. But the recent New Horizons spacecraft revealed that this distant world holds plenty of scientific mysteries. Sure, Pluto might be small, but it has a nitrogen atmosphere, giant glaciers, towering ice mountains, frozen plains, and red snow. Like other planets of any size, Pluto has also been bombarded by space rocks over its lifetime, but there aren't as many craters as you might presume (I mean, if you're into presuming). When people ask me if it's a planet, I say it's no longer what I call one of the "traditional planets." Instead, it could be the first of a whole new class of objects, a "plutoid." An icy object out around the orbit of Neptune and beyond, with enough gravity to crunch it down into a ball. I confess I like the word "plutoid"; it can help us understand the big picture of our solar system.

➤ If you get enough gas and dust into a small enough space, gravity works to pull it all together into one of those round balls called spheres. Our Sun is a sphere. So are the major planets and moons. Most asteroids don't have enough mass or rock packed into them for gravity to turn them into spheres. So they can be jagged, irregular, and hard to land a spacecraft on. Although Pluto is massive enough to be spherical, by the time we managed to get the New Horizons spacecraft out to Pluto, it was shooting by too fast for a landing. Anyway, Pluto is special. In a Plutonian kinda way.

The Moons

➤ In recent decades, it has become clear that some of the most interesting and complex worlds in our solar system are not the planets themselves, but their moons—objects that orbit planets and asteroids. Here are a few favorites.

Europa

This moon of Jupiter hides a deep, salty ocean beneath its ice-encrusted surface. That ice shell is several kilometers (a few miles) thick, so we don't know for certain, but evidence suggests that the ocean below could be 100 kilometers (60 miles) deep. The ocean stays liquid, too, because Europa is constantly getting squeezed and stretched by Jupiter's gravitational pull. This motion warms the ocean. Why are we so interested in this place? Because with its warm, deep, salty ocean, and plenty of time—4.5 billion years—for life to develop and change, Europa may be home to some fascinating aquatic aliens.

Enceladus

Although it's only the sixth largest moon of Saturn, Enceladus [Enn-SELL-uh-duss] is named after one of the giants in Greek mythology. And it's a truly fascinating distant moon. That's why we mentioned it in the astrobiology chapter. Geysers on the icy surface shoot plumes of water vapor and ice into the atmosphere, suggesting that an ocean lurks beneath the surface. Scientists also believe this moon might have hydrothermal vents below that ice—the same structures that pump hot minerals into the water on the ocean floor here on Earth. We already know life thrives near these hydrothermal vents on our own planet. Could similar life-forms be alive in the waters of Enceladus? Let's design, build, and send a spacecraft to find out!

Io

Named after a young lady who was changed into a cow (you gotta love those kooky ancient storytellers), Jupiter's moon Io has hundreds of volcanos. It's the most volcanically active body in the solar system. Some of its volcanos spew fountains of lava dozens of kilometers (or miles) high. Lava lakes stretch across the surface, too, but Io doesn't appear to have any water. It's too hot.

Titan

If you were to walk around on the surface of Saturn's Titan, you'd see clouds, rain, rivers, lakes, seas, waves, coastlines, and dunes. The atmosphere is so thick and the gravity so low that if you had on the right space suit, you could fly by flapping your arms! The rivers of Titan are running with the chemicals ethane and methane, not water. Could there be alien life-forms near the surface? As I write, we are planning to send the Dragonfly spacecraft to Titan, to launch in 2026 and arrive around 2034. This explorer will have eight propellers. Instead of a "quad-copter," it's an "octo-copter." It's going to be amazing!

> " We live in a special time. The next series of missions that are going to go to and visit Enceladus aren't targeting whether there was life. They're literally going on a bug hunt to see if there's life there now."
>
> —PLANETARY SCIENTIST ALEXANDER HAYES

TRY THIS!

Motion, Heat, Moon!

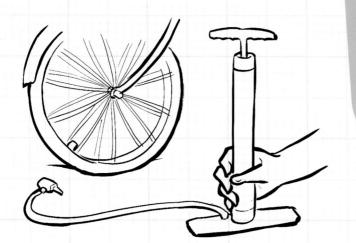

WHAT YOU NEED:

Car or bike tire that needs air

Bicycle pump

WHAT YOU DO:

1. If the tire is not already low, let some air out. (The more air you let out, the more you'll detect this effect.)

2. Wrap your hand around the base of the pump; feel its temperature.

3. Attach the pump and pump the tire back up.

4. Feel the temperature again. It's warmer.

RESULTS: The pump gets warm because you've taken air with its moving molecules and squeezed the energy of all that motion into a smaller space at the bottom of the pump, before it gets driven into the tire. That's what happens to moons of Jupiter as they get squeezed by gravity during each orbit.

Notice that the pump doesn't get warm because of the piston sliding up and down. It's the squeezed-up molecular motion that causes the warmth. Don't believe me? Try pumping the pump a few dozen times, while it's not connected to any tire. Just let the pumped air out into the air around you. The pump will hardly get warm at all.

Uh-Oh:
The Future of the Sun

" The Sun is growing an inch a year, and in 200 million years it will be so big and so bright that it will be too hot on Earth to sustain life. So at that point we'll have to move to Mars or some other planet."

—ASTROPHYSICIST J. J. ELDRIDGE

WHOA, DUDE, IT'S ALL CONNECTED.

Let's Get Planetary!

Planetary science might have the widest mix of scientists of any fields. To understand all these other worlds, we need astronomers to find them and astrophysicists to tell us how they got there. Oceanographers are important, because some of these spots have oceans. Chemists and geochemists, too, so we understand the ingredients. Then we need geologists and geophysicists and volcanologists to tell us what's happening on the surface. Not to mention engineers to build the instruments and robots to study all these things. When it comes to studying planets, every field of science is playing a part!

Our Moon

Our closest neighbor is still hiding a few secrets. Scientists who study the Moon are called selenologists; the word comes from a figure in Greek mythology named Selene. She was believed to be the goddess of the Moon. Okay, right, but what exactly is that disk in the night sky? The Moon has a solid inner core. A fluid layer surrounds that. The rest is mantle and crust—kind of like Earth, only different. Earth's crust is divided into plates. And these plates are slowly but steadily either spreading apart, or crunching together. The Moon's crust is just one giant unbroken shell, like a Moon egg. Which is weird, but important, because that solid outer crust or eggshell can give us clues about what's going on inside. Selenologists really want those clues. Sure, astronauts have been to the Moon. Humans have flown spacecraft around it. We've landed more than 100 robots and rovers there, but we still have a lot of unanswered questions. As my selenologist pal Tom Watters told me: "There's a lot about the Moon we're still working to try to understand."

Contrary to what you might have heard, the Moon does not have a "dark side." Instead, it has a "far side" that we can see only with cameras on spacecraft. And the far side gets blasted with sunlight every month, when the Moon is on the Sun's side of Earth. It's hardly dark. It's a common thing for people to get not quite right.

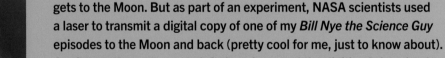

ADVENTURES IN THE SOLAR SYSTEM

The Science Guy on the Moon

➤ Yeah, I've been there. Not physically. Not in the way an astronaut gets to the Moon. But as part of an experiment, NASA scientists used a laser to transmit a digital copy of one of my *Bill Nye the Science Guy* episodes to the Moon and back (pretty cool for me, just to know about). A reflector that astronauts left there bounced the digitized show back to receiving stations here on Earth. The scientists were trying to find a better way to communicate between Earth and the Moon, in case we ever build a base there. Lasers don't send messages any faster than the radio waves we normally use. But laser light's frequency is around 100 times higher than a typical spacecraft radio frequency (check on light, ol' chapter 9). So we can pack more information into those messages than ever—including informational science shows!

To-Do List:
Build a Moon Base

A Moon base could be a pretty good launchpad for missions to other locations in the solar system. Astronauts on their way to Mars could stop off at a Moon base, restock their supplies, and maybe even switch ships. The whole journey could be safer and it may be not much more expensive than going straight (on a curved orbital path) to the Red Planet. A Moon base would still have to supply warmth, water, and food for its guests. But we couldn't just set up camp anywhere. The lunar surface gets pounded by space rocks and zapped with powerful cosmic rays—high-energy particles from deep space. Any style of Moon hotel would have to protect its guests. Here are two potential locations for a Moon base that could limit a few of these dangers.

First footprint on the Moon.
NASA Apollo 11, 20 July 1969.

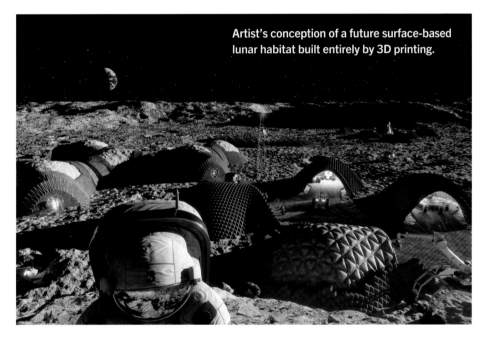

Artist's conception of a future surface-based lunar habitat built entirely by 3D printing.

1. Inside Lava Tubes

At one point, the Moon was an active volcanic object. Molten rock flowed up from below the cool crust and spilled across the surface as lava. Most of the evidence suggests that the main volcanic activity stopped about a billion years ago. Whether in Hawaii or on the Moon, lava tubes form when a stream of lava cools to a solid on top, while liquid lava drains away underneath. On the Moon, the surface of a lava stream was exposed to the icy blackness of space, so it solidified pretty quickly. When that lunar lava flow stopped, the streambed, along with its cooled-off roof, became a hollow tube. Building a Moon base inside one of these underground tunnels could protect astronauts from solar flares, cosmic rays, and space rocks. Mission planners would have to find a lava tube without too many moonquakes. Careful. Careful.

2. On the Surface

I know, I know. Maybe this whole thing sounds like a terrible idea. Rocks and particles slam into the surface all the time, and we definitely don't want them hitting astronauts or space tourists. One idea suggests sending construction robots and building materials to the Moon before astronauts. These machines could set up living spaces, then cover them with lunar rocks and dust. I mean, how hard (or expensive) could it be?

Rock Blanket
We call the top layer of rock on a moon or planet its "regolith," from the Greek words for "blanket" and "rock." Regolith is a planet or moon's cozy stone covering.

Rocky regolith material could be piled high onto our Moon motels, providing extra protective shielding. Then you could pick a spot where moonquakes aren't too common, and you might have yourself a base.

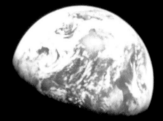

Earthrise. Apollo 8 astronauts shared this photograph of Earth during their first manned mission to the Moon on 24 December 1968.

MOON DEPARTMENT

1. Is the Moon Shrinking?

In the early days of the Moon, before it grew up and went to middle school and started washing its own laundry, this ball of rock and dust was as hot and fiery as a roiling sphere of magma. Then it gradually began to cool. As it cooled, it started to shrink. And if it has been shrinking, then there should be cracks all through the crust, like those cookies you baked at the end of chapter 13. In recent years, scientists have begun to discover more and more of these cracks, suggesting that the Moon might still be shrinking even today.

2. What Causes Moonquakes?

Astronauts left sensors on the Moon that detect the occasional moonquake (like an earthquake but on a moon). Some moonquakes set the surface rumbling enough to make scientists worry (just a little bit) about how we're going to build safe bases on the Moon. But what causes these moonquakes? The Moon doesn't have spreading, crunching plates, with oozing magma on its surface. So is Earth's gravity doing the work? Does it have something to do with those cracks? Meteorites? Or is it all of the above? Go figure that out, would ya? Call some selenologists when you're done.

TRY THIS!

Discovering Moons

WHAT YOU NEED:

Telescope or binoculars

Piece of paper

Pencil or pen

Four hours

WHAT YOU DO:

1. On a clear night, observe Jupiter through the telescope or binoculars.

2. Make a drawing of what you see.

3. Come back four hours later, and make another drawing.

RESULTS: You will have seen the very bright disk of Jupiter plus two, three, or four bright dots nearby, its moons—once again, they're Calisto, Io, Ganymede, and Europa. With a small telescope, you won't be sure which is which, but you'll see the moons move over just a few hours. This is how the famous Italian astronomer Galileo Galilei studied Jupiter's moons. At first, people didn't believe other planets could have moons. Well, they do. Lots of them.

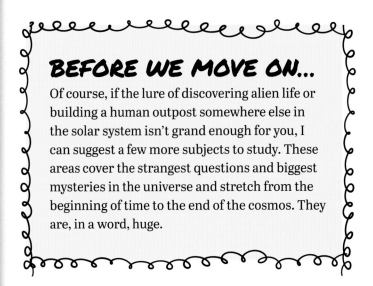

" We will go to the planets of this solar system. Probably in this century. What could be more fascinating than to be an active part of this effort, and be the new explorers of the future? You don't even have to be a scientist. You could be a lawyer in an outer space colony. You could be a chef who tries to develop new foods for other planets. No matter what kind of activity you pursue, it could be useful in understanding and exploring the universe."

—PLANETARY SCIENTIST THOMAS NAVARRO

BEFORE WE MOVE ON...

Of course, if the lure of discovering alien life or building a human outpost somewhere else in the solar system isn't grand enough for you, I can suggest a few more subjects to study. These areas cover the strangest questions and biggest mysteries in the universe and stretch from the beginning of time to the end of the cosmos. They are, in a word, huge.

chapter 18

Huge
Cosmology, Astrophysics, and a Few Unsolved Mysteries of the Universe

▶ **Now we're going big.** I'm talking cosmic, the grandest of the grand, a few steps short of infinite. This is the realm of cosmology, the study of how stars and galaxies are born, change with time, crash into each other, and move around the universe.

Even though we've gently skipped from pushing a book across the table to stars smashing into one another, the three laws of our old friend Newton still apply. Inertia, force, and action-reaction—these laws guide the cosmic stuff, too. But his apple-tree-inspired theory of universal gravitation starts to show its limits. Cosmology is where Albert Einstein's view of gravity, summed up in his general theory of relativity, shows its amazing power to predict the motions of objects everywhere in the cosmos. The players in this cosmic game include all kinds of fantastic, exotic objects.

The happenings around the supergiant V838 Monocerotis star, captured by the Hubble Space Telescope.

< Stars

Sure, we all know stars. Those bright white dots in the night sky. Our Sun is a star, and all stars are actually nuclear-fusing balls of atoms like hydrogen and helium crushed by gravity into very hot, very round spheres. (Not perfect spheres, but slightly flattened because they're spinning. We say they're a bit "oblate" [oh-BLATE], like our own Earth.) As gravity pulls all those atoms inward, toward each other, it forces the tiny particles to smash together. The gravitational smashing releases energy that eventually, after a few more stellar astrophysical shenanigans, causes a star to shine.

What kind of light does a star throw out across the universe? That's right! IROYGBIVU (chapter 9 again). Oh, and speaking of the U at the end there, don't forget sunscreen. And sunglasses. That energetic invisible ultraviolet light will get ya.

Spiral Galaxy M81 seen in ultraviolet light by the Galex space telescope.

< Galaxies

When gravity holds billions of stars together, we call this huge group a galaxy. Most galaxies aren't even on their own, though. Gravity invisibly binds them to other nearby galaxies. The enormously gigantic groups of galaxies can be part of larger families called clusters. And the clusters are organized into superclusters. Here on Earth we've figured out that we're in the Milky Way galaxy, which is part of what we call the Local Group. This group is a member of an even larger supercluster of galaxies called Laniakea [Lah-Nee-ah-KAY-uh].

Your Cosmic Address

If you ever get lost in space, and a friendly alien offers to send a letter home, this is the address you should give him. Or her. Or it.

20 cents

Earth
The Solar System
Milky Way
The Local Group
Laniakea

Any alien could figure it out from there. Laniakea means "enormous heaven" in Hawaiian, by the way.

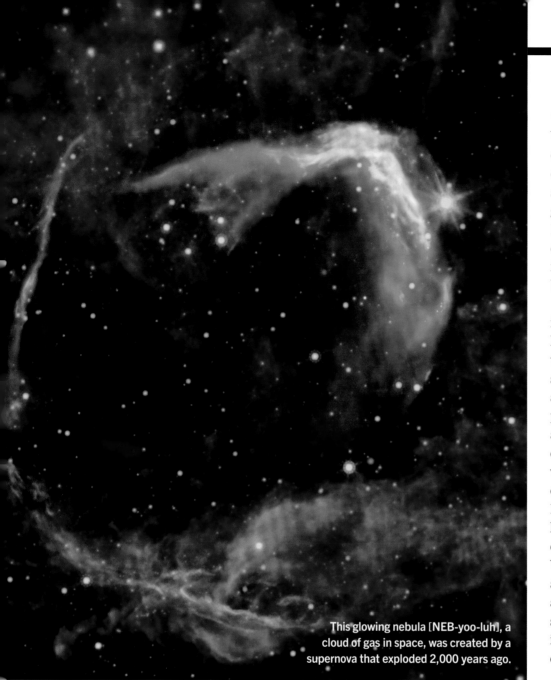

This glowing nebula [NEB-yoo-luh], a cloud of gas in space, was created by a supernova that exploded 2,000 years ago.

< Supernovas

When our cars run out of gasoline, or when the battery in my electric car runs low on charge, the motor stops spinning, and the car stops going. Stars need fuel to burn, too. Normally a star kicks out enough energy to push back against the inward pull of gravity, so it's nice and balanced and shining brightly.

When a star runs out of fuel, and it can't crank out enough heat and light, gravity takes over, squeezing the star into a smaller and smaller space. If a star gets to be eight times as massive as our Sun, the inner part, the core, becomes packed into an amazingly small ball. The star's energy gets smashed into a small volume so fast that the outer shell of the star gets thrown outward. It explodes, sending bursts of light and particles flying into the cosmos. We call this a supernova. With very sensitive telescopes and a worldwide coordinated effort, astronomers detect about 15 supernovas (sometimes supernovae) in distant regions of the cosmos every month. Wow!

Black Holes >

Gravity gives some stars such an enormously powerful inward-from-all-directions-at-once hug that they collapse. They become completely black, invisible stars that act like a hole in space. In a black hole, so much matter is jammed into such a tiny space and gravity becomes so strong that not even light can escape. We can figure out where they are out there in deep space by measuring how rays of light from other stars get bent by the enormous gravity of these objects. The largest black holes hide 10 billion, or more, times as much matter as our Sun.

The shadow of a black hole is the closest scientists have come to an image of a black hole itself, a completely dark object from which light cannot escape.

Loops and blobs of cosmic dust lie hidden in the giant elliptical galaxy NGC 1316.

∧ Dust

Right. This one probably doesn't sound all that exciting. But these tiny particles get scattered all through space when stars explode. Gravity brings the scattered atoms back together—gravity pulls on everything, everywhere, across the universe—and we get new stars, new planets, new asteroids, and comets. Oh, and more dust, too. Nowadays, the universe seems to be filled with stars and their ancestors' dust. There's so much dust out there that we can't see most of our own Milky Way galaxy, even on a very clear night. But that's no reason not to clean the dust off all those bookshelves in your room. Absolutely no reason.

ADVENTURES IN ASTROPHYSICS

Scientists have been studying supernovas for centuries, but new ones are always appearing. In 2011, a 10-year-old Canadian girl named Kathryn Gray discovered a supernova of her own. This particular supernova happened 240 million light-years away in the constellation of Camelopardalis. But there were no camels present, as far as I know. I've only ridden one camel. He didn't have much to say about supernovas. Probably because they're hard to eat, let alone carry home to one's camel room.

❝ I wanted to be an astrophysicist because I just love understanding the universe. It's so huge, and the more I research, the more I realize we have no idea what's going on. My friends are always saying you're so smart, you know everything about the universe, and I think, well, actually, as scientists we've realized that we don't know anything. That's one of the reasons I love it."

—ASTROPHYSICIST MAGGIE LIEU

1

MOST OF THE MATTER IN THE UNIVERSE IS INVISIBLE.

The stuff you see all around you every day is pretty important to you—your room, the food you eat, and your socks. And if you look up at the night sky, you'll see an uncountable number of stars and planets, and they seem like a big deal, too. But when it comes to the cosmos, all those stars and planets are actually a pretty small deal, because you're not seeing everything. You can't. We can't. As I mentioned earlier, a huge amount of the visible matter in the universe is just dust that's hard to see. But even when you add up all the dust you figure you can't detect, and all the planets, and all the billions and billions of stars, you don't get close to the total amount of matter that seems to be lurking out there. We figure we only see about 5% of all the stuff that there is in the cosmos. The rest is what we are currently calling dark matter. This strange stuff has enough gravity to pull on galaxies, so we know it's there. But right now, dark matter has us in the dark (sorry). Perhaps you'll become the astrophysicist who figures out what we're seeing when we can't see dark matter. If you do go into astrophysics, and you do indeed solve this problem, keep me posted. Or maybe I'll find out on my own if you find the secret, since you'll be quite famous! I should probably book you for a new episode of my show right now, just to get ahead of everyone else. When you're ready, ask your people to call my people.

Using the Hubble Space Telescope and the Chandra X-ray Telescope—two amazing instruments in orbit around Earth, astronomers have proven that there's something we can't see out there that has a lot of gravity. They detect it when galaxies collide.

2

WHEN YOU LOOK OUT AND UP, YOU'RE LOOKING BACK IN TIME.

I know. I know. We already went over this, in our chapter on light, and your brain exploded, and then you put it back together again, carefully, and you really don't want it to do that again, at least not at this time. But seriously: Think about this once again. That galaxy you're looking at in the night sky? The light might have traveled for hundreds of millions of years before it reached your eyes, or the lens of your telescope. In that time, a star in that galaxy could have burned out or exploded. Or maybe it only burns out and explodes here, when its light gets here. Whoa.

> "Astrophysics is a way to explore the universe. It's about nature and the universe and how things work on the biggest scales possible. It also takes a lot of creativity. You have to dream and imagine and come up with new questions to help us understand nature a little better."
>
> —ASTROPHYSICIST
> CHIARA MINGARELLI

A "zombie" star like the one imagined here just won't die, even after exploding.

3

SOMEDAY THE STARS WILL STOP SHINING.

This isn't the title of my new young adult romance novel. It's science! The universe is expanding. Our own galaxy is on the run. This expansion is getting faster and faster, too. At some point in the future, the stars in our night sky might be so far away, and moving so quickly, that their light won't reach us. It won't be tomorrow. Or even in 100 years, or 1 million years, or 100 million years. But it's going to happen at some time way, way off in the future. Some people are very troubled by this discovery. Other people, like me and you, I hope, think it's cool. We are part of something much bigger than ourselves. As we live and breathe, you and I are at least one way that the cosmos understands itself.

TRY THIS!

Dark Matter Decoded

WHAT YOU NEED:

Loose change

Two Mason jars with lids

Water

WHAT YOU DO:

1. Drop some change into each jar.

2. Fill one jar all the way to the very top with water.

3. Screw the lids of both jars down tight.

4. Move several steps back.

5. Have a friend turn both jars upside down at the same time, so they end up on their lids.

6. Watch how the coins move.

RESULTS: Did the coins in the empty jar move differently than the change in the water-filled one? When you study each jar from back where you're standing, they don't look very different from each other. From a distance, we don't really notice the water. In the same way, astrophysicists can't see dark matter. But we know the one jar is filled with water (because you filled it, duh . . .). But also, you can see that the coins move differently in the different jars. This is like astrophysicists realizing that dark matter must be out there, because distant galaxies are moving in unexpected ways.

< Jupiter

The fifth planet from the Sun is a big one. Bundle up all the other planets in the solar system and Jupiter would still be twice as massive. A year on Jupiter is the same as about 12 years here on Earth, and the planet is known as one of the gas giants. The surface isn't exactly solid like ours. But it isn't a gas, either. It's in a not quite liquid, maybe sorta soupy state, and it's amazingly hot. Scientists think the temperature near Jupiter's core could be 24,000°C (43,000°F)—or even way hotter. Weird, I know. But science does get a little strange out there in the far reaches of the solar system, at least by our standards. Here's one other Jovian (that means having to do with Jupiter) oddity: The planet has at least 79 moons! Galileo Galilei discovered the first four, Ganymede, Calisto, Io, and Europa, way back in 1610, with a telescope.

< Saturn

Another gas giant, Saturn is sixth in line, out beyond Jupiter. The planet itself is a big ball of two common elements, hydrogen and helium. It has the lowest density of all the planets. So low, in fact, that if you somehow plopped Saturn in a gigantic cosmic bathtub, the planet would float. Of course, I'm not sure where you'd get all the gravity you'd need for that adventure. Hmm. And oh, the rings! Those beautiful rings. There are seven major ones in all, and they're made of little grains of ice and rock. Saturn has at least 82 moons—take that, Jupiter. And thanks to the Cassini mission, which orbited the planet nearly 300 times over 13 years, scientists discovered new moons forming inside the rings. Please, please, please find yourself a telescope, or a friend with one, and observe these rings some clear night. They astonish everyone who sees them. You might want to hurry, though. The rings may be gone in 100 million years.

TRY THIS!

Pulsar Flash Rate with a Phone

WHAT YOU NEED:

Phone with a light

String

Tape

Doorway

WHAT YOU DO:

1. Tie your phone to a string. (Same knots you might use to tie ribbon on a birthday present.)

2. Hang it from a doorway using plenty of tape.

3. Let the phone spin on the string.

4. Get as far away as you can, and count how many flashes you see in, say, every 10 seconds.

RESULTS: The flashes you see are like the karate chop beams of energy from a pulsar.

SUPER COOL SCIENTIST:

Jocelyn Bell

When British astrophysicist Jocelyn Bell was a student in the 1960s, she helped build an unusual kind of telescope to pick up radio waves from distant parts of the universe. She was startled to find that some of those waves arrived in perfectly regular bursts. At first Bell and her coworkers wondered if she might be getting a radio signal from a distant civilization. Were aliens sending us a note in the form of radio pulses like the dots and dashes in some kind of Morse code of the cosmos? Uh, well . . . apparently not. Eventually Bell figured out that she'd discovered a new kind of cosmic object (well, it's ancient actually), a star that has collapsed so much and so fast that it produces a repeating karate chop of radio waves and light, beaming in one direction, instead of a uniform glow in all directions. And it's spinning. When we observe this type of star from here on Earth, we detect the chop as a nonstop sequence of flashes or pulses, so we call this star a pulsar. Many people feel Dr. Bell should have received a Nobel Prize for her work. And many years after publishing her paper, Bell was awarded the $3 million Special Breakthrough Prize in Fundamental Physics. She made a huge discovery.

One of the wonderful LIGO detectors.

Black Hole Fights

Astrophysicists use a variety of tools to figure out how the universe works. I love the Laser Interferometer Gravitational-Wave Observatory, or LIGO. The observatories detectors are amazing, beautiful, gigantic, L-shaped precision instruments, 4 kilometers (2½ miles) on a side and thousands of kilometers apart, that measure ripples in space and time. Wait . . . what?

You heard me . . . or read me: Einstein's discoveries predict that gravity bends and warps space itself. He predicted some weird effects. According to Einstein's idea, major cosmic events, such as two black holes crashing into one another, would kick out superstrong waves of gravity, in all directions. Then these gravitational ripples would radiate through the cosmos like waves through the ocean. They would travel for hundreds of millions, even billions, of years at the speed of pure energy—the speed of light. What would these waves do? Not much, really. You certainly wouldn't feel one. Or be able to surf it. The idea seemed like more of a dream than reality, because such waves, strong as they may be, are still gravity (chapter 11). So they would be fantastically weak—a tiny amount of energy that would be spread so thin that they'd be hard to detect at all, let alone measure.

In 2001, scientists finished building the first LIGO, which was designed to pick up the tiny motions that would tell scientists a gravitational wave has rolled through the cosmos all the way to our planet. They waited. For years, they discovered nothing, but they kept tuning and improving the instruments, making them more and more sensitive. Today, the system can detect a deflection smaller than 1/10,000 the width of a proton. Sure enough, in 2015, the LIGO system found its first evidence of a gravitational wave, resulting from colliding black holes. Einstein's wild ideas were right. Who knows where this discovery may lead one day?

Artist's conception of gravitational waves and light as two orbiting neutron stars coalesce. The image on the left can give you an idea of how space-time gets distorted near the collisions.

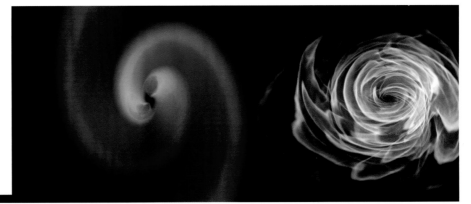

COSMIC
DEPARTMENT

1. What is dark energy?

As if dark matter weren't weird enough, astrophysicists are convinced that there is a mysterious force pushing the universe apart faster and faster. For years, scientists were pretty sure gravity would be pulling things together, slowing the expansion of the universe down, grabbing hold of distant galaxies, and at least stopping them from racing away from each other. But the pull of gravity is not enough. Something is working against gravity, and no one really knows what it is or how it works. Right now, we just call it dark energy. So get on that one, too. Okay?

Long after the big bang, the expansion of the universe is accelerating. Is it due to dark energy?

2. What's at the center of a black hole?

Astrophysicists have made amazing discoveries about black holes. They've learned about how they're formed, how they function, how they swallow up stars. But still—no one knows what's going on deep inside of a black hole, that spot where all the matter and light from former stars is trapped. Could the center of a black hole connect to other parts of the cosmos at other times? Black holes are weird enough already, but that would be some kinda science fiction something. Would you mind figuring that one out? Great. Thanks. And if it does involve time travel, please go back to when I was writing this book, and give me the answer, so I can fill in all your fellow readers and time travelers.

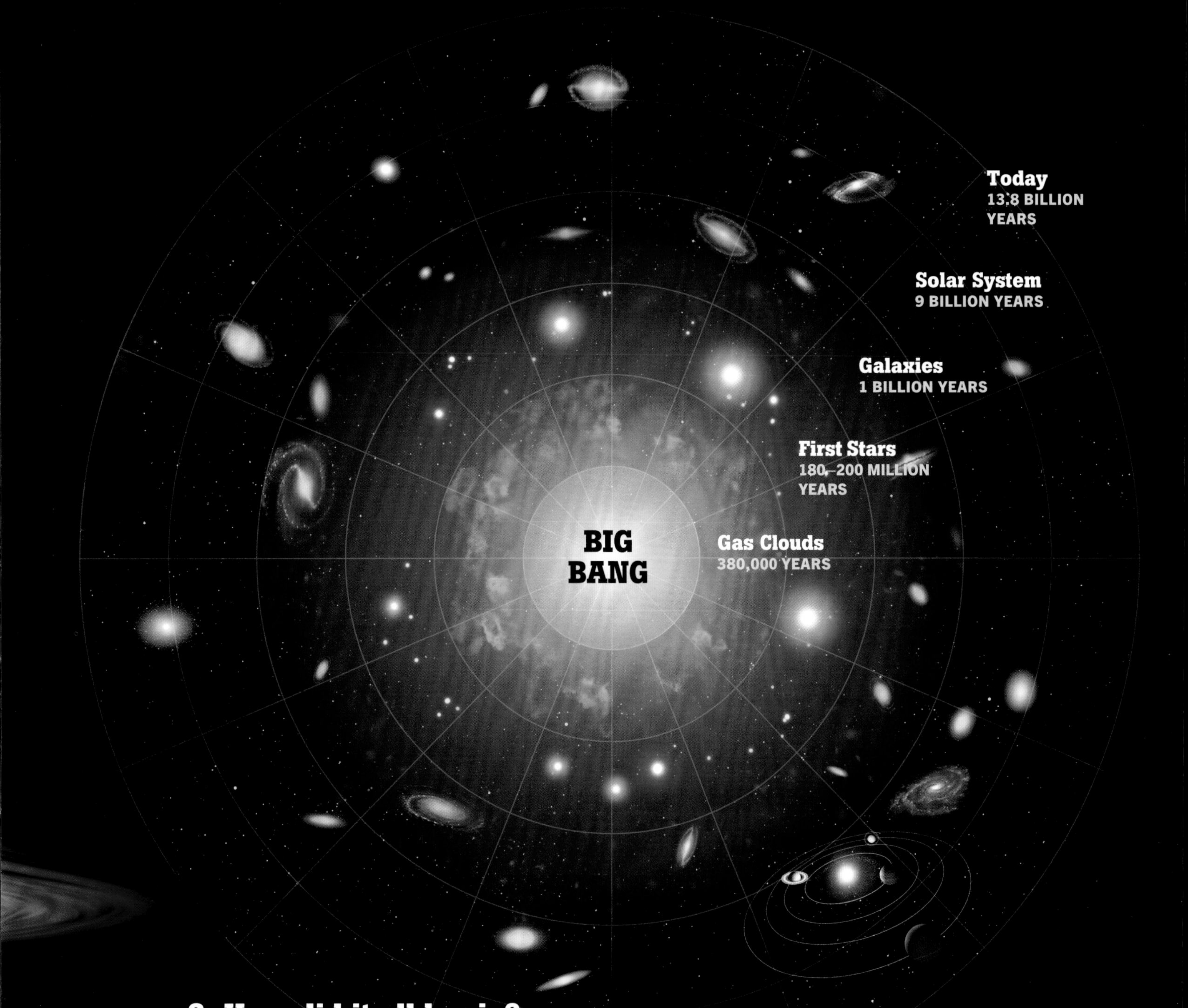

Today
13.8 BILLION
YEARS

Solar System
9 BILLION YEARS

Galaxies
1 BILLION YEARS

First Stars
180–200 MILLION
YEARS

**BIG
BANG**

Gas Clouds
380,000 YEARS

3. How did it all begin?

Since we've reached the end, we might as well journey back to the beginning. All the way
back to the beginning of time. How did the universe start? Scientists have determined
that our universe is right around 13.8 billion years old. They figure it started with a
bang, too—a really big bang. Not only that, because everything is moving apart so evenly,
astronomers figure ours is the only universe we can ever detect or know much about.
Remember how we said that energy cannot be created or destroyed? Well, all the energy
in our universe today was all there at the very beginning, crammed into a tiny point that's
much, much smaller than the head of a pin. This head-scratching big bang theory has
always puzzled me. Is this really the way it all started? Once you finish saving and changing
the world by solving all the other mysteries and problems I've laid out in this book, I'd
appreciate it if you'd turn to this next. Come to think of it, you could start with this one.

THE BIG FINISH

➤ Now that you know everything about everything and, more important, have started to watch, listen, and think about the world around you like a scientist, I have one final piece of advice: Wash your hands. Actually, that's good advice, but it's not quite what I meant.

Here's the real really big tip: Stay curious.

Or maybe it's not so much a piece of advice as it is a plea. Some of us adult people lose our sense of wonder somewhere along the way. We become set in our ways of thinking; we stop being curious and stop exploring. Well, don't let that be you. Ask questions about the world around you and the stars beyond. Think, think, think. Be curious now, and stay curious as your telomeres shorten. That right there would be something fantastic. A world full of curious, interested people. Let's go there together. Let's change the world.

"TELOMERES"
We didn't talk about telomeres? Seriously? Yikes. You're the scientist now, kid. Go find out about them for yourself.